A BRAN[...]
A PROMI[...]

Enter Sydney Omarr[...] [...]te day-by-day predictions for every aspect of your life. With expert readings and forecasts, you can chart a course to romance, adventure, good health, or career opportunities while gaining valuable insight into yourself and others. Offering a daily outlook for 18 full months, this fascinating guide shows you:

- The important dates in your life
- What to expect from an astrological reading
- How the stars can help you stay healthy and fit
- Your lucky lottery numbers
  And more!

Let this expert's sound advice guide you through a year of heavenly possibilities—for today and for every day of 2003!

SYDNEY OMARR'S DAY-BY-DAY ASTROLOGICAL GUIDE FOR

ARIES—March 21–April 19
TAURUS—April 20–May 20
GEMINI—May 21–June 20
CANCER—June 21–July 22
LEO—July 23–August 22
VIRGO—August 23–September 22
LIBRA—September 23–October 22
SCORPIO—October 23–November 21
SAGITTARIUS—November 22–December 21
CAPRICORN—December 22–January 19
AQUARIUS—January 20–February 18
PISCES—February 19–March 20

IN 2003

SYDNEY OMARR'S

DAY-BY-DAY ASTROLOGICAL GUIDE FOR

GEMINI

MAY 21–JUNE 20

2003

A SIGNET BOOK

SIGNET
Published by New American Library, a division of
Penguin Putnam Inc., 375 Hudson Street,
New York, New York 10014, U.S.A.
Penguin Books Ltd, 80 Strand,
London WC2R 0RL, England
Penguin Books Australia Ltd, Ringwood,
Victoria, Australia
Penguin Books Canada Ltd, 10 Alcorn Avenue,
Toronto, Ontario, Canada M4V 3B2
Penguin Books (N.Z.) Ltd, 182–190 Wairau Road,
Auckland 10, New Zealand

Penguin Books Ltd, Registered Offices:
Harmondsworth, Middlesex, England

First published by Signet, an imprint of New American Library,
a division of Penguin Putnam Inc.

First Printing, June 2002
10 9 8 7 6 5 4 3 2 1

CONTENTS

INTRODUCTION

Astrology Comes of Age

In times of change, people throughout the ages have looked to astrology for answers and explanations, searching the stars for portents of the future, hoping for a favorable prediction. Today, more people are searching for a deeper, more personal meaning, asking what astrology can tell them about themselves and their purpose in life, and how to handle current events.

Astrology now has evolved into a tool for self-knowledge, which has come of age in our time and is being validated by scholarly research. It is good news for astrology fans that there is an accredited college of astrology in Seattle, which will raise standards and serve as a focal point for the latest research. In France, astrologer Elizabeth Tessier presented her thesis in astrology at the Sorbonne and was granted a degree, making history at this prestigious institution. Internet websites give everyone instant access to sophisticated computer software and the thinking of top astrologers around the world.

Like millions of Americans who turn to astrology for fun, curiosity, or guidance, you're in for a fascinating experience as you explore the cosmos this unique way. Unlike other arts or sciences, astrology can give you specific details on who you are and where you're going, with immediate practical advice on how to deal with the whole range of problems and situations that crop up in daily life. It's no wonder that the lure of discovering a real human connection with the universe has kept people in all walks of life, from tycoons to the man on the street, intrigued with astrology for millennia.

This book is dedicated to helping you make astrology your own. As you discover astrology for yourself, you'll learn that, far from being a vague, intuitive art shrouded in mystery, it is quite a precise language that communicates in a very orderly and specific way. Yet it retains a sense of wonder and mystery. We marvel how those faraway planets can tell us so much about ourselves with such uncanny accuracy!

Haven't there been times when you feel an unexplained "pull" in a certain direction, times when everything seems to be going haywire, times when nobody seems to understand you, and other times when you seem to hit a lucky roll? Astrology offers explanations to these baffling conditions, points out trends and cycles, and suggests solutions to difficulties or alternative courses to take. Astrology brings the happenings in the universe down to human terms without dictating a moral code or involving a religion.

This book will give you basic tools for taking a voyage through your personal galaxy. Your most important tool is your own horoscope, a map of the heavens based on the happenings at the moment you were born. This tells you about your potential in every area of life, what talents to develop, where to look for a profitable career, even what kind of partner to choose for business and love. It can target your trouble spots in relationships, giving you clues about why you have difficulty communicating with someone and how to improve the situation. It offers heavenly help to improve the quality of your life, to make the most of your strengths, protect yourself from stress, even how to decorate your home.

Then there is the matter of timing. Astrology helps you pick the perfect moment to initiate a plan, sign a contract, go to a party, meet someone special, or close a deal. It's all based on an understanding of the way the energies of the planets are acting and interacting at a given time. This book will reveal which planet affects your communications for better or worse and what the 2003 outlook will be. You'll learn which phase of the moon is best for starting new ventures, and when to expect a major transition in your life. Starting with the groundwork of astrology, you'll learn to speak its language and discover what those exotic symbols really mean.

For your day-to-day living, there are eighteen months of

personal predictions. Each day, there are highlights of the planetary, lunar, and numerical cycles as they relate to your sign with custom-blended interpretations. What's more, you'll find the daily moon sign and lucky numbers for significant days.

So whether you're new to astrology or a regular reader, let this guide put you on the right celestial path for 2003. May the stars light your way to the happiest, healthiest year ever!

CHAPTER 1

2003: A Year of Changes

Uranus Moves to Pisces

When a slow-moving planet changes astrological signs, it is a major event, marking a total change in direction for at least seven years—a whole new generation. This year, the slow-moving planet Uranus moves into Pisces, bringing about a powerful change in group consciousness. In the astrological drama, Uranus plays the oddball, the rebellious rule breaker who is often called the "Great Awakener," for the way it operates in sudden, surprising ways. Uranus is likely to hit your life when and where you least expect, jolting you out of complacency and comfort. Uranus is also associated with technological experimentation and breakthroughs.

Since 1996, Uranus has been in a power position traveling through Aquarius, the sign it rules. It signaled the rise of the Internet, when the dot coms ruled the stock market and computers became part of our daily lives. As Aquarius is also the sign of social consciousness, associated with the eleventh house of the horoscope, the Uranus transit there has forced us to be aware of the dissension in the global community, with cataclysmic results in the Middle East. The surprise attack on the World Trade Center on September 11, 2001 was a tragic example of Uranus's influence.

Uranus dips its toe into Pisces on March 10, 2003 and spends six months there before retrograding back to Aquarius on September 14. Uranus will move finally into Pisces on December 30, where it will remain until the year 2011. The early six-month visit of Uranus in Pisces gives us a preview of coming trends for the next seven years.

The emphasis now changes to the mysterious mystical sign of Pisces—a sign of secrets, all that is hidden, stealthy,

5

beneath the surface, and behind the scenes. It is a sign of "losing one's self" in spirituality, of merging with the divine via meditation or ecstatic religious practices, of tapping the deep waters of the unconscious. During previous episodes of Uranus in Pisces, great religions and spiritual movements have come into being, most recently Mormonism and Christian fundamentalism.

Pisces is associated with the twelfth house of the horoscope, where we have no limits or boundaries. Athletes know it as the "zone," the euphoria that comes when they feel at one with their sport. Pisces represents places of voluntary or involuntary confinement via monasteries, prisons, and hospitals, where we no longer need take responsibility for our actions. It is where we escape from reality via addictions of all kinds, including alcohol and drugs.

In its most positive mode, Pisces promotes imagination and creativity, the art of illusion in theater and film, the inspiration of great artists. A water sign, Pisces is naturally associated with all things liquid—oceans, oil, alcohol—and with those creatures that live in water—fish, the fishing industry, fish habitats. Pisces also rules the underdog, the enslaved, and the disenfranchised, whose status has been illuminated in previous Uranus in Pisces periods.

The last time Uranus was in Pisces was early in the twentieth century from 1919 to 1927, during the "roaring 20s." Prohibition of alcohol (Pisces-ruled) began in 1920, causing secret bootleg industries and speakeasy clubs where racy dancing and upbeat music signaled the "Jazz Age." A unique American music evolved, with great musicians like Louis Armstrong and George Gershwin. It was a time of creativity in film and theater, which extended to the electronic inventions of radio and television. In literature, the "Lost Generation" of American writers began publishing. Socially, the underdog triumphed. Women finally won the right to vote in 1920. Gandhi began the peaceful noncooperation movement against the British in India. Yet the underworld also thrived, such as the Mafia's secret "Cosa Nostra" and the precursor of the IRA in Ireland.

The nineteenth-century period of Uranus in Pisces, from 1836 to 1843, might also give us a preview of what to expect. At that time, as the Victorian Era began, there were rumblings of women's rights. Victoria Woodhull, who would later be the first female to run for U.S. President, was born. The underdog issues of slavery were coming to a head. The slave ship *Amistad* mutinied and ran aground on Long Island, New York, in 1839. A legal battle ensued that went to the Supreme Court, where former President John Quincy Adams argued for the rebel slaves' freedom and won. The saga of the *Amistad* has inspired books, an opera, and a major film. The Cherokee "Vail of Tears" march to Oklahoma was another dramatic and sorrowful episode. Baseball was invented. Financier J. P. Morgan and John D. Rockefeller, founder of Standard Oil, were born. Many great artists and composers, such as Cézanne, Monet, Renoir, Winslow Homer, and Tchaikovsky, were born. The Cunard Line celebrated its first Atlantic crossing. There were great inventions in photography, such as the stereoscope and the daguerreotype. The Opium Wars erupted in China. Wars between the Afghans and the British resulted in the British being driven from Afghanistan. In America, Mexicans defeated 182 Texans at the Alamo.

These moments from history could give us clues about what to expect. Perhaps the first woman president will be elected, and the emancipation of women in Arab countries will proceed. With the Pisces emphasis this year revved up by Mars, the planet of action and war, which is also transiting Pisces for much of the year, we can expect a continuing emphasis on stealth and terrorist activities. Pisces rules the prenatal phase of life, which is related to regenerative medicine. Researchers dream of replacing body parts with new ones grown from embryonic stem cells. Legal issues, which now present obstacles to this type of research, may be overcome during the Uranus transit. If so, our dream of perfect health may be within reach.

Petroleum issues, both in the oil-producing countries and offshore oil drilling, will come to a head. Uranus in Pisces suggests that development of new hydroelectric sources may provide the power we need to continue our current power-thirsty lifestyle.

In previous eras, there was a flourishing of the arts, particularly new forms such as film, photography, poetry, and painting. We are seeing many new artistic forms developing

7

now, such as computer-created actors and special effects. The sky's the limit on this influence.

Those who have problems with Uranus are those who resist change, so the key is to embrace the future. Those born in early Pisces, February 18 to 20, are most likely to have Uranian changes in their lives this year. Go with the flow!

Pluto in Sagittarius: Religious Intensity

The slow-moving planet Pluto is our guide to life-changing, long-term trends. Pluto brings about a heightened consciousness and transformation of matters related to the sign it is passing through. In Sagittarius until 2008, Pluto is emphasizing everything associated with this sign to prepare us philosophically and spiritually for things to come. Those born from December 10–13 will be feeling the force of Pluto this year.

Perhaps the most pervasive sign of Pluto in Sagittarius over the past few years has been globalization in all its forms. We are re-forming boundaries, creating new forms of travel that will definitely include space travel. At this writing, the $60 billion space station is under way, a joint venture between the United States, Russia, Japan, Europe, and Canada. It is scheduled for completion in 2006 and will be one of the brightest objects in the sky.

In true Sagittarius fashion, Pluto will shift our emphasis away from acquiring wealth to a quest for the meaning of it all, as upward strivers discover that money and power are not enough and religious extremists assert themselves. Sagittarius is the sign of linking everything together. Therefore, the trend will be to find ways to interconnect on a spiritual, philosophical, and intellectual level.

The spiritual emphasis of Pluto in Sagittarius has already filtered down to our home lives. Home altars and private sanctuaries are becoming a part of our personal environment. The oriental art of feng shui has moved westward, giving rise to a more harmonious, spiritual atmosphere in offices and homes, which also promotes luck and prosperity.

Sagittarius are known for their love of animals, especially horses, and people have never been more pet-happy than now. Look for extremes related to animal welfare, such as vegetarianism, which will become even more popular and widespread as a lifestyle. As habitats are destroyed, the care, feeding, and control of wild animals will become a larger issue, especially where there are deer, bears, and coyotes in the backyard.

The Sagittarius love of the outdoors combined with Pluto's power has already promoted extreme sports, especially those that require strong legs, like rock climbing, trekking, or snowboarding. Rugged, sporty all-terrain vehicles continue to be popular. Expect the trend toward more adventurous travel as well as fitness or sports-oriented vacations to accelerate. Exotic hiking trips to unexplored territories, mountain-climbing expeditions, spa vacations, and sports-associated resorts are part of this trend.

Publishing, which is associated with Sagittarius, has been transformed by the new electronic media, with an enormous variety of books available in print and sold over the Internet. The Internet bookstore will continue to prosper under Pluto in Sagittarius. It is fascinating that the online bookstore Amazon.com took the Sagittarius-influenced name of the fierce female tribe of archer–warriors who went to the extreme of removing their right breasts to better shoot their arrows.

Jupiter: Who Is on a Roll This Year?

Good fortune, expansion, and big money opportunities are associated with the movement of Jupiter, the planet that embodies the principle of expansion. Jupiter has a 12-year cycle, staying in each sign for approximately one year.

When Jupiter enters a sign, the fields associated with that sign usually provide excellent opportunities. Areas of speculation associated with the sign Jupiter is passing through will have the hottest market potential—the ones that currently arouse excitement and enthusiasm.

The flip side of Jupiter is that there are no limits. You can expand off the planet under a Jupiter transit, which is why the planet is often called the "Gateway to Heaven." If something is going to burst (such as an artery) or overextend or go over the top in some way, it could happen under a supposedly "lucky" Jupiter transit . . . so be aware.

In 2003, Jupiter will finish its journey through Leo in late August, then move into Virgo for the remainder of the year. So sun sign Leos and Virgos or those with strong Leo or Virgo influence in their horoscopes should have abundant growth opportunities during the year. Those born under Aquarius and Pisces may find their best opportunities working with partners this year, since Jupiter will be transiting their seventh house of relationships.

Tense Times

Be especially cautious in late August. At that time Jupiter, the sun, and Mercury all in Virgo are at odds with Uranus and Mars in Pisces. There may be great impatience to change things, tense boundary issues, and a lack of clear vision. It will be important to communicate well and to understand what each partner in a relationship requires. Most of all, what is needed then is patience. There is still some unfinished business to resolve, which should happen in the fall. There may be responsibilities to others (Aquarius) that must be attended to before you can move ahead and a workable plan for the future can be developed. Play the waiting game.

Saturn Puts on the Brakes in Gemini

Saturn keywords are focus, time, commitment, accomplishment, discipline, restriction. If Jupiter gives you a handout, then Saturn hands you the bill. With Saturn, nothing's free—you work for what you get. So it's always a good idea to find the areas (or houses) of your horoscope where Saturn is passing through in order to learn where to focus your energy on lasting value. With Saturn, you must be sure to finish what you start, be responsible, put in the hard work, and stick with it.

Saturn finishes up its two-year transit of Gemini in June 2003. Over the last two years, the normally light-spirited Geminis have had to deal with a serious, sobering influence of Saturn, just after they enjoyed the expansive period of Jupiter in Gemini in 2000 and 2001. Geminis have to back up the risks they took then, and will be required to deliver on promises made. It'll be a powerful challenge for changeable Geminis, who must now pay the piper.

In the world at large, Saturn in Gemini has impacted communications. Talk must be followed up by action now. We'll be finishing up Gemini issues of lower education and literacy, reforming the lower educational system. Since Gemini is an air sign, which rules the lungs, there will be further controversy and restriction surrounding air pollution, air-born viruses, and the tobacco industry.

After Saturn moves into Cancer on June 3, 2003, the emphasis will switch to Cancer-related issues. Bear in mind that the United States is a Cancer country, born July 4, 1776, and that George W. Bush was born under Cancer (July 7, 1946). So this country is likely to experience the restrictive influence of Cancer.

Other Cancer areas are: domesticity, the home and homeland, the food supply, digestion, motherhood, milk, dairy products, hotels, restaurants, boating, cruise ships, waterways, water-related industries, crabs, sea fowl, the tides, the moon.

Neptune in Aquarius

Where there is Neptune, look for imagination and creativity. And, since Neptune is the planet of deception and illusion, scams and scandals will continue, especially in the high-tech area associated with Aquarius. Neptune is also associated with hospitals, which are acquiring a Neptunian glamour, as well as cutting-edge technology. The atmosphere of many hospitals is already changing from the intimidating sterile surgical environment of the past to that of a health-promoting spa, with alternative therapies such as massage, diet counseling, and aromatherapy. New procedures in plastic surgery, also a Neptunian glamour field, and antiaging therapies should restore the bloom and the body of youth.

There are two Neptune times to watch in 2003: in mid-February and again in the first week of June, when Neptune opposes expansive Jupiter in Leo. There may be a feeling of great optimism on one hand but a lack of direction on the other. Since judgment may be clouded and personal goals are likely unrealistic and too ego-centered, avoid making long-term decisions until the path ahead clears early in 2004. Instead, focus on spiritual growth and on making a positive contribution to the community, be it local or global.

CHAPTER 2

How to Find Your Best Times

Have you ever wanted to coordinate your schedule with the cosmos, as many of the rich and famous who have personal astrologers do? You can practice the art of prediction by studying the movement of the planets, then using this information to pick the perfect time for upcoming events in your life. For instance, when mischievous Mercury creates havoc with communications, you'll back up your vital computer files, read between the lines of contracts, and put off closing that deal until you have double-checked all the information. When Venus in your sign makes you the romantic flavor of the month, you've got maximum sex appeal. Why not get a knockout new outfit or hairstyle, then ask someone you'd like to know better to dinner? Venus timing can also help you win over the competition with a stunning sales pitch or make an offer they won't refuse.

To find out for yourself if there's truth to the saying "timing is everything," mark your own calendar for love, career moves, vacations, and important events, using the information in this chapter and in Chapter 4 on the planets, as well as the moon sign listings under your daily forecast. Here are the happenings to note on your agenda:

- Dates of your sun sign (high-energy period)
- The month previous to your sun sign (low-energy period)
- Dates of planets in your sign this year
- Full and new moons (Pay special attention when these fall in your sun sign)
- Eclipses
- Moon in your sun sign every month, as well as moon in the opposite sign (listed in daily forecast)

13

- Mercury retrogrades
- Other retrograde periods

Your Annual Prime Time

Every birthday starts a cycle of solar energy for you. You should feel a new surge of vitality as the powerful sun enters your sign. This is the time when predominant energies are most favorable to you. So go for it! Start new projects, make your big moves (especially when the new moon is in your sign, doubling your charisma). You'll get the recognition you deserve now, when everyone is attuned to your sun sign. Look in the tables in this book to see if other planets will also be passing through your sun sign at this time. Venus (love, beauty), Mars (energy, drive), and Mercury (communication, mental sharpness) reinforce the sun and give an extra boost to your life in the areas they affect. Venus will rev up your social and love life, making you seem especially attractive. Mars gives you extra energy and drive. Mercury fuels your brainpower and helps you communicate. Jupiter signals an especially lucky period of expansion.

There are two "down" times related to the sun. During the month before your birthday period, when you are winding up your annual cycle, you could be feeling especially vulnerable and depleted. So at that time get extra rest, watch your diet, and take it easy. Don't overstress yourself. Use this time to gear up for a big "push" when the sun enters your sign.

Another "down" time is when the sun is in a sign opposite your sun sign (six months from your birthday). That's when the prevailing energies are very different from yours. You may feel at odds with the world. You'll have to work harder for recognition because people are not on your wavelength. However, this could be a good time to work on a team, in cooperation with others, or behind the scenes.

Plan Your Day Using the Moon's Phase and Sign

Working with the phases of the moon is as easy as looking up at the night sky. During the new moon, when both the sun and moon are in the same sign, begin new ventures—especially activities that are favored by that sign. Then you'll utilize the powerful energies pulling you in the same direction. You'll be focused outward, toward action, and in a doing mode. Postpone breaking off, terminating, deliberating, or reflecting—activities that require introspection and passive work. These are better suited to a later moon phase.

Get your project under way during the first quarter. Then go public at the full moon, a time of high intensity, when feelings come out into the open. This is your time to shine—to express yourself. Be aware, however, that because pressures are being released, other people will also be letting off steam. Since confrontations are possible, take advantage of this time either to air grievances or to avoid arguments. Traditionally, astrologers often advise against surgery at this time, which could produce heavier bleeding.

From the last quarter of the moon to the next new moon, it's a winding-down phase, a time to cut off unproductive relationships, do serious thinking, and focus on inward-directed activities.

You'll feel some new and full moons more strongly than others, especially those new moons that fall in your sun sign and full moons in your opposite sign. Because that full moon happens at your low-energy time of year, it is likely to be an especially stressful time in a relationship, when any hidden problems or unexpressed emotions could surface.

Full and New Moons in 2003

New Moon—January 2 in Capricorn
Full Moon—January 18 in Cancer

New Moon—February 1 in Aquarius
Full Moon—February 16 in Leo

15

New Moon—March 2 in Pisces
Full Moon—March 18 in Virgo

New Moon—April 1 in Aries
Full Moon—April 16 in Libra

New Moon—May 1 in Taurus
Full Moon—May 15 in Scorpio
New Moon—May 30 in Gemini

Full Moon—June 14 in Sagittarius
New Moon—June 29 in Cancer

Full Moon—July 13 in Capricorn
New Moon—July 29 in Leo

Full Moon—August 11 in Aquarius
New Moon—August 27 in Virgo

Full Moon—September 10 in Pisces
New Moon—September 25 in Libra

Full Moon—October 10 in Aries
New Moon—October 25 in Scorpio

Full Moon—November 8 in Taurus
New Moon—November 23 in Sagittarius

Full Moon—December 8 in Gemini
New Moon—December 23 in Capricorn

Moon Sign Timing

To forecast the daily emotional "weather," to determine
your monthly high and low days, or to synchronize your
activities with the cycles of the moon, take note of the
moon's sign under your daily forecast at the end of the
book. Here are some of the activities favored and the
moods you are likely to encounter under each moon sign.

Moon in Aries

Get moving! The new moon in Aries is an ideal time to start new projects. Everyone is pushy, raring to go, rather impatient, and short-tempered. Leave details and follow-up for later. Competitive sports or martial arts are great ways to let off steam. Quiet types could use some assertiveness, but it's a great day for dynamos. Be careful not to step on too many toes.

Moon in Taurus

It's time to lay the foundations for success. Do solid, methodical tasks like follow-through or backup work. Make investments, buy real estate, do appraisals, do some hard bargaining. Attend to your property. Get out in the country or spend some time in your garden. Enjoy creature comforts, music, a good dinner, sensual love-making. Forget starting a diet—this is a day when you'll feel self-indulgent.

Moon in Gemini

Talk means action today. Telephone, write letters, fax! Make new contacts, stay in touch with steady customers. You can juggle lots of tasks today. It's a great time for mental activity of any kind. Don't try to pin people down—they, too, are feeling restless. Keep it light. Flirtations and socializing are good. Watch gossip—and don't give away secrets.

Moon in Cancer

This is a moody, sensitive, emotional time. People respond to personal attention, to mothering. Stay at home, have a family dinner, call your mother. Nostalgia, memories, and psychic powers are heightened. You'll want to hang on to people and things (don't clean out your closets now). You could have shrewd insights into what others really need and want. Pay attention to dreams, intuition, and gut reactions.

Moon in Leo

Everybody is in a much more confident, warm, generous mood. It's a good day to ask for a raise, show what you can do, dress like a star. People will respond to flattery, enjoy a bit of drama and theater. You may be extravagant, treat yourself royally, and show off a bit—don't break the bank! Be careful you don't promise more than you can deliver.

Moon in Virgo

Do practical down-to-earth chores. Review your budget, make repairs, be an efficiency expert. Not a day to ask for a raise. Tend to personal care and maintenance. Have a health checkup, go on a diet, buy vitamins or health food. Make your home spotless. Take care of details and piled-up chores. Reorganize your work and life so they run more smoothly and efficiently. Save money. Be prepared for others to be in a critical, faultfinding mood.

Moon in Libra

Attend to legal matters. Negotiate contracts. Arbitrate. Do things with your favorite partner. Socialize. Be romantic. Buy a special gift, a beautiful object. Decorate yourself or your surroundings. Buy new clothes. Throw a party. Have an elegant, romantic evening. Smooth over any ruffled feathers. Avoid confrontations. Stick to civilized discussions.

Moon in Scorpio

This is a day to do things with passion. You'll have excellent concentration and focus. Try not to get too intense emotionally. Avoid sharp exchanges with loved ones. Others may tend to go to extremes, get jealous, overreact.

Great for troubleshooting, problem solving, research, scientific work—and making love. Pay attention to those psychic vibes.

Moon in Sagittarius

A great time for travel, philosophical discussions, setting long-range career goals. Work out, do sports, buy athletic equipment. Others will be feeling upbeat, exuberant, and adventurous. Risk taking is favored. You may feel like taking a gamble, betting on the horses, visiting a local casino, buying a lottery ticket. Teaching, writing, and spiritual activities also get the green light. Relax outdoors. Take care of animals.

Moon in Capricorn

You can accomplish a lot today, so get on the ball! Attend to business. Issues concerning your basic responsibilities, duties, family, and elderly parents could crop up. You'll be expected to deliver on promises. Weed out the deadwood from your life. Get a dental checkup. Not a good day for gambling or taking risks.

Moon in Aquarius

A great day for doing things with groups—clubs, meetings, outings, politics, parties. Campaign for your candidate. Work for a worthy cause. Deal with larger issues that affect humanity—the environment and metaphysical questions. Buy a computer or electronic gadget. Watch TV. Wear something outrageous. Try something you've never done before. Present an original idea. Don't stick to a rigid schedule—go with the flow. Take a class in meditation, mind control, yoga.

Moon in Pisces

This can be a very creative day, so let your imagination work overtime. Film, theater, music, ballet could inspire you. Spend some time alone, resting and reflecting, reading or writing poetry. Daydreams can also be profitable. Help those less fortunate. Lend a listening ear to someone who may be feeling blue. Don't overindulge in self-pity or escapism, however. People are especially vulnerable to substance abuse now. Turn your thoughts to romance and someone special.

How to Handle Eclipses

One of the most amazing phenomena, which many of us take for granted, is the spatial relationship between the sun and moon. How many of us have ever noticed or marveled that, relative to our viewpoint here on earth, both the largest source of energy (the sun) and the smallest (the moon) appear to be almost exactly the same size? Or wondered what would happen if the moon's orbit became closer to earth or farther away?

This fascinating relationship is most evident to us at the time of the solar eclipse, when the moon is directly aligned with the sun and so nearly covers it that scientists use the moment of eclipse to study solar flares. The darkening of the sun has been used in history and mythology to indicate dire happenings ahead. In some parts of the world, people hide in their homes during the darkening of the sun. When the two most powerful forces in astrology—the sun and moon—are lined up, we're sure to feel the effects both in world events and in our personal lives. Both solar and lunar eclipses are times when our natural rhythms are changed, depending on where the eclipse falls in your horoscope. If the eclipse falls on or close to your birthday, you're going to have important changes in your life, perhaps a turning point.

Lunar Eclipses

Lunar eclipse: A momentary "turn off" that could help us turn our lives around.

A lunar eclipse happens during a full moon when the

earth moves exactly between the sun and moon, breaking their natural monthly opposition. Normally, the earth is not on a level plane; otherwise, eclipses would occur every month. During a lunar eclipse, the earth "short circuits" the connection between the sun and moon. The effect on us can be either confusion or clarity. Our subconscious lunar energies, which normally respond to the rhythmic cycle of opposing sun and moon, are momentarily turned off. This could cause a bewildering disorientation that intensifies our insecurities. On the other hand, this moment of clarity might give us insights that could help change destructive emotional patterns such as addictions.

Solar Eclipses

Solar eclipse: Deep feelings come to the surface.

The solar eclipse occurs during the new moon. This time, the moon blocks the sun's energies as it passes exactly between the sun and the earth. In astrological interpretation, the moon darkens the objective, conscious force, represented by the sun, allowing subconscious lunar forces, which activate our deepest emotions, to dominate. Emotional truths can be revealed or emotions can run wild, as our solar objectivity is cut off. If your sign is affected, you may find yourself beginning a period of work on a deep inner level. And you may have psychic experiences or deep feelings that come to the surface.

You'll start feeling the energies of an upcoming eclipse a few days after the previous new or full moon. The energy continues to intensify until the actual eclipse, then disperses for three or four days. So plan ahead at least a week or more before an eclipse, then allow several days afterward for the natural rhythms to return. Try not to make major moves during this period. (It's not a great time to get married, change jobs, or buy a home, for instance.)

Eclipses in 2003

There are four eclipses this year.

Full Moon and Lunar Eclipse—May 15 in Scorpio

New Moon and Solar Eclipse—May 30 in Gemini
Full Moon and Lunar Eclipse—November 8 in Taurus
New Moon and Solar Eclipse—November 23 in Sagittarius

When the Planets Go Backward

All the planets, except for the sun and moon, have times when they appear to move backward—or retrograde—as it seems from our point of view on earth. At these times, planets do not work as they normally do. So it's best to "take a break" from that planet's energies in our life and to do some work on an inner level.

Mercury Retrograde: Taming the Trickster

Mercury goes retrograde most often, and its effects can be especially irritating. When it reaches a short distance ahead of the sun several times a year, it seems to move backward from our point of view. Astrologers often compare retrograde motion to the optical illusion that occurs when we ride on a train that passes another train traveling at a different speed—the second train appears to be moving in reverse.

What this means to you is that the Mercury-ruled areas of your life—analytical thought processes, communications, scheduling—are subject to all kinds of confusion. Be prepared. People may change their minds, renege on commitments. Communications equipment can break down. Schedules may be changed on short notice. People are late for appointments or don't show up at all. Traffic is terrible. Major purchases malfunction, don't work out, or get delivered in the wrong color. Letters don't arrive or are delivered to the wrong address. Employees will make errors that have to be corrected later. Contracts don't work out or must be renegotiated.

Since most of us can't put our lives on "hold" during Mercury retrogrades, we should learn to tame the trickster and make it work for us. The key is in the prefix *re-*. This is the time to go back over things in your life, *re*flect on what you've done during the previous months. Now you can get deeper insights, spot errors you've missed. So take time to *re*view and *re*evaluate what has happened. *Re*st and *re*ward yourself—it's a good time to take a vacation, especially if you *re*visit a favorite place. *Re*organize your work and finish up projects that are backed up. Clean out your desk and closets. Throw away what you can't *re*cycle. If you must sign contracts or agreements, do so with a contingency clause that lets you *re*evaluate the terms later.

Postpone major purchases or commitments for the time being. Don't get married (unless you're *re*marrying the same person). Try not to *re*ly on other people keeping appointments, contracts, or agreements to the letter; have several alternatives. Double-check and *re*ad between the lines. Don't buy anything connected with communications or transportation (if you must, be sure to cover yourself).

Mercury retrograding through your sun sign will intensify its effect on your life.

If Mercury was retrograde when you were born, you may be one of the lucky people who don't suffer the frustrations of this period. If so, your mind probably works in a very intuitive, insightful way.

The sign in which Mercury is retrograding can give you an idea of what's in store—as well as the sun signs that will be especially challenged.

MERCURY RETROGRADES IN 2003
Mercury has four retrograde periods this year.
    January 2 to January 22 in Capricorn
    April 26 to May 20 in Taurus
    August 28 to September 20 in Virgo
    December 17 to January 6, 2004 in Capricorn

Venus Retrograde

Retrograding Venus can cause your relationships to take a backward step, or it can make you extravagant and impractical. Shopping till you drop and buying what you cannot afford are trip-ups at this time. It's *not* a good time to redecorate—you'll hate the color of the walls later. Postpone getting a new hairstyle. Try not to fall in love either. But if you wish to make amends in an already troubled relationship, make peaceful overtures at this time.

VENUS RETROGRADES IN 2003
There is no Venus retrograde period in 2003.

Mars Tips: When to Push and When to Hold Back!

Mars shows how and when to get where you want to go. Timing your moves with Mars on your side can give you a big push. On the other hand, pushing Mars the wrong way can guarantee that you'll run into frustrations in every corner. Your best times to forge ahead are during the weeks when Mars is traveling through your sun sign or your Mars sign (look these up at the end of Chapter 4 on the planets). Also consider times when Mars is in a compatible sign (fire with air signs, or earth with water signs). You'll be sure to have planetary power on your side.

In 2003, Mars spends six months in Pisces from June 17 to December 16. This is especially significant because the movements of Mars will be activating the volatile planet Uranus (the planet of awakenings), which is in the process of making a major move from Aquarius to Pisces. As Uranus dips its toe in the watery sign of Pisces, Mars will be on hand to give it a warm welcome! This could be quite an unstable time, as we make a leap into the future. Be alert for sudden changes around June 23 and again in mid-September, when these two volatile planets align.

MARS RETROGRADE
Hold your fire when Mars retrogrades in 2003, especially if you are a Pisces. Be especially careful around the ocean or bodies of water. Since this happens during the warm beachtime months of August and September, beware of dangerous tides and prowling sharks. Now is the time to exercise patience. Let someone else run with the ball, especially if it's the opposing team. You may feel you're not accomplishing

much, but that's the right idea. Slow down and work off any frustrations at the gym. It's also best to postpone buying mechanical devices, which are Mars-ruled, and to take extra care when handling sharp objects.

Be sure to use the appropriate protective gear when playing sports, especially foot gear. Don't take unnecessary chances. This is not the time for daredevil moves! Pace yourself. Pay extra attention to your health, since you may be especially vulnerable at this time.

MARS RETROGRADES IN 2003
Mars retrogrades in 2003 for almost two months: July 29 to September 27 in Pisces.

When Other Planets Retrograde

The slower-moving planets stay retrograde for months at a time (Saturn, Jupiter, Neptune, Uranus, and Pluto). When Saturn is retrograde, it's an uphill battle with self-discipline. You may feel more like hanging out at the beach than getting things done. Neptune retrograde promotes a dreamy escapism from reality, when you may feel you're in a fog (Pisces will feel this, especially). Uranus retrograde may mean setbacks in areas where there have been sudden changes, when you may be forced to regroup or reevaluate the situation. Since Mars is activating Uranus this year, it could be a significantly unstable time. Think of this as an adjustment period, a time to think things over and allow new ideas to develop. Pluto retrograde is a time to work on establishing proportion and balance in areas where there have been recent dramatic transformations.

When the planets move forward again, there's a shift in the atmosphere. Activities connected with each planet start moving ahead, plans that were stalled get rolling. Make a special note of those days on your calendar and proceed accordingly.

OTHER RETROGRADES IN 2003
The five slower-moving planets all go retrograde in 2003.

Jupiter retrogrades from December 4, 2002 to April 4, 2003 in Leo.

Saturn retrogrades from October 11, 2002 to February 22, 2003, and again from October 25, 2003 to March 7, 2004.

Uranus retrogrades from June 6 in Pisces back to Aquarius on September 15, then turns direct on November 8 in Aquarius.

Neptune retrogrades from May 15 to November 22 in Aquarius.

Pluto retrogrades from March 22 to August 28 in Sagittarius.

CHAPTER 3

A Crash Course in Astrology: What You Need to Know

Could you be your own astrologer? You may be wondering if you can access this special realm of knowledge without years of study. Even though astrology is a very precise art that uses an ancient language of symbols, the basic principles are not difficult to learn. And once you know the basics, you can penetrate beyond the realm of your sun sign into the realm of the other planets. The more you know, the more you'll want to know.

Here's a nontechnical guide to help you find your way around the world of astrology.

Where the Signs Are

First, let's get our "sign language" straight because, for most readers, that's the starting point of astrology.

Signs are actually a type of celestial real estate, located on the *zodiac,* an imaginary 360-degree belt circling the earth. This belt is divided into twelve equal 30-degree portions, and these are the signs. There's confusion about the difference between the *signs* and the *constellations* of the zodiac. Constellations are patterns of stars that originally marked the twelve divisions, like signposts. Though a sign is named after the constellation that once marked the same area, the constellations are no longer in the same place relative to the earth they were centuries ago. Over hundreds of years, the earth's orbit has shifted, so that from our point of view here on earth the constellations moved.

However, the signs remain in place. Most Western astrologers use the twelve-equal-part division of the zodiac. However, there are some methods of astrology that do still use the constellations instead of the signs.

Most people think of themselves in terms of their *sun sign*. A sun sign refers to the sign the sun is orbiting through at a given moment (from our point of view here on earth). For instance "I'm an Aries" means that the sun was passing through Aries when that person was born. However, there are nine other planets (plus asteroids, fixed stars, and sensitive points) that also form our total astrological personality, and some or many of these will be located in other signs. No one is completely "Aries," with all their astrological components in one sign! (Please note that, in astrology, the sun and moon are usually referred to as "planets," though of course they're not.)

As mentioned before, the sun signs are areas on the zodiac. They do not *do* anything (planets are the doers). However, they are associated with many things, depending on their location.

What Makes a Sign Special?

What makes Aries the sign of go-getters, Taurus savvy with money, Gemini talk a blue streak, and Sagittarius footloose? Definitions of the signs are not accidental. They are derived from different combinations of four concepts: a sign's *element, quality, polarity,* and *place (order)* on the zodiac.

Take the element of fire: it's hot, passionate. Then add the active cardinal mode. Give it a jolt of positive energy, and place it first in line. And doesn't that sound like the active, me-first, driving, hotheaded, energetic Aries?

Then take the element of earth: it's practical, sensual, where things grow. Add the fixed, stable mode. Give it energy that reacts to its surroundings, that settles in. Put it after Aries. Now you've got a good idea of how sensual, earthy Taurus operates.

Another way to grasp the idea is to pretend you're doing

a magical puzzle based on the numbers that can divide into twelve (the number of signs): 4, 3, and 2. There are four "building blocks" or elements, three ways a sign operates (qualities), and two polarities. These alternate in turn around the zodiac, with a different combination coming up for each sign.

The Four Elements

First, consider the four elements that describe the physical concept of the sign. Is it *fiery* (dynamic), *earthy* (practical), *airy* (mental), *watery* (emotional)? Therefore, there are three zodiac signs of each of the four elements: *fire* (Aries, Leo, Sagittarius); *earth* (Taurus, Virgo, Capricorn); *air* (Gemini, Libra, Aquarius); *water* (Cancer, Scorpio, Pisces). These are the same elements that make up our planet: earth, air, fire, and water. But astrology uses the elements as *symbols* that link our body and psyche to the rhythms of the planets.

Fire signs spread warmth and enthusiasm. They are able to fire up or motivate others. They have hot tempers. These are people who make ideas catch fire and spring into existence. Earth signs are the builders of the zodiac who follow through after the initiative of fire signs to make things happen. These people are solid, practical realists who enjoy material things and sensual pleasures. They are interested in ideas that can be used to achieve concrete results. Air signs are mental people, great communicators. Following the consolidating earth signs, they'll reach out to inspire others through the use of words, social contacts, discussion, and debate. Water signs complete each four-sign series adding the ingredients of emotion, compassion, and imagination. Water sign people are nonverbal communicators who attune themselves to their surroundings and react through the medium of feelings.

The Three Qualities

The second consideration when defining a sign is how it will operate. Will it take the initiative, or move slowly and deliberately, or adapt easily? It's *quality* (or modality) will tell. There are three qualities and four signs of each quality: cardinal, fixed, and mutable.

Cardinal signs are the start-up signs that begin each season (Aries, Cancer, Libra, Capricorn). These people love to be active, involved in projects. They are usually on the fast track to success, impatient to get things under way. *Fixed signs* (Taurus, Leo, Scorpio, Aquarius) move steadily, always in control. They happen in the middle of a season, after the initial character of the season is established. Fixed signs are naturally more centered. They tend to move more deliberately, do things more slowly but thoroughly. They govern parts of your horoscope where you take root and integrate your experiences. *Mutable signs* (Gemini, Virgo, Sagittarius, Pisces) embody the principle of distribution. These are the signs that break up the cycle, then prepare the way for a change by distributing the energy to the next group. Mutables are flexible, adaptable, communicative. They can move in many directions easily, darting around obstacles.

The Two Polarities

In addition to an element and a quality, each sign has a *polarity,* either a positive or a negative electrical charge that generates energy around the zodiac, like a giant battery. Polarity refers to opposites, which you could also define as masculine/feminine, yin/yang, active/reactive. Alternating around the zodiac, the six fire and air signs are positive, active, masculine, and yang in polarity. These signs are open, expanding outward. The six earth and water signs are reactive, negative, and yin in polarity. They are nurturing and receptive, which allows the energy to develop and take shape. All positive energy would be like a car without brakes. All negative energy would be like a stalled vehicle, going nowhere. Both polarities are needed in balanced proportion.

The Order of the Signs: Their Place

Finally we must consider the *order* of the signs—that is the *place* each sign occupies in the zodiac. This consideration is vital to the balance of the zodiac and the transmission of energy throughout the zodiac. Each sign is quite different from its neighbors on either side. Yet each seems to grow out of its predecessor like links in a chain. And each transmits a synthesis of energy gathered along the chain to the following sign—beginning with the fiery, active, positive, cardinal sign of Aries and ending with the watery, mutable, reactive Pisces.

The table shows how the signs shape up according to the four characteristics discussed.

How the Signs Add Up

Sign	Element	Quality	Polarity	Place
Aries	fire	cardinal	masculine	first
Taurus	earth	fixed	feminine	second
Gemini	air	mutable	masculine	third
Cancer	water	cardinal	feminine	fourth
Leo	fire	fixed	masculine	fifth
Virgo	earth	mutable	feminine	sixth
Libra	air	cardinal	masculine	seventh
Scorpio	water	fixed	feminine	eighth
Sagittarius	fire	mutable	masculine	ninth
Capricorn	earth	cardinal	feminine	tenth
Aquarius	air	fixed	masculine	eleventh
Pisces	water	mutable	feminine	twelfth

The Houses and the Horoscope Chart

A horoscope chart is a map of the heavens at a given moment in time. It looks somewhat like a wheel divided with twelve spokes. In between each of the "spokes" is a section called a *house*. Each house deals with a different area of life and is influenced by a special sign and a planet. In addition, the house is governed by the sign passing over the spoke (or cusp of the house) at that particular moment. For example, the first house is naturally associated with Aries and Mars. However, if Capricorn was the sign passing over the house cusp at the time the chart was cast, that house would have a Capricorn influence as well.

The houses start at the left center spoke (the number 9 position if you were reading a clock) and are read *counterclockwise* around the chart. Astrologers look at the houses to tell in what area of life an event is happening or about to happen.

The First House: Home of Aries and Mars

This is the house of "firsts"—the first impression you make, how you initiate matters, the image you choose to project. This is where you advertise yourself, where you project your personality. Planets that fall here will intensify the way you come across to others. Often the first house will project an entirely different type of personality than the sun sign. For instance, a Capricorn with Leo in the first house will come across as much more flamboyant than the average Capricorn. The sign passing over the first house at the time of your birth is known as your *ascendant*, or *rising sign*.

The Second House: Home of Taurus and Venus

This house is where you experience the material world—what you value. Here are your attitudes about money, possessions, finances, whatever belongs to you, and what you own, as well as your earning and spending capacity. On a deeper level, this house reveals your sense of self-worth, the inner values that draw wealth in various forms.

The Third House: Home of Gemini and Mercury

This house describes how you communicate with others, how you reach out to others nearby, and how you interact with the immediate environment. It shows how your thinking process works and the way you express your thoughts. Are you articulate or tongue-tied? Can you think on your feet? This house also shows your first relationships, your experiences with brothers and sisters, and how you deal with people close to you such as your neighbors or pals. It's where you take short trips, write letters, or use the telephone. It shows how your mind works in terms of left-brain logical and analytical functions.

The Fourth House: Home of Cancer and the Moon

The fourth house shows the foundation of life, the psychological underpinnings. At the bottom of the chart, this house shows how you are nurtured and made to feel secure—your roots! It shows your early home environment and the circumstances at the end of your life (your final "home") as well as the place you call home now. Astrologers look here for information about the parental nurturers in your life.

The Fifth House: Home of Leo and the Sun

The fifth house, the Leo house, is where the creative potential develops. Here you express yourself and procreate in the sense that children are outgrowths of your creative ability. But this house most represents your inner childlike self who delights in play. If your inner security has been established by the time you reach this house, you are now free to have fun, romance, and love affairs and to give of yourself. This is also the place astrologers look for playful love affairs, flirtations, and brief romantic encounters (rather than long-term commitments).

The Sixth House: Home of Virgo and Mercury

The sixth house has been called the "repair and maintenance" department. This house shows how you take care of your body and organize yourself to perform efficiently in the world. Here is where you get things done, where you look after others, and fulfill service duties such as taking care of pets. Here is your daily survival, your "job" (as opposed to your career, which is the domain of the tenth house), your diet, and your health and fitness regimens.

The Seventh House: Home of Libra and Venus

This house shows your attitude toward partners and those with whom you enter commitments, contracts, or agreements. Here is the way you relate to others, as well as your close, intimate, one-on-one relationships (including open enemies—those you "face off" with). Open hostilities, lawsuits, divorces, and marriages happen here. If the first house represents the "I," the seventh or opposite house is the "not-I"—the complementary partner you attract by the way you come across. If you are having trouble with partnerships, consider what you are attracting by the energies of your first and seventh house.

The Eighth House: Home of Scorpio and Pluto (also Mars)

The eighth house refers to how you merge with something or someone, and how you handle power and control. This is one of the most mysterious and powerful houses, where your energy transforms itself from "I" to "we." As you give up power and control by uniting with something or someone, two kinds of energies merge and become something greater, leading to a regeneration of the self on a higher level. Here are your attitudes toward sex, shared resources, taxes (what you share with the government). Because this house involves what belongs to others, you face issues of control and power struggles, or undergo a deep psychological transformation as you bond with another. Here you transcend yourself with dreams, drugs, and occult or psychic experiences that reflect the collective unconscious.

The Ninth House: Home of Sagittarius and Jupiter

The ninth house shows your search for wisdom and higher knowledge—your belief system. As the third house represents the "lower mind," its opposite on the wheel, the ninth house, is the "higher mind"—the abstract, intuitive, spiritual mind that asks "big" questions like "Why are we here?" After the third house has explored what was close at hand, the ninth stretches out to broaden you mentally with higher education and travel. Here you stretch spiritually with religious activity. Since you are concerned with how everything is related, you tend to push boundaries, take risks. Here is where you express your ideas in a book or thesis, where you pontificate, philosophize, or preach.

The Tenth House: Home of Capricorn and Saturn

The tenth house is associated with your public life and high-profile activities. Located directly overhead at the "high noon" position on the horoscope wheel, this is the most "visible" house in the chart, the one where the world sees you. It deals with your career (but not your routine "job") and your reputation. Here is where you go public, take on responsibilities (as opposed to the fourth house, where you stay home). This will affect the career you choose and your "public relations." This house is also associated with your father figure or the main authority figure in your life.

The Eleventh House: Home of Aquarius and Uranus

The eleventh house is where you extend yourself to a group, a goal, or a belief system. This house is where you define what you really want, the kinds of friends you have, your political affiliations, and the kind of groups you identify with as an equal. Here is where you become concerned with "what other people think" or where you rebel against social conventions. Here is where you could become a socially conscious humanitarian or a partygoing social butterfly. It's where you look to others to stimulate you and discover your kinship to the rest of humanity. The sign on this house can help you understand what you gain and lose from friendships.

The Twelfth House: Home of Pisces and Neptune

The twelfth house is where the boundaries between yourself and others become blurred, and you become selfless. Old-fashioned astrologers used to put a rather negative spin on this house, calling it the "house of self-undoing." When we "undo ourselves," we surrender control, boundaries, limits, and rules. But instead of being self-undoing, the twelfth house can be a place of great creativity and talent. It is the place where you can tap into the collective unconscious, where your imagination is limitless.

In your trip around the zodiac, you've gone from the "I" of self-assertion in the first house to the final house symbolizing the dissolution that happens before rebirth. It's where accumulated experiences are processed in the unconscious. Spiritually oriented astrologers look to this house for evidence of past lives and karma. Places where we go for solitude or to do spiritual or reparatory work such as retreats, religious institutions, and hospitals belong to the twelfth house. Here is also where we withdraw from society voluntarily or involuntarily, put to prison because of antisocial activity. Selfless giving through charitable acts is part of this house, as is helpless receiving or dependence on charity.

In your daily life, the twelfth house reveals your deepest intimacies, your best-kept secrets, especially those you hide from yourself and keep repressed deep in the unconscious. It is where we surrender a sense of a separate self to a deep feeling of wholeness, such as selfless service in religion or any activity that involves merging with the greater whole. Many sports stars have important planets in the twelfth house that enable them to play in the "zone," finding an inner, almost mystical, strength that transcends their limits.

Who's Home in Your Houses?

Houses are stronger or weaker depending on how many planets are inhabiting them. If there are many planets in a given house, it follows that the activities of that house will be especially important in your life. If the planet that rules the house is also located there, this too adds power to the house.

In the next chapter we will visit the planets.

CHAPTER 4

The Guide to Your Galaxy: Visit All Your Planets

Your personal galaxy includes nine other planets besides the sun (the moon is also regarded as a "planet"). Each planet represents a basic force in your life, and the sign where it is placed represents how this force will manifest. Visit all your planets, not just your sun sign, for a complete picture of your astrological personality.

It may be easiest to imagine the planet as a person with a choice of twelve different roles to play. In some roles the planet will be more outgoing and aggressive; in other roles the more thoughtful or spiritual side of its nature will be expressed.

Whether a planet will play a starring or supporting role depends on its position in your horoscope. A planet in the first house, especially one that's close to your rising sign, is sure to be a featured player. Planets that are grouped together usually operate like a team, playing off each other, rather than expressing their energy singularly. A planet that stands alone, away from the others, is usually outstanding and sometimes calls the shots.

Each planet has two signs where it is especially at home. These are called its *dignities*. The most favorable place for a planet is in the sign or signs it rules; the next best place is in a sign where it is *exalted,* or especially harmonious. On the other hand, there are places in the horoscope where a planet has to work harder to play its role. These places are called the planets *detriment* and *fall.* The sign opposite a planet's rulership, which embodies the opposite area of life, is its *detriment.* The sign opposite its exaltation is its *fall.* Though these terms may suggest unfortunate circumstances for the planet, that is not always true. In fact, a planet that is debilitated can actually be more complete because it must stretch itself to meet the challenges of living in a more difficult sign. Like world leaders who've had to struggle for greatness, this planet may actually develop great strength and character.

Here's a list of the best places for each planet to be. Note that, as new planets were discovered, they replaced the traditional rulers of signs which best complemented their energies.

ARIES—Mars
TAURUS—Venus, in its most sensual form
GEMINI—Mercury, in its communicative role
CANCER—the moon
LEO—the sun
VIRGO—also Mercury, this time in its more critical capacity
LIBRA—also Venus, in its more aesthetic, judgmental form
SCORPIO—Pluto, replacing Mars, the sign's original ruler
SAGITTARIUS—Jupiter
CAPRICORN—Saturn
AQUARIUS—Uranus, replacing Saturn, its original ruler
PISCES—Neptune, replacing Jupiter, its original ruler

A person who has many planets in exalted signs is lucky indeed, for here is where the planet can accomplish the most and be its most influential and creative.

SUN—exalted in Aries, where its energy creates action
MOON—exalted in Taurus, where instincts and reactions operate on a highly creative level
MERCURY—exalted in Aquarius, where it can reach analytical heights
VENUS—exalted in Pisces, a sign whose sensitivity encourages love and creativity
MARS—exalted in Capricorn, a sign that puts energy to work productively
JUPITER—exalted in Cancer, where it encourages nurturing and growth

SATURN—at home in Libra, where it steadies the scales of justice and promotes balanced, responsible judgment

URANUS—powerful in Scorpio, where it promotes transformation

NEPTUNE—especially favored in Cancer, where it gains the security to transcend to a higher state

PLUTO—exalted in Pisces, where it dissolves the old cycle to make way for transition to the new

The Sun Is Always Top of the List

Your sun sign is the part of you that shines brightest. Then other planets add special coloration that sets you apart from other members of your sign. If you know a person's sun sign, you already know some useful generic qualities. But when you know all the planets, you have a much more accurate profile and can predict more accurately how that individual will act. The sun is just one card in your hand. When you know the other planets, you can really play to win!

Since the sun is always the first consideration, it is important to treat it as the star of the show. It is your conscious ego. It is always center stage, even when sharing a house or a sign with several other planets. This is why sun sign astrology works for so many people. In chart interpretations, the sun can also play the parental role.

The sun rules the sign of Leo, gaining strength through the pride, dignity, and confidence of this fixed, fiery personality. It is exalted in "me-first" Aries. In its detriment, Aquarius, the sun ego is strengthened through group participation and social consciousness rather than through self-centeredness. Note how many Aquarius people are involved in politics, social work, public life, and follow the demands of their sun sign to be spokesperson for a group. In its fall, Libra, the sun needs the strength of a partner—an "other"—to enhance balance and self-expression.

Like your sun sign, each of the other nine planet's personalities is colored by the sign it is passing through at the time. For example, Mercury, the planet that rules the way you communicate, will express itself in a dynamic, headstrong Aries way if it is passing through the sign of Aries when you were born. You will communicate in a much different way if it is passing through the slower, more patient sign of Taurus. And so on through the list. Here's a rundown of the planets and how they behave in every sign.

The Moon Expresses Your Inner Feelings

The moon can teach you about the inner side of yourself, your needs and secrets, as well as those of others. It is your most personal planet—the receptive, reflective, female, nurturing side of you. And it reflects who you were nurtured by—the "mother" or mother figure in your chart. In a man's chart, the moon position also describes his female, receptive, emotional side as well as the woman in his life who will have the deepest effect. (Venus reveals the kind of woman who attracts him physically.)

The sign the moon was passing through at your birth reflects your instinctive emotional nature, what appeals to you subconsciously. Since accurate moon tables are too extensive for this book, check through these descriptions to find the moon sign that feels most familiar. Or, better yet, have your chart calculated by a computer service to get your accurate moon placement.

The moon rules maternal Cancer and is exalted in Taurus—both comforting, home-loving signs where the natural emotional energies of the moon are easily and productively expressed. But when the moon is in the opposite signs—in its Capricorn detriment and its Scorpio fall—it leaves the comfortable nest and deals with emotional issues of power and achievement in the outside world. Those of you with the moon in these signs will find your emotional role more challenging in life.

Moon in Aries

You are an idealistic, impetuous person who falls in and out of love easily. This placement makes you both independent and ardent. You love a challenge, but could cool once your quarry is captured. You should cultivate patience and tolerance. Otherwise, you might gravitate toward those who treat you rough, just for the sake of challenge and excitement.

Moon in Taurus

You are a sentimental soul who is very fond of the good life. You gravitate toward solid, secure relationships. You like displays of affection and creature comforts—all the tangible trappings of a cozy, safe, calm atmosphere. You are sensual and steady emotionally, but very stubborn and determined. You can't be pushed and tend to dislike changes. You should make an effort to broaden your horizons and to take a risk sometimes.

Moon in Gemini

You crave mental stimulation and variety in life, which you usually get through an ever-varied social life or the excitement of flirtation, or multiple professional involvements— or all of these. You may marry more than once and have a rather chaotic emotional life due to your difficulty with commitment and settling down. Be sure to find a partner who is as outgoing as you are. You will have to learn at some point to focus your energies because you tend to be somewhat fragmented—to do two things at once, to have two homes, even to have two lovers. If you can find a creative way to express your many-faceted nature, you'll be ahead of the game.

Moon in Cancer

This is the most powerful lunar position. It is sure to make a deep imprint on your character. Your needs are very much associated with your reaction to the needs of others. You are very sensitive and self-protective, though some of you may mask this with a hard shell. This placement also gives an excellent memory, keen intuition, and an uncanny ability to perceive the needs of others. All of the lunar phases will affect you, especially full moons and eclipses, so you would do well to mark them on your calendar. Because you're happiest at home, you may work at home or turn your office into a second home where you can nurture and comfort people. (You may tend to "mother the world.") With natural psychic and intuitive ability, you might be drawn to occult work in some way. Or you may get professionally involved with providing food and shelter to others.

Moon in Leo

This warm, passionate moon takes everything to heart. You are attracted to all that is noble, generous, and aristocratic in life (and may be a bit of a snob). You have an innate ability to take command emotionally, but you do need strong support, loyalty, and loud applause from those you love. You are possessive of your loved ones and your turf, and will roar if anyone threatens to take over your territory.

Moon in Virgo

You are rather cool until you decide if others measure up. But once someone or something meets your ideal standards, you hold up your end of the arrangement perfectly. You may, in fact, drive yourself too hard to attain some notion of perfection. Try to be a bit easier on yourself and others. Don't always act the censor! You love to be the teacher. You are drawn to situations where you can change others for the better, but sometimes you must learn to accept others for what they are. Enjoy what you have!

Moon in Libra

A partnership-oriented moon, you may find it difficult to be alone or to do things alone. After you have learned emotional balance by leaning on yourself first, you can have excellent relationships. It is best for you to avoid extremes, which set your scales swinging and can make your love life precarious. You thrive in a rather conservative, traditional, romantic relationship where you receive attention and flattery—but not possessiveness—from your partner. You'll be your most charming in an elegant, harmonious atmosphere.

Moon in Scorpio

This is a moon that enjoys and responds to intense, passionate feelings. You may go to extremes and have a very dramatic emotional life, full of ardor, suspicion, jealousy, and obsession. It would be much healthier to channel your need for power and control into meaningful work. This is a good position for anyone in the fields of medicine, police work, research, the occult, psychoanalysis, or intuitive work, because life-and-death situations don't faze you. However, you do take personal disappointments very hard.

Moon in Sagittarius

You take life's ups and downs with good humor and the proverbial grain of salt. You'll love 'em and leave 'em, taking off on a great adventure at a moment's notice. "Born free" could be your slogan. Attracted by the exotic, you have wanderlust mentally and physically. You may be too much in search of new mental and spiritual stimulation to ever settle down.

Moon in Capricorn

Are you ever accused of being too cool and calculating? You have an earthy side, but you take prestige and position very seriously. Your strong drive to succeed extends to your romantic life where you will be devoted to improving your lifestyle and rising to the top. A structured situation where you can advance methodically makes you feel wonderfully secure. You may be attracted to someone older or very much younger or from a different social world. It may be difficult to look at the lighter side of emotional relationships. However, the "up" side of this moon in the sign of its detriment is that you tend to be very dutiful and responsible to those you care for.

Moon in Aquarius

You are a people collector with many friends of all backgrounds. You are happiest surrounded by people and may feel uneasy when left alone. Though you usually stay friends with lovers, intense emotions and demanding one-on-one relationships turn you off. You don't like anything to be too rigid or scheduled. Though tolerant and understanding, you can be emotionally unpredictable and may opt for an unconventional love life. With plenty of space, you will be able to sustain relationships with liberal, freedom-loving types.

Moon in Pisces

You are very responsive and empathetic to others, especially if they have problems or are the underdog. (Be on guard against attracting too many people with sob stories!) You'll be happiest if you can express your creative imagination in the arts or in the spiritual or healing professions. Because you may tend to escape in fantasies or overreact to the moods of others, you need an emotional anchor to help you keep a firm foothold in reality. Steer clear of too much escapism (especially in alcohol) or reclusiveness. Places near water soothe your moods. Working in a field that gives you emotional variety will also help you be productive.

Close Neighbors: Mercury, Venus, and Mars

These planets work in your immediate personal life.

Mercury affects how you communicate and how your mental processes work. Are you a quick study who grasps information rapidly? Or do you learn more slowly and thoroughly? How is your concentration? Can you express yourself easily? Are you a good writer? All these questions can be answered by your Mercury placement.

Venus shows what you react to. What turns you on? What appeals to you aesthetically? Are you charming to others? Are you attractive to look at? Your taste, your refinement, your sense of balance and proportion are all Venus-ruled.

Mars is your outgoing energy, your drive and ambition. Do you reach out for new adventures? Are you assertive? Are you motivated? Self-confident? Hot-tempered? How you channel your energy and drive is revealed by your Mars placement.

Mercury Says It All

Since Mercury never travels far from the sun, read Mercury in your sun sign, then the sign preceding and following it. Then decide which reflects the way your mind works.

Mercury in Aries

Your mind is very active and assertive. You never hesitate to say what you think, never shy away from a battle. In fact, you may relish a verbal confrontation. Tact is not your strong point, so you may have to learn not to trip over your tongue.

Mercury in Taurus

Though you may be a slow learner, you have good concentration and mental stamina. You want to make your ideas really happen. You'll attack a problem methodically and consider every angle thoroughly, never jumping to conclusions. You'll stick with a subject until you master it.

Mercury in Gemini

You are a wonderful communicator with great facility for expressing yourself both verbally and in writing. You talk and talk, and you love gathering all kinds of information. You probably finish other people's sentences, and talk with hand gestures. You can talk to anybody anytime . . . and probably have phone and e-mail bills to prove it. You read anything from sci-fi to Shakespeare, and might need an extra room just for your book collection. Though you learn fast, you may lack focus and discipline. Watch a tendency to jump from subject to subject.

Mercury in Cancer

You rely on intuition more than logic. Your mental processes are usually colored by your emotions, so you may seem shy or hesitant to voice your opinions. However, this placement gives you the advantage of great imagination and empathy in the way you communicate with others.

Mercury in Leo

You are enthusiastic and very dramatic in the way you express yourself. You like to hold the attention of groups, and could be a great public speaker. Your mind thinks big, so you prefer to deal with the overall picture rather than with the details.

Mercury in Virgo

This is one of the best places for Mercury. It should give you critical ability, attention to details, and thorough analysis. Your mind focuses on the practical side of things. This type of thinking is very well suited to being a teacher or editor.

Mercury in Libra

You're either a born diplomat who smoothes over ruffled feathers or a talented debater. However, since you're forever weighing the pros and cons of a situation, you may vacillate when making decisions.

Mercury in Scorpio

This is an investigative mind that stops at nothing to get the answers. You may have a sarcastic, stinging wit or a gift for the cutting remark. There's always a grain of truth to your verbal sallies, thanks to your penetrating insight.

Mercury in Sagittarius

You are a supersalesman with a tendency to expound. Though you are very broad-minded, you can be dogmatic when it comes to telling others what's good for them. You won't hesitate to tell the truth as you see it, so watch a tendency toward tactlessness. On the plus side, you have a great sense of humor. This position of Mercury is often considered by astrologers to be at a disadvantage because Sagittarius opposes Gemini, the sign Mercury rules, and squares off with Virgo, another Mercury-ruled sign. What often happens is that Mercury in Sagittarius oversteps its bounds and loses sight of the facts in a situation. Do a reality check before making promises you may not be able to deliver.

Mercury in Capricorn

This placement endows good mental discipline. You have a love of learning and a very orderly approach to your subjects. You will patiently plod through the facts and figures until you have mastered the tasks. You grasp structured situations easily, but may be short on creativity.

Mercury in Aquarius

An independent, original thinker, you'll have more cutting-edge ideas than the average person. You will be quick to check out any unusual opportunities. Your opinions are so well-researched and grounded that once your mind is made up, it is difficult to change.

Mercury in Pisces

You have the psychic and intuitive mind of a natural poet. Learn to make use of your creative imagination. You may think in terms of helping others, but check a tendency to be vague and forgetful of details.

Venus Relates

Venus tells how you relate to others and to your environment. It shows where you receive pleasure, what you love to do. Find your Venus placement from the charts at the end of this chapter (pages 78–85) by looking for the year of your birth in the left-hand column. Then follow the line of that year across the page until you reach the time period of your birthday. The sign heading that column will be your Venus. If you were born on a day when Venus was changing signs, check the signs preceding or following that day to determine if that sign feels more like your Venus nature.

Venus in Aries

You can't stand to be bored, confined, or ordered around. But a good challenge, maybe even a rousing row, turns you on. Confess—don't you pick a fight now and then just to get someone stirred up? You're attracted by the chase, not the catch, which could cause some problems in your love life if the object of your affection becomes too attainable. You like to wear red and be first with the latest fashion. You'll spot a trend before anyone else.

Venus in Taurus

All your senses work in high gear. You love to be surrounded by glorious tastes, smells, textures, sounds, and visuals. Austerity is not for you! Neither is being rushed. You like time to enjoy your pleasures. Soothing surroundings with plenty of creature comforts are your cup of tea. You like to feel secure in your nest, with no sudden jolts or surprises. You like familiar objects—in fact, you may hate to let anything or anyone go.

Venus in Gemini

You are a lively, sparkling personality who thrives in a situation that affords a constant variety and a frequent change of scenery. A varied social life is important to you, with plenty of stimulation and a chance to engage in some light flirtation. Commitment may be difficult, because playing the field is so much fun.

Venus in Cancer

An atmosphere where you feel protected, coddled, and mothered is best for you. You love to be surrounded by children in a cozy, homelike situation. You are attracted to those who are tender and nurturing, who make you feel secure and well provided for. You may be quite secretive about your emotional life, or attracted to clandestine relationships.

Venus in Leo

First-class attention in large doses turns you on, and so does the glitter of real gold and the flash of mirrors. You like to feel like a star at all times, surrounded by your admiring audience. The side effect is that you may be attracted to flatterers and tinsel, while the real gold requires some digging.

Venus in Virgo

Everything neatly in its place? On the surface, you are attracted to an atmosphere where everything is in perfect order, but underneath are some basic, earthy urges. You are attracted to those who appeal to your need to teach, to be of service, or to play out a Pygmalion fantasy. You are at your best when you are busy doing something useful.

Venus in Libra

Elegance and harmony are your key words. You can't abide an atmosphere of contention. Your taste tends toward the classic, with light harmonies of color—nothing clashing, trendy, or outrageous. You love doing things with a partner, and should be careful to pick one who is decisive but patient enough to let you weigh the pros and cons. And steer clear of argumentative types!

Venus in Scorpio

Hidden mysteries intrigue you. In fact, anything that is too open and aboveboard is a bit of a bore. You surely have a stack of whodunits by the bed, along with an erotic magazine or two. You like to solve puzzles, and may also be fascinated with the occult, crime, or scientific research. Intense, all-or-nothing situations add spice to your life, and you love to ferret out the secrets of others. But you could get burned by your flair for living dangerously. The color black, spicy food, dark wood furniture, and heady perfume all get you in the right mood.

Venus in Sagittarius

If you are not actually a world traveler, your surroundings are sure to reflect your love of faraway places. You like a casual outdoor atmosphere and a dog or two to pet. There should be plenty of room for athletic equipment and suitcases. You're attracted to kindred souls who love to travel and who share your freedom-loving philosophy of life. Athletics and spiritual or New Age pursuits could be other interests.

Venus in Capricorn

No fly-by-night relationships for you! You want substance in life, and you are attracted to whatever will help you get where you are going. Status objects turn you on. And so do those who have a serious, responsible, businesslike approach as well as those who remind you of a beloved parent. It is characteristic of this placement to be attracted to someone of a different generation. Antiques, traditional clothing, and dignified behavior favor you.

Venus in Aquarius

This Venus wants to make friends more than to make love. You like to be in a group, particularly one pushing a worthy cause. You feel quite at home surrounded by people, remaining detached from any intense commitment. Original ideas and unpredictable people fascinate you. You don't like everything to be planned out in advance, preferring spontaneity and delightful surprises.

Venus in Pisces

This Venus loves to give of yourself, and you find plenty of takers. Stray animals and people appeal to your heart and your pocketbook, but be careful to look at their motives realistically once in a while. You are extremely vulnerable to sob stories of all kinds. Fantasy, theater, and psychic or spiritual activities also speak to you.

Mars Moves and Shakes

Mars is the mover and shaker in your life. It shows how you pursue your goals, whether you have energy to burn or proceed in a slow, steady pace. It will also show how you get angry. Do you explode or do a slow burn or hold everything inside, then get revenge later?

To find your Mars, turn to the charts on pages 86–94. Then find your birth year in the left-hand column and trace the line across horizontally until you come to the column headed by the month of your birth. There you will find an abbreviation of your Mars sign. If the description of your Mars sign doesn't ring true, read the description of the sign preceding and following it. You may have been born on a day when Mars was changing signs, and your Mars would then be in the adjacent sign.

Mars in Aries

In the sign it rules, Mars shows its brilliant fiery nature. You have an explosive temper and can be quite impatient. On the other hand, you have tremendous courage, energy, and drive. You'll let nothing stand in your way as you race to be first! Obstacles are met head-on and broken through by force. However, those that require patience and persistence can have you exploding in rage. You're a great starter, but not necessarily around for the finish.

Mars in Taurus

Slow, steady, concentrated energy gives you staying power. You have great stamina, and you never give up. Your tactic is to wear away obstacles with your persistence. Often you come out a winner because you've had the patience to hang in there. When angered, you do a slow burn.

Mars in Gemini

You can't sit still for long. This Mars craves variety. You often have two or more things going on at once—it's all an amusing game to you. Your life can get very complicated, but that only adds spice and stimulation. What drives you into a nervous, hyper state? Boredom, sameness, routine, and confinement. You can do wonderful things with your hands, and you have a way with words.

Mars in Cancer

You rarely attack head-on. Instead, you'll keep things to yourself, make plans in secret, and always cover your actions. This might be interpreted by some as manipulative, but you are only being self-protective. You get furious when anyone knows too much about you. But you do like to know all about others. Your mothering and feeding instincts can be put to good use if you work in the food, hotel, or child-care businesses. You may have to overcome your fragile sense of security, which prompts you not to take risks and to get physically upset when criticized. Don't take things so personally!

Mars in Leo

You have a very dominant personality that takes center stage. Modesty is not one of your traits, nor is taking a backseat. You prefer giving the orders, and have been known to make a dramatic scene if they are not obeyed. Properly used, this Mars confers leadership ability, endurance, and courage.

Mars in Virgo

You are the faultfinder of the zodiac. You notice every detail. Mistakes of any kind make you very nervous. You may worry, even if everything is going smoothly. You may not express your anger directly, but you sure can nag. You have definite likes and dislikes, and you are sure you can do the job better than anyone else. You are certainly more industrious and detail-oriented than other signs. Your Mars energy is often most positively expressed in some kind of teaching role.

Mars in Libra

This Mars will have a passion for beauty, justice, and art. Generally, you will avoid confrontations at all costs. You prefer to spend your energy finding diplomatic solutions or weighing pros and cons. Your other techniques are passive aggression or exercising your well-known charm to get people to do what you want.

Mars in Scorpio

This is a powerful placement, so intense that it demands careful channeling into worthwhile activities. Otherwise, you could become obsessed with your sexuality or might use your need for power and control to manipulate others. You are strong-willed, shrewd, and very private about your affairs, and you'll usually have a secret agenda behind your actions. Your great stamina, focus, and discipline would be excellent assets for careers in the military or medical fields, especially research or surgery. When angry, you don't get mad—you get even!

Mars in Sagittarius

This expansive Mars often propels people into sales, travel, athletics, or philosophy. Your energies function well when you are on the move. You have a hot temper, and are inclined to say what you think before you consider the consequences. You shoot for high goals—and talk endlessly about them—but you may be weak on groundwork. This Mars needs a solid foundation. Watch a tendency to take unnecessary risks.

Mars in Capricorn

This is an ambitious Mars with an excellent sense of timing. You have an eye for those who can be of use to you, and you may dismiss people ruthlessly when you're angry. But you drive yourself hard and deliver full value. This is a good placement for an executive. You'll aim for status and a high material position in life, and you'll keep climbing despite the odds. A great Mars to have!

Mars in Aquarius

This is the most rebellious Mars. You seem to have a drive to assert yourself against the status quo. You may enjoy provoking people, shocking them out of traditional views. Or this placement could express itself in an offbeat sex life. Somehow you often find yourself in unconventional situations. You enjoy being a leader of an active group, which pursues forward-looking studies, politics, or goals.

Mars in Pisces

This Mars is a good actor who knows just how to appeal to the sympathies of others. You create and project wonderful fantasies, or you use your sensitive antennae to crusade for those less fortunate. You get what you want through creating a veil of illusion and glamour. This is a good Mars for someone in the creative fields—a dancer, performer, photographer, or someone in motion pictures. Many famous film stars have this placement. Watch a tendency to manipulate by making others feel sorry for you.

Jupiter Gives You the Breaks

Jupiter is the planet in your horoscope that makes you want *more*. This big, bright, swirling mass of gases is associated with abundance, prosperity, and the kind of windfall you get without too much hard work. You're optimistic under Jupiter's influence, when anything seems possible. You'll travel, expand your mind with higher education, and publish to share your knowledge widely. On the other hand, Jupiter's influence is neither discriminating nor disciplined. It represents the principle of growth without judgment. Therefore, if not kept in check, it could result in extravagance, weight gain, laziness, and carelessness.

Be sure to look up your Jupiter in the tables in this book. When the current position of Jupiter is favorable, you may get that lucky break. This is a great time to try new things, take risks, travel, or get more education. Opportunities seem to open up easily, so take advantage of them.

Once a year, Jupiter changes signs. That means you are due for an expansive time every twelve years, when Jupiter travels through your sun sign. You'll also have "up" periods every four years, when Jupiter is in the same element as your sun sign.

Jupiter in Aries

You are the soul of enthusiasm and optimism. Your luckiest times are when you are getting started on an exciting project or selling an idea that you really believe in. You may have to watch a tendency to be arrogant with those who do not share your enthusiasm. You follow your impulses, often ignoring budget or other commonsense limitations. To produce real, solid benefits, you'll need patience and follow-through wherever this Jupiter falls in your horoscope.

Jupiter in Taurus

You'll spend on beautiful material things, especially those that come from nature—items made of rare woods, natural fabrics, or precious gems, for instance. You can't have too much comfort or too many sensual pleasures. Watch a tendency to overindulge in good food, or to overpamper yourself with nothing but the best. Spartan living is not for you! You may be especially lucky in matters of real estate.

Jupiter in Gemini

You are the great talker of the zodiac, and you may be a great writer, too. But restlessness could be your weak point. You jump around, talk too much, and could be a jack-of-all-trades. Keeping a secret is especially difficult, so you'll also have to watch a tendency to spill the beans. Since you love to be at the center of a beehive of activity, you'll have a vibrant social life. Your best opportunities will come through your talent for language—speaking, writing, communicating, and selling.

Jupiter in Cancer

You are luckiest in situations where you can find emotional closeness or deal with basic security needs such as food, nurturing, or shelter. You may be a great collector. Or you may simply love to accumulate things—you are the one who stashes things away for a rainy day. You probably have a very good memory and love children. In fact, you may have many children to care for. The food, hotel, child-care, and shipping businesses hold good opportunities for you.

Jupiter in Leo

You are a natural showman who loves to live in a larger-than-life way. Yours is a personality full of color that always finds its way into the limelight. You can't have too much attention or applause. Show biz is a natural place for you, and so is any area where you can play to a crowd. Exercising your flair for drama, your natural playfulness, and your romantic nature brings you good fortune. But watch a tendency to be overly extravagant or to monopolize center stage.

Jupiter in Virgo

You actually love those minute details others find boring. To you, they make all the difference between the perfect and the ordinary. You are the fine craftsman who spots every flaw. You expand your awareness by finding the most efficient methods and by being of service to others. Many of you will be drawn to medical or teaching fields. You'll also have luck in publishing, crafts, nutrition, and service professions. Watch out for a tendency to overwork.

Jupiter in Libra

This is an other-directed Jupiter that develops best with a partner. The stimulation of others helps you grow. You are also most comfortable in harmonious, beautiful situations, and you work well with artistic people. You have a great sense of fair play and an ability to evaluate the pros and cons of a situation. You usually prefer to play the role of diplomat rather than adversary.

Jupiter in Scorpio

You love the feeling of power and control, of taking things to their limit. You can't resist a mystery. Your shrewd, penetrating mind sees right through to the heart of most situations and people. You have luck in work that provides for solutions to matters of life and death. You may be drawn to undercover work, behind-the-scenes intrigue, psychotherapy, the occult, and sex-related ventures. Your challenge will be to develop a sense of moderation and tolerance for other beliefs. This Jupiter can be fanatical. You may have luck in handling other people's money—insurance, taxes, and inheritance can bring you a windfall.

Jupiter in Sagittarius

Independent, outgoing, and idealistic, you'll shoot for the stars. This Jupiter compels you to travel far and wide, both physically and mentally, via higher education. You may have luck while traveling in an exotic place. You also have luck with outdoor ventures, exercise, and animals, particularly horses. Since you tend to be very open about your opinions, watch a tendency to be tactless and to exaggerate. Instead, use your wonderful sense of humor to make your point.

Jupiter in Capricorn

Jupiter is much more restrained in Capricorn, the sign of rules and authority. Here, Jupiter can make you overwork and heighten any ambition or sense of duty you may have. You'll expand in areas that advance your position, putting you farther up the social or corporate ladder. You are lucky working within the establishment in a very structured situation where you can show off your ability to organize and reap rewards for your hard work.

Jupiter in Aquarius

This is another freedom-loving Jupiter, with great tolerance and originality. You are at your best when you are working for a humanitarian cause and in the company of many supporters. This is a good Jupiter for a political career. You'll relate to all kinds of people on all social levels. You have an abundance of original ideas, but you are best off away from routine and any situation that imposes rigid rules. You need mental stimulation!

Jupiter in Pisces

You are a giver whose feelings and pocketbook are easily touched by others, so choose your companions with care. You could be the original sucker for a hard-luck story. Better find a worthy hospital or a charity that will appreciate your selfless support. You have a great creative imagination. You may attract good fortune in fields related to oil, perfume, pharmaceuticals, petroleum, dance, footwear, and alcohol. But beware of overindulgence in alcohol—focus on a creative outlet instead.

Saturn Puts on the Brakes

Jupiter speeds you up with *lucky breaks,* then along comes Saturn to slow you down with the *disciplinary brakes.* Saturn has unfairly been called a malefic planet, one of the bad guys of the zodiac. On the contrary, Saturn is one of our best friends, the kind who tells you what you need to hear even if it's not good news. Under a Saturn transit, we grow up, take responsibility for our lives, and emerge from whatever test this planet has in store as far wiser, more capable, and mature human beings.

When Saturn hits a critical point in your horoscope, you can count on an experience that will make you slow up, pull back, and reexamine your life. It is a call to eliminate what is not working and to shape up. By the end of its twenty-eight-year trip around the zodiac, Saturn will have tested you in all areas of your life. The major tests happen in seven-year cycles, when Saturn passes over the *angles* of your chart—your rising sign, midheaven, descendant, and nadir. This is when the real life-changing experiences happen. But you are also in for a testing period whenever Saturn passes a *planet* in your chart or stresses that planet from a distance. Therefore, it is useful to check your planetary positions with the timetable of Saturn to prepare in advance, or at least to brace yourself.

When Saturn returns to its location at the time of your birth, at approximately age twenty-eight, you'll have your first Saturn return. At this time, a person usually takes stock or settles down to find his or her mission in life and assumes full adult duties and responsibilities.

Another way Saturn helps us is to reveal the karmic lessons from previous lives and to give us the chance to overcome them. So look at Saturn's challenges as much-needed opportunities for self-improvement. Under a Jupiter influence, you'll have more fun. But Saturn gives you solid, long-lasting results.

Look up your natal Saturn in the tables in this book for clues on where you need work.

Saturn in Aries

Saturn here puts the brakes on Aries natural drive and enthusiasm. You don't let anyone push you around, and you know what's best for yourself. Following orders is not your strong point, and neither is diplomacy. You tend to be quick to go on the offensive in relationships, attacking first, before anyone attacks you. Because no one quite lives up to your standards, you often wind up doing everything yourself. You'll have to learn to cooperate and tone down self-centeredness.

Saturn in Taurus

A big issue is getting control of the cash flow. There will be lean periods that can be frightening, but you have the patience and endurance to stick them out and the methodical drive to prosper in the end. Learn to take a philosophical attitude, like Ben Franklin who also had this placement and who said, "A penny saved is a penny earned."

Saturn in Gemini

You are a serious student of life, but you may have difficulty communicating or sharing your knowledge. You may be shy, speak slowly, or have fears about communicating, like Eleanor Roosevelt. You dwell in the realms of science, theory, or abstract analysis—even when you are dealing with the emotions, like Sigmund Freud who also had this placement.

Saturn in Cancer

Your tests come with establishing a secure emotional base. In doing so, you may have to deal with some very basic fears centering on your early home environment. Most of your Saturn tests will have emotional roots in those early childhood experiences. You may have difficulty remaining objective in terms of what you try to achieve. So it will be especially important for you to deal with negative feelings such as guilt, paranoia, jealousy, resentment, and suspicion. Galileo and Michelangelo also navigated these murky waters.

Saturn in Leo

This is an authoritarian Saturn—a strict, demanding parent who may deny the pleasure principle in your zeal to see that rules are followed. Though you may feel guilty about taking the spotlight, you are very ambitious and loyal. You have to watch a tendency toward rigidity, also toward overwork and holding back affection. Joseph Kennedy and Billy Graham share this placement.

Saturn in Virgo

This is a cautious, exacting Saturn. You are intensely hard on yourself. Most of all, you give yourself the roughest time with your constant worries about every little detail, often making yourself sick. You may have difficulties setting priorities and getting the job done. Your tests will come in learning tolerance and understanding of others. Charles de Gaulle, Mae West, and Nathaniel Hawthorne had this meticulous Saturn.

Saturn in Libra

Saturn is exalted here, which makes this planet an ally. You may choose very serious, older partners in life, perhaps stemming from a fear of dependency. You need to learn to stand solidly on your own before you commit to another. You are extremely cautious as you deliberate every involvement—with good reason. It is best that you find an occupation that makes good use of your sense of duty and honor. Steer clear of fly-by-night situations. Both Khrushchev and Mao Tse-tung had this placement.

Saturn in Scorpio

You have great staying power. This Saturn tests you in situations involving the control of others. You may feel drawn to some kind of intrigue or undercover work, like J. Edgar Hoover. Or there may be an air of mystery surrounding your life and death, like Marilyn Monroe and Robert Kennedy who both had this placement. There are lessons to be learned from your sexual involvements. Often sex is used for manipulation or is somehow out of the ordinary. The Roman emperor Caligula and the transvestite Christine Jorgensen are extreme cases.

Saturn in Sagittarius

Your challenges and lessons will come from tests of your spiritual and philosophical values, as happened to Martin Luther King and Gandhi. You are high-minded and sincere with this reflective, moral placement. Uncompromising in your ethical standards, you could become a benevolent despot.

Saturn in Capricorn

With the help of Saturn at maximum strength, your judgment will improve with age. And, like Spencer Tracy's screen image, you'll be the gray-haired hero with a strong sense of responsibility. You advance in life slowly but steadily, always with a strong hand at the helm and an eye for the advantageous situation. Like Pat Robertson, you're likely to stand for conservative values. Negatively, you may be a loner, prone to periods of melancholy.

Saturn in Aquarius

Your tests come from relationships with groups. Do you care too much about what others think? Do you feel like an outsider, like Greta Garbo? You may fear being different from others and therefore slight your own unique, forward-looking gifts. Or, like Lord Byron and Howard Hughes, you may take the opposite tack and rebel in the extreme. You can apply discipline to accomplish great humanitarian goals, as Albert Schweitzer did.

Saturn in Pisces

Your fear of the unknown and the irrational may lead you to the safety and protection of an institution. You may go on the run like Jesse James, who had this placement, to avoid looking too deeply inside. Or you might go in the opposite, more positive direction and develop a disciplined psychoanalytic approach, which puts you more in control of your feelings. Some of you will take refuge in work with hospitals, charities, or religious institutions. Queen Victoria, who had this placement, symbolized an era when institutions of all kinds were sustained. Discipline applied to artistic work, especially poetry and dance, or to spiritual work, such as yoga or meditation, might be helpful.

Uranus, Neptune, and Pluto Affect Your Whole Generation

These three planets remain in signs such a long time that a whole generation bears the imprint of the sign. Mass movements, great sweeping changes, fads that characterize a generation, even the issues of the conflicts and wars of the time are influenced by these "outer three" planets. When one of these distant planets changes signs, there is a definite shift in the atmosphere, the feeling of the end of an era.

Since these planets are so far away from the sun—too distant to be seen by the naked eye—they pick up signals from the universe at large. These planetary receivers literally link the sun with distant energies, and then perform a similar function in your horoscope by linking your central character with intuitive, spiritual, transformative forces from the cosmos. Each planet has a special domain, and will reflect this in the area of your chart where it falls.

Uranus Wakes You Up

There is nothing ordinary about this quirky green planet that seems to be traveling on its side, surrounded by a swarm of moons. Is it any wonder that astrologers assigned it to Aquarius, the most eccentric and gregarious sign? Uranus seems to wend its way around the sun, marching to its own tune.

Significantly, Uranus follows Saturn, the planet of limitations and structures. Often we get caught up in the structures we have created to give ourselves a sense of security. However, if we lose contact with our spiritual roots, then Uranus is likely to jolt us out of our comfortable rut and wake us up.

Uranus energy is electrical, happening in sudden flashes. It is not influenced by karma or past events, nor does it regard tradition, sex, or sentiment. The Uranian key words are surprise and awakening. Suddenly, there's that flash of inspiration, that bright idea, that totally new approach to revolutionize whatever scheme you were undertaking. A Uranus event takes you by surprise; it happens from out of the blue, for better or for worse. The Uranus place in your life is where you awaken and become your own person, leaving the structures of Saturn behind. And it is probably the most unconventional place in your chart.

Look up the sign of Uranus at the time of your birth and see where you follow your own tune.

Uranus in Aries

Birth Dates:
    March 31, 1927–November 4, 1927
    January 13, 1928–June 6, 1934
    October 10, 1934–March 28, 1935

Your generation is original, creative, pioneering. It developed the computer, the airplane, and the cyclotron. You let nothing hold you back from exploring the unknown, and you have a powerful mixture of fire and electricity behind you. Women of your generation were among the first to be liberated. You were the unforgettable style-setters. You have a surprise in store for everyone. Like Yoko Ono, Grace Kelly, and Jacqueline Onassis, your life may be jolted by sudden and violent changes.

Uranus in Taurus

Birth Dates:
    June 6, 1934–October 10, 1934
    March 28, 1935–August 7, 1941
    October 5, 1941–May 15, 1942

World War II began during your generation. You are probably self-employed or would like to be. You have original ideas about making money, and you brace yourself for sudden changes of fortune. This Uranus can cause shake-ups, particularly in finances, but it can also make you a born entrepreneur.

Uranus in Gemini

Birth Dates:
August 7, 1941–October 5, 1941
May 15, 1942–August 30, 1948
November 12, 1948–June 10, 1949

You were the first children to be influenced by television. Now, in your adult years, your generation stocks up on answering machines, cell phones, computers, and fax machines—any new way you can communicate. You have an inquiring mind, but your interests may be rather short-lived. This Uranus can be easily fragmented if there is no structure and focus.

Uranus in Cancer

Birth Dates:
August 30, 1948–November 12, 1948
June 10, 1949–August 24, 1955
January 28, 1956–June 10, 1956

This generation came at a time when divorce was becoming commonplace, so your home image is unconventional. You may have an unusual relationship with your parents; you may have come from a broken home or an unconventional one. You'll have unorthodox ideas about parenting, intimacy, food, and shelter. You may also be interested in dreams, psychic phenomena, and memory work.

Uranus in Leo

Birth Dates:
August 24, 1955–January 28, 1956
June 10, 1956–November 1, 1961
January 10, 1962–August 10, 1962

This generation understood how to use electronic media. Many of your group are now leaders in the high-tech industries, and you also understand how to use the new media to promote yourself. Like Isadora Duncan, you may have a very eccentric kind of charisma and a life that is sparked by unusual love affairs. Your children, too, may have traits that are out of the ordinary. Where this planet falls in your chart, you'll have a love of freedom, be a bit of an egomaniac, and show the full force of your personality in a unique way, like tennis great Martina Navratilova.

Uranus in Virgo

Birth Dates:
November 1, 1961–January 10, 1962
August 10, 1962–September 28, 1968
May 20, 1969–June 24, 1969

You'll have highly individual work methods. Many of you will be finding newer, more practical ways to use computers. Like Einstein, who had this placement, you'll break the rules brilliantly. Your generation came at a time of student rebellions, the civil rights movement, and the general acceptance of health foods. Chances are, you're concerned about pollution and cleaning up the environment. You may also be involved with nontraditional healing methods. Heavyweight champ Mike Tyson has this placement.

Uranus in Libra

Birth Dates:
  September 28, 1968–May 20, 1969
  June 24, 1969–November 21, 1974
  May 1, 1975–September 8, 1975

Your generation will be always changing partners. Born during the era of women's liberation, you may have come from a broken home and have no clear image of what a marriage entails. There will be many sudden splits and experiments before you settle down. Your generation will be much involved in legal and political reforms and in changing artistic and fashion looks.

Uranus in Scorpio

Birth Dates:
  November 21, 1974–May 1, 1975
  September 8, 1975–February 17, 1981
  March 20, 1981–November 16, 1981

Interest in transformation, meditation, and life after death signaled the beginning of New Age consciousness. Your generation recognizes no boundaries, no limits, and no external controls. You'll have new attitudes toward death and dying, psychic phenomena, and the occult. Like Mae West and Casanova, you'll shock 'em sexually, too.

Uranus in Sagittarius

Birth Dates:
  February 17, 1981–March 20, 1981
  November 16, 1981–February 15, 1988
  May 27, 1988–December 2, 1988

Could this generation be the first to travel in outer space? An earlier generation with this placement included Charles Lindbergh and a time when the first Zeppelins and the Wright Brothers were conquering the skies. Uranus here forecasts great discoveries, mind expansion, and long-distance travel. Like Galileo and Martin Luther, those born in these years will generate new theories about the cosmos and man's relation to it.

Uranus in Capricorn

Birth Dates:
  December 20, 1904–January 30, 1912
  September 4, 1912–November 12, 1912
  February 15, 1988–May 27, 1988
  December 2, 1988–April 1, 1995
  June 9, 1995–January 12, 1996

This generation, now growing up, will challenge traditions with the help of electronic gadgets. In these years, we got organized with the help of technology put to practical use. The Internet was born following the great economic boom of the 1990s. Great leaders, who were movers and shakers of history, like Julius Caesar and Henry VIII, were born under this placement.

Uranus in Aquarius

Birth Dates:
  January 30, 1912–September 4, 1912
  November 12, 1912–April 1, 1919
  August 16, 1919–January 22, 1920
  April 1, 1995–June 9, 1995
  January 12, 1996–March 10, 2003
  September 15, 2003–December 30, 2003

The last generation with this placement produced great innovative minds such as Leonard Bernstein and Orson Welles. The next will become another radical breakthrough generation, much concerned with global issues that involve all humanity. Already this is a time of experimentation on every level, when home computers are becoming as ubiquitous as television.

Uranus in Pisces

Birth Dates:
    April 1, 1919–August 16, 1919
    January 22, 1920–March 31, 1927
    November 4, 1927–January 12, 1928
    March 10, 2003–September 15, 2003
    December 30, 2003–May 28, 2010

Uranus moves into Pisces during 2003, ushering in a new generation that will surely spark new intuitions, innovations, and creativity in the arts as well as in the sciences. In the past century, Uranus in Pisces focused attention on the rise of such electronic entertainment as radio and the cinema as well as on the secretiveness of Prohibition. This produced a generation of idealists exemplified by Judy Garland's theme, "Somewhere Over the Rainbow."

Neptune Takes You Out of This World

Under Neptune's influence, you see what you want to see. But Neptune also encourages you to create, to let your fantasies and daydreams run free. Neptune is often maligned as the planet of illusions, drugs, and alcohol where you can't bear to face reality. But it also embodies the energy of glamour, subtlety, mystery, and mysticism. It governs anything that takes you beyond the mundane world, including out-of-body experiences.

Neptune acts to break through and transcend your ordinary perceptions to take you to another level of reality where you experience either confusion or ecstasy. Neptune's force can pull you off course, but only if you allow this to happen. Those who use Neptune wisely can translate their daydreams into poetry, theater, design, or inspired moves in the business world, avoiding the tricky "con artist" side of this planet.

Find your Neptune listed below.

Neptune in Cancer

Birth Dates:
  July 19, 1901–December 25, 1901
  May 21, 1902–September 23, 1914
  December 14, 1914–July 19, 1915
  March 19, 1916–May 2, 1916

Dreams of the homeland, idealistic patriotism, and glamorization of the nurturing assets of women characterized this time. You who were born here have unusual psychic ability and deep insights into basic needs of others.

Neptune in Leo

Birth Dates:
  September 23, 1914–December 14, 1914
  July 19, 1915–March 19, 1916
  May 2, 1916–September 21, 1928
  February 19, 1929–July 24, 1929

Neptune in Leo brought us the glamour and high living of the 1920s and the big spenders of that time. Neptunian temptations of gambling, seduction, theater, and lavish entertaining distracted from the realities of the age. Those born in that generation also made great advances in the arts.

Neptune in Virgo

Birth Dates:
  September 21, 1928–February 19, 1929
  July 24, 1929–October 3, 1942
  April 17, 1943–August 2, 1943

Neptune in Virgo encompassed the Great Depression and World War II. Those born under this placement spread the gospel of health and fitness as they matured in a changing world. This generation's devotion to spending hours at the office inspired the term "workaholic."

Neptune in Libra

Birth Dates:
    October 3, 1942–April 17, 1943
    August 2, 1943–December 24, 1955
    March 12, 1956–October 19, 1956
    June 15, 1957–August 6, 1957

Neptune in Libra was the romantic generation who would later be concerned with relating. As this generation matured, there was a new trend toward marriage and commitment. Racial and sexual equality become important issues, as they redesigned traditional roles to suit modern times.

Neptune in Scorpio

Birth Dates:
    December 24, 1955–March 12, 1956
    October 19, 1956–June 15, 1957
    August 6, 1957–January 4, 1970
    May 3, 1970–November 6, 1970

Neptune in Scorpio brought in a generation that would become interested in transformative power. Born in an era that glamorized sex, drugs, rock and roll, and Eastern religion, they matured in a more sobering time of AIDS, cocaine abuse, and New Age spirituality. As they evolve, they will become active in healing the planet from the results of the abuse of power.

Neptune in Sagittarius

Birth Dates:
    January 4, 1970–May 3, 1970
    November 6, 1970–January 19, 1984
    June 23, 1984–November 21, 1984

Neptune in Sagittarius was the time when space and astronaut travel became a reality. The Neptune influence glamorized new approaches to mysticism, religion, and mind expansion. This generation will take a new approach to spiritual life, with emphasis on visions, mysticism, and clairvoyance.

Neptune in Capricorn

Birth Dates:
  January 19, 1984–June 23, 1984
  November 21, 1984–January 29, 1998

Neptune in Capricorn brought a time when delusions about material power were first glamorized, then dashed on the rocks of reality. It was also a time when the psychic and occult worlds spawned a new category of business enterprise, and sold services on television.

Neptune in Aquarius

Birth Dates:
  January 29, 1998–April 4, 2111

This should continue to be a time of breakthroughs. Here the creative influence of Neptune reaches a universal audience. This is a time of dissolving barriers, of globalization—when we truly become one world.

Pluto Transforms You

Pluto is a mysterious little planet with a strange elliptical orbit that occasionally runs inside the orbit of its neighbor Neptune. Because of its eccentric path, the length of time Pluto stays in any given sign can vary from thirteen to thirty-two years. It covered only seven signs in the last century. Though it is a tiny planet, its influence is great. When Pluto zaps a strategic point in your horoscope, your life changes dramatically.

This little planet is the power behind the scenes. It affects you at deep levels of consciousness, causing events to come to the surface that will transform you and your generation. Nothing escapes, or is sacred, with this probing planet. Its purpose is to wipe out the past so something new can happen. The Pluto place in your horoscope is where you have invisible power (Mars governs the visible power)—where you can transform, heal, and affect the unconscious needs of the masses. Pluto tells lots about how your generation projects power, what makes it seem "cool" to others. And when Pluto changes signs, there's a whole new concept of what's "cool."

Pluto in Gemini

Birth Dates:
    Late 1800s–May 28, 1914

This was a time of mass suggestion and breakthroughs in communications, a time when many brilliant writers such as Ernest Hemingway and F. Scott Fitzgerald were born. Henry Miller, D. H. Lawrence, and James Joyce scandalized society by using explicit sexual images and language in their literature. "Muckraking" journalists exposed corruption. Pluto-ruled Scorpio President Theodore Roosevelt said, "Speak softly, but carry a big stick." This generation had an intense need to communicate and made major breakthroughs in knowledge. A compulsive restlessness and a thirst for a variety of experiences characterized many of this generation.

Pluto in Cancer

Birth Dates:
    May 26, 1914–June 14, 1939

Dictators and mass media arose to wield emotional power over the masses. Women's rights was a popular issue. Deep sentimental feelings, acquisitiveness, and possessiveness characterized these times and people. Most of the great stars of the Hollywood era that embodied the American image were born during this period: Grace Kelly, Esther Williams, Frank Sinatra, Lana Turner, etc.

Pluto in Leo

Birth Dates:
    June 14, 1939–August 19, 1957

The performing arts played on the emotions of the masses. Mick Jagger, John Lennon, and rock and roll were born at this time. So were "baby boomers" like Bill and Hillary Clinton. Those born here tend to be self-centered, powerful, and boisterous. This generation does its own thing, for better or for worse.

Pluto in Virgo

Birth Dates:
August 19, 1957–October 5, 1971
April 17, 1972–July 30, 1972

This is the "yuppie" generation that sparked a mass movement toward fitness, health, and career. It is a much more sober, serious, driven generation than the fun-loving Pluto in Leo. During this time, machines were invented to process detail work efficiently. Inventions took a practical turn with answering machines, fax machines, car phones, and home office equipment—all making the workplace far more efficient.

Pluto in Libra

Birth Dates:
October 5, 1971–April 17, 1972
July 30, 1972–November 5, 1983
May 18, 1984–August 27, 1984

A mellower generation, people born at this time are concerned with partnerships, working together, and finding diplomatic solutions to problems. Marriage is important to this generation, and they will redefine it by combining traditional values with equal partnership. This was a time of women's liberation, gay rights, ERA, and legal battles over abortion, all of which transformed our ideas about relationships.

Pluto in Scorpio

Birth Dates:
November 5, 1983–May 18, 1984
August 27, 1984–January 17, 1995

Pluto was in its ruling sign for a comparatively short period of time. In 1989, it was at its perihelion, or closest point to the sun and earth. We have all felt the transforming power somewhere in our lives. This was a time of record achievements, destructive sexually transmitted diseases, nuclear power controversies, and explosive political issues. Pluto destroys in order to create new understanding—the phoenix rising from the ashes—which should be some consolation for those of you who felt Pluto's force before 1995. Sexual shockers were par for the course during these intense years when black clothing, transvestites, body piercing, tattoos, and sexually explicit advertising pushed the boundaries of good taste.

Pluto in Sagittarius

Birth Dates:
　January 17, 1995–April 20, 1995
　November 10, 1995–January 27, 2008

During our current Pluto transit, we are being pushed to expand our horizons, to find deeper spiritual meaning in life. Pluto's opposition with Saturn in 2001 brought an enormous conflict between traditional societies and the forces of change.

For many of us, this Pluto transit will mean rolling down the information superhighway into the future. For others, it signals a time of spiritual emphasis when religious convictions will exert more power in our political life as well.

Since Sagittarius is the sign that rules travel, there's a good possibility that Pluto, the planet of extremes, will make space travel a reality for some of us. Discovery of life on Mars, traveling here on meteors, could transform our ideas about where we came from.

New dimensions in electronic publishing, concern with animal rights and the environment, and an increasing emphasis on extreme forms of religion are other signs of these times. Look for charismatic religious leaders to arise now. We'll also be developing far-reaching philosophies designed to elevate our lives with a new sense of purpose.

VENUS SIGNS 1901–2003

	Aries	Taurus	Gemini	Cancer	Leo	Virgo
1901	3/29–4/22	4/22–5/17	5/17–6/10	6/10–7/5	7/5–7/29	7/29–8/23
1902	5/7–6/3	6/3–6/30	6/30–7/25	7/25–8/19	8/19–9/13	9/13–10/7
1903	2/28–3/24	3/24–4/18	4/18–5/13	5/13–6/9	6/9–7/7	7/7–8/17
						9/6–11/8
1904	3/13–5/7	5/7–6/1	6/1–6/25	6/25–7/19	7/19–8/13	8/13–9/6
1905	2/3–3/6	3/6–4/9	7/8–8/6	8/6–9/1	9/1–9/27	9/27–10/21
	4/9–5/28	5/28–7/8				
1906	3/1–4/7	4/7–5/2	5/2–5/26	5/26–6/20	6/20–7/16	7/16–8/11
1907	4/27–5/22	5/22–6/16	6/16–7/11	7/11–8/4	8/4–8/29	8/29–9/22
1908	2/14–3/10	3/10–4/5	4/5–5/5	5/5–9/8	9/8–10/8	10/8–11/3
1909	3/29–4/22	4/22–5/16	5/16–6/10	6/10–7/4	7/4–7/29	7/29–8/23
1910	5/7–6/3	6/4–6/29	6/30–7/24	7/25–8/18	8/19–9/12	9/13–10/6
1911	2/28–3/23	3/24–4/17	4/18–5/12	5/13–6/8	6/9–7/7	7/8–11/8
1912	4/13–5/6	5/7–5/31	6/1–6/24	6/24–7/18	7/19–8/12	8/13–9/5
1913	2/3–3/6	3/7–5/1	7/8–8/5	8/6–8/31	9/1–9/26	9/27–10/20
	5/2–5/30	5/31–7/7				
1914	3/14–4/6	4/7–5/1	5/2–5/25	5/26–6/19	6/20–7/15	7/16–8/10
1915	4/27–5/21	5/22–6/15	6/16–7/10	7/11–8/3	8/4–8/28	8/29–9/21
1916	2/14–3/9	3/10–4/5	4/6–5/5	5/6–9/8	9/9–10/7	10/8–11/2
1917	3/29–4/21	4/22–5/15	5/16–6/9	6/10–7/3	7/4–7/28	7/29–8/21
1918	5/7–6/2	6/3–6/28	6/29–7/24	7/25–8/18	8/19–9/11	9/12–10/5
1919	2/27–3/22	3/23–4/16	4/17–5/12	5/13–6/7	6/8–7/7	7/8–11/8
1920	4/12–5/6	5/7–5/30	5/31–6/23	6/24–7/18	7/19–8/11	8/12–9/4
1921	2/3–3/6	3/7–4/25	7/8–8/5	8/6–8/31	9/1–9/25	9/26–10/20
	4/26–6/1	6/2–7/7				
1922	3/13–4/6	4/7–4/30	5/1–5/25	5/26–6/19	6/20–7/14	7/15–8/9
1923	4/27–5/21	5/22–6/14	6/15–7/9	7/10–8/3	8/4–8/27	8/28–9/20
1924	2/13–3/8	3/9–4/4	4/5–5/5	5/6–9/8	9/9–10/7	10/8–11/12
1925	3/28–4/20	4/21–5/15	5/16–6/8	6/9–7/3	7/4–7/27	7/28–8/21

Libra	Scorpio	Sagittarius	Capricorn	Aquarius	Pisces
8/23–9/17	9/17–10/12	10/12–1/16	1/16–2/9	2/9–3/5	3/5–3/29
			11/7–12/5	12/5–1/11	
10/7–10/31	10/31–11/24	11/24–12/18	12/18–1/11	2/6–4/4	1/11–2/6
					4/4–5/7
8/17–9/6	12/9–1/5			1/11–2/4	2/4–2/28
11/8–12/9					
9/6–9/30	9/30–10/25	1/5–1/30	1/30–2/24	2/24–3/19	3/19–4/13
		10/25–11/18	11/18–12/13	12/13–1/7	
10/21–11/14	11/14–12/8	12/8–1/1/06			1/7–2/3
8/11–9/7	9/7–10/9	10/9–12/15	1/1–1/25	1/25–2/18	2/18–3/14
	12/15–12/25	12/25–2/6			
9/22–10/16	10/16–11/9	11/9–12/3	2/6–3/6	3/6–4/2	4/2–4/27
			12/3–12/27	12/27–1/20	
11/3–11/28	11/28–12/22	12/22–1/15			1/20–2/4
8/23–9/17	9/17–10/12	10/12–11/17	1/15–2/9	2/9–3/5	3/5–3/29
			11/17–12/5	12/5–1/15	
10/7–10/30	10/31–11/23	11/24–12/17	12/18–12/31	1/1–1/15	1/16–1/28
				1/29–4/4	4/5–5/6
11/19–12/8	12/9–12/31		1/1–1/10	1/11–2/2	2/3–2/27
9/6–9/30	1/1–1/4	1/5–1/29	1/30–2/23	2/24–3/18	3/19–4/12
	10/1–10/24	10/25–11/17	11/18–12/12	12/13–12/31	
10/21–11/13	11/14–12/7	12/8–12/31		1/1–1/6	1/7–2/2
8/11–9/6	9/7–10/9	10/10–12/5	1/1–1/24	1/25–2/17	2/18–3/13
	12/6–12/30	12/31			
9/22–10/15	10/16–11/8	1/1–2/6	2/7–3/6	3/7–4/1	4/2–4/26
		11/9–12/2	12/3–12/26	12/27–12/31	
11/3–11/27	11/28–12/21	12/22–12/31		1/1–1/19	1/20–2/13
8/22–9/16	9/17–10/11	1/1–1/14	1/15–2/7	2/8–3/4	3/5–3/28
		10/12–11/6	11/7–12/5	12/6–12/31	
10/6–10/29	10/30–11/22	11/23–12/16	12/17–12/31	1/1–4/5	4/6–5/6
11/9–12/8	12/9–12/31		1/1–1/9	1/10–2/2	2/3–2/26
9/5–9/30	1/1–1/3	1/4–1/28	1/29–2/22	2/23–3/18	3/19–4/11
	9/31–10/23	10/24–11/17	11/18–12/11	12/12–12/31	
10/21–11/13	11/14–12/7	12/8–12/31		1/1–1/6	1/7–2/2
8/10–9/6	9/7–10/10	10/11–11/28	1/1–1/24	1/25–2/16	2/17–3/12
	11/29–12/31				
9/21–10/14	1/1	1/2–2/6	2/7–3/5	3/6–3/31	4/1–4/26
	10/15–11/7	11/8–12/1	12/2–12/25	12/26–12/31	
11/13–11/26	11/27–12/21	12/22–12/31		1/1–1/19	1/20–2/12
8/22–9/15	9/16–10/11	1/1–1/14	1/15–2/7	2/8–3/3	3/4–3/27
		10/12–11/6	11/7–12/5	12/6–12/31	

VENUS SIGNS 1901–2003

	Aries	Taurus	Gemini	Cancer	Leo	Virgo
1926	5/7–6/2	6/3–6/28	6/29–7/23	7/24–8/17	8/18–9/11	9/12–10/5
1927	2/27–3/22	3/23–4/16	4/17–5/11	5/12–6/7	6/8–7/7	7/8–11/9
1928	4/12–5/5	5/6–5/29	5/30–6/23	6/24–7/17	7/18–8/11	8/12–9/4
1929	2/3–3/7	3/8–4/19	7/8–8/4	8/5–8/30	8/31–9/25	9/26–10/19
	4/20–6/2	6/3–7/7				
1930	3/13–4/5	4/6–4/30	5/1–5/24	5/25–6/18	6/19–7/14	7/15–8/9
1931	4/26–5/20	5/21–6/13	6/14–7/8	7/9–8/2	8/3–8/26	8/27–9/19
1932	2/12–3/8	3/9–4/3	4/4–5/5	5/6–7/12	9/9–10/6	10/7–11/1
			7/13–7/27	7/28–9/8		
1933	3/27–4/19	4/20–5/28	5/29–6/8	6/9–7/2	7/3–7/26	7/27–8/20
1934	5/6–6/1	6/2–6/27	6/28–7/22	7/23–8/16	8/17–9/10	9/11–10/4
1935	2/26–3/21	3/22–4/15	4/16–5/10	5/11–6/6	6/7–7/6	7/7–11/8
1936	4/11–5/4	5/5–5/28	5/29–6/22	6/23–7/16	7/17–8/10	8/11–9/4
1937	2/2–3/8	3/9–4/13	7/7–8/3	8/4–8/29	8/30–9/24	9/25–10/18
	4/14–6/3	6/4–7/6				
1938	3/12–4/4	4/5–4/28	4/29–5/23	5/24–6/18	6/19–7/13	7/14–8/8
1939	4/25–5/19	5/20–6/13	6/14–7/8	7/9–8/1	8/2–8/25	8/26–9/19
1940	2/12–3/7	3/8–4/3	4/4–5/5	5/6–7/4	9/9–10/5	10/6–10/31
			7/5–7/31	8/1–9/8		
1941	3/27–4/19	4/20–5/13	5/14–6/6	6/7–7/1	7/2–7/26	7/27–8/20
1942	5/6–6/1	6/2–6/26	6/27–7/22	7/23–8/16	8/17–9/9	9/10–10/3
1943	2/25–3/20	3/21–4/14	4/15–5/10	5/11–6/6	6/7–7/6	7/7–11/8
1944	4/10–5/3	5/4–5/28	5/29–6/21	6/22–7/16	7/17–8/9	8/10–9/2
1945	2/2–3/10	3/11–4/6	7/7–8/3	8/4–8/29	8/30–9/23	9/24–10/18
	4/7–6/3	6/4–7/6				
1946	3/11–4/4	4/5–4/28	4/29–5/23	5/24–6/17	6/18–7/12	7/13–8/8
1947	4/25–5/19	5/20–6/12	6/13–7/7	7/8–8/1	8/2–8/25	8/26–9/18
1948	2/11–3/7	3/8–4/3	4/4–5/6	5/7–6/28	9/8–10/5	10/6–10/31
			6/29–8/2	8/3–9/7		
1949	3/26–4/19	4/20–5/13	5/14–6/6	6/7–6/30	7/1–7/25	7/26–8/19
1950	5/5–5/31	6/1–6/26	6/27–7/21	7/22–8/15	8/16–9/9	9/10–10/3
1951	2/25–3/21	3/22–4/15	4/16–5/10	5/11–6/6	6/7–7/7	7/8–11/9

Libra	Scorpio	Sagittarius	Capricorn	Aquarius	Pisces
10/6–10/29	10/30–11/22	11/23–12/16	12/17–12/31	1/1–4/5	4/6–5/6
11/10–12/8	12/9–12/31	1/1–1/7	1/8	1/9–2/1	2/2–2/26
9/5–9/28	1/1–1/3	1/4–1/28	1/29–2/22	2/23–3/17	3/18–4/11
	9/29–10/23	10/24–11/16	11/17–12/11	12/12–12/31	
10/20–11/12	11/13–12/6	12/7–12/30	12/31	1/1–1/5	1/6–2/2
8/10–9/6	9/7–10/11	10/12–11/21	1/1–1/23	1/24–2/16	2/17–3/12
	11/22–12/31				
9/20–10/13	1/1–1/3	1/4–2/6	2/7–3/4	3/5–3/31	4/1–4/25
	10/14–11/6	11/7–11/30	12/1–12/24	12/25–12/31	
11/2–11/25	11/26–12/20	12/21–12/31		1/1–1/18	1/19–2/11
8/21–9/14	9/15–10/10	1/1–1/13	1/14–2/6	2/7–3/2	3/3–3/26
		10/11–11/5	11/6–12/4	12/5–12/31	
10/5–10/28	10/29–11/21	11/22–12/15	12/16–12/31	1/1–4/5	4/6–5/5
11/9–12/7	12/8–12/31		1/1–1/7	1/8–1/31	2/1–2/25
9/5–9/27	1/1–1/2	1/3–1/27	1/28–2/21	2/22–3/16	3/17–4/10
	9/28–10/22	10/23–11/15	11/16–12/10	12/11–12/31	
10/19–11/11	11/12–12/5	12/6–12/29	12/30–12/31	1/1–1/5	1/6–2/1
8/9–9/6	9/7–10/13	10/14–11/14	1/1–1/22	1/23–2/15	2/16–3/11
	11/15–12/31				
9/20–10/13	1/1–1/3	1/4–2/5	2/6–3/4	3/5–3/30	3/31–4/24
	10/14–11/6	11/7–11/30	12/1–12/24	12/25–12/31	
11/1–11/25	11/26–12/19	12/20–12/31		1/1–1/18	1/19–2/11
8/21–9/14	9/15–10/9	1/1–1/12	1/13–2/5	2/6–3/1	3/2–3/26
		10/10–11/5	11/6–12/4	12/5–12/31	
10/4–10/27	10/28–11/20	11/21–12/14	12/15–12/31	1/1–4/5	4/6–5/5
11/9–12/7	12/8–12/31		1/1–1/7	1/8–1/31	2/1–2/24
9/3–9/27	1/1–1/2	1/3–1/27	1/28–2/20	2/21–3/16	3/17–4/9
	9/28–10/21	10/22–11/15	11/16–12/10	12/11–12/31	
10/19–11/11	11/12–12/5	12/6–12/29	12/30–12/31	1/1–1/4	1/5–2/1
8/9–9/6	9/7–10/15	10/16–11/7	1/1–1/21	1/22–2/14	2/15–3/10
	11/8–12/31				
9/19–10/12	1/1–1/4	1/5–2/5	2/6–3/4	3/5–3/29	3/30–4/24
	10/13–11/5	11/6–11/29	11/30–12/23	12/24–12/31	
11/1–11/25	11/26–12/19	12/20–12/31		1/1–1/17	1/18–2/10
8/20–9/14	9/15–10/9	1/1–1/12	1/13–2/5	2/6–3/1	3/2–3/25
		10/10–11/5	11/6–12/5	12/6–12/31	
10/4–10/27	10/28–11/20	11/21–12/13	12/14–12/31	1/1–4/5	4/6–5/4
11/10–12/7	12/8–12/31		1/1–1/7	1/8–1/31	2/1–2/24

VENUS SIGNS 1901–2003

	Aries	Taurus	Gemini	Cancer	Leo	Virgo
1952	4/10–5/4	5/5–5/28	5/29–6/21	6/22–7/16	7/17–8/9	8/10–9/3
1953	2/2–3/3	3/4–3/31	7/8–8/3	8/4–8/29	8/30–9/24	9/25–10/18
	4/1–6/5	6/6–7/7				
1954	3/12–4/4	4/5–4/28	4/29–5/23	5/24–6/17	6/18–7/13	7/14–8/8
1955	4/25–5/19	5/20–6/13	6/14–7/7	7/8–8/1	8/2–8/25	8/26–9/18
1956	2/12–3/7	3/8–4/4	4/5–5/7	5/8–6/23	9/9–10/5	10/6–10/31
			6/24–8/4	8/5–9/8		
1957	3/26–4/19	4/20–5/13	5/14–6/6	6/7–7/1	7/2–7/26	7/27–8/19
1958	5/6–5/31	6/1–6/26	6/27–7/22	7/23–8/15	8/16–9/9	9/10–10/3
1959	2/25–3/20	3/21–4/14	4/15–5/10	5/11–6/6	6/7–7/8	7/9–9/20
					9/21–9/24	9/25–11/9
1960	4/10–5/3	5/4–5/28	5/29–6/21	6/22–7/15	7/16–8/9	8/10–9/2
1961	2/3–6/5	6/6–7/7	7/8–8/3	8/4–8/29	8/30–9/23	9/24–10/17
1962	3/11–4/3	4/4–4/28	4/29–5/22	5/23–6/17	6/18–7/12	7/13–8/8
1963	4/24–5/18	5/19–6/12	6/13–7/7	7/8–7/31	8/1–8/25	8/26–9/18
1964	2/11–3/7	3/8–4/4	4/5–5/9	5/10–6/17	9/9–10/5	10/6–10/31
			6/18–8/5	8/6–9/8		
1965	3/26–4/18	4/19–5/12	5/13–6/6	6/7–6/30	7/1–7/25	7/26–8/19
1966	5/6–6/31	6/1–6/26	6/27–7/21	7/22–8/15	8/16–9/8	9/9–10/2
1967	2/24–3/20	3/21–4/14	4/15–5/10	5/11–6/6	6/7–7/8	7/9–9/9
					9/10–10/1	10/2–11/9
1968	4/9–5/3	5/4–5/27	5/28–6/20	6/21–7/15	7/16–8/8	8/9–9/2
1969	2/3–6/6	6/7–7/6	7/7–8/3	8/4–8/28	8/29–9/22	9/23–10/17
1970	3/11–4/3	4/4–4/27	4/28–5/22	5/23–6/16	6/17–7/12	7/13–8/8
1971	4/24–5/18	5/19–6/12	6/13–7/6	7/7–7/31	8/1–8/24	8/25–9/17
1972	2/11–3/7	3/8–4/3	4/4–5/10	5/11–6/11		
			6/12–8/6	8/7–9/8	9/9–10/5	10/6–10/30
1973	3/25–4/18	4/18–5/12	5/13–6/5	6/6–6/29	7/1–7/25	7/26–8/19
1974						
	5/5–5/31	6/1–6/25	6/26–7/21	7/22–8/14	8/15–9/8	9/9–10/2
1975	2/24–3/20	3/21–4/13	4/14–5/9	5/10–6/6	6/7–7/9	7/10–9/2
					9/3–10/4	10/5–11/9

Libra	Scorpio	Sagittarius	Capricorn	Aquarius	Pisces
9/4–9/27	1/1–1/2	1/3–1/27	1/28–2/20	2/21–3/16	3/17–4/9
	9/28–10/21	10/22–11/15	11/16–12/10	12/11–12/31	
10/19–11/11	11/12–12/5	12/6–12/29	12/30–12/31	1/1–1/5	1/6–2/1
8/9–9/6	9/7–10/22	10/23–10/27	1/1–1/22	1/23–2/15	2/16–3/11
	10/28–12/31				
9/19–10/13	1/1–1/6	1/7–2/5	2/6–3/4	3/5–3/30	3/31–4/24
	10/14–11/5	11/6–11/30	12/1–12/24	12/25–12/31	
11/1–11/25	11/26–12/19	12/20–12/31		1/1–1/17	1/18–2/11
8/20–9/14	9/15–10/9	1/1–1/12	1/13–2/5	2/6–3/1	3/2–3/25
		10/10–11/5	11/6–12/6	12/7–12/31	
10/4–10/27	10/28–11/20	11/21–12/14	12/15–12/31	1/1–4/6	4/7–5/5
11/10–12/7	12/8–12/31		1/1–1/7	1/8–1/31	2/1–2/24
9/3–9/26	1/1–1/2	1/3–1/27	1/28–2/20	2/21–3/15	3/16–4/9
	9/27–10/21	10/22–11/15	11/16–12/10	12/11–12/31	
10/18–11/11	11/12–12/4	12/5–12/28	12/29–12/31	1/1–1/5	1/6–2/2
8/9–9/6	9/7–12/31		1/1–1/21	1/22–2/14	2/15–3/10
9/19–10/12	1/1–1/6	1/7–2/5	2/6–3/4	3/5–3/29	3/30–4/23
	10/13–11/5	11/6–11/29	11/30–12/23	12/24–12/31	
11/1–11/24	11/25–12/19	12/20–12/31		1/1–1/16	1/17–2/10
8/20–9/13	9/14–10/9	1/1–1/12	1/13–2/5	2/6–3/1	3/2–3/25
		10/10–11/5	11/6–12/7	12/8–12/31	
10/3–10/26	10/27–11/19	11/20–12/13	2/7–2/25	1/1–2/6	4/7–5/5
			12/14–12/31	2/26–4/6	
11/10–12/7	12/8–12/31		1/1–1/6	1/7–1/30	1/31–2/23
9/3–9/26	1/1	1/2–1/26	1/27–2/20	2/21–3/15	3/16–4/8
	9/27–10/21	10/22–11/14	11/15–12/9	12/10–12/31	
10/18–11/10	11/11–12/4	12/5–12/28	12/29–12/31	1/1–1/4	1/5–2/2
8/9–9/7	9/8–12/31		1/1–1/21	1/22–2/14	2/15–3/10
9/18–10/11	1/1–1/7	1/8–2/5	2/6–3/4	3/5–3/29	3/30–4/23
	10/12–11/5	11/6–11/29	11/30–12/23	12/24–12/31	
	11/25–12/18	12/19–12/31		1/1–1/16	1/17–2/10
10/31–11/24					
8/20–9/13	9/14–10/8	1/1–1/12	1/13–2/4	2/5–2/28	3/1–3/24
		10/9–11/5	11/6–12/7	12/8–12/31	
			1/30–2/28	1/1–1/29	
10/3–10/26	10/27–11/19	11/20–12/13	12/14–12/31	3/1–4/6	4/7–5/4
			1/1–1/6	1/7–1/30	1/31–2/23
11/10–12/7	12/8–12/31				

VENUS SIGNS 1901–2003

	Aries	Taurus	Gemini	Cancer	Leo	Virgo
1976	4/8–5/2	5/2–5/27	5/27—6/20	6/20–7/14	7/14–8/8	8/8–9/1
1977	2/2–6/6	6/6–7/6	7/6–8/2	8/2–8/28	8/28–9/22	9/22–10/17
1978	3/9–4/2	4/2–4/27	4/27–5/22	5/22–6/16	6/16–7/12	7/12–8/6
1979	4/23–5/18	5/18–6/11	6/11–7/6	7/6–7/30	7/30–8/24	8/24–9/17
1980	2/9–3/6	3/6–4/3	4/3–5/12 6/5–8/6	5/12–6/5 8/6–9/7	9/7–10/4	10/4–10/30
1981	3/24–4/17	4/17–5/11	5/11–6/5	6/5–6/29	6/29–7/24	7/24–8/18
1982	5/4–5/30	5/30–6/25	6/25–7/20	7/20–8/14	8/14–9/7	9/7–10/2
1983	2/22–3/19	3/19–4/13	4/13–5/9	5/9–6/6	6/6–7/10 8/27–10/5	7/10–8/27 10/5–11/9
1984	4/7–5/2	5/2–5/26	5/26–6/20	6/20–7/14	7/14–8/7	8/7–9/1
1985	2/2–6/6	6/7–7/6	7/6–8/2	8/2–8/28	8/28–9/22	9/22–10/16
1986	3/9–4/2	4/2–4/26	4/26–5/21	5/21–6/15	6/15–7/11	7/11–8/7
1987	4/22–5/17	5/17–6/11	6/11–7/5	7/5–7/30	7/30–8/23	8/23–9/16
1988	2/9–3/6	3/6–4/3	4/3–5/17 5/27–8/6	5/17–5/27 8/28–9/22	9/7–10/4 9/22–10/16	10/4–10/29
1989	3/23–4/16	4/16–5/11	5/11–6/4	6/4–6/29	6/29–7/24	7/24–8/18
1990	5/4–5/30	5/30–6/25	6/25–7/20	7/20–8/13	8/13–9/7	9/7–10/1
1991	2/22–3/18	3/18–4/13	4/13–5/9	5/9–6/6	6/6–7/11 8/21–10/6	7/11–8/21 10/6–11/9
1992	4/7–5/1	5/1–5/26	5/26–6/19	6/19–7/13	7/13–8/7	8/7–8/31
1993	2/2–6/6	6/6–7/6	7/6–8/1	8/1–8/27	8/27–9/21	9/21–10/16
1994	3/8–4/1	4/1–4/26	4/26–5/21	5/21–6/15	6/15–7/11	7/11–8/7
1995	4/22–5/16	5/16–6/10	6/10–7/5	7/5–7/29	7/29–8/23	8/23–9/16
1996	2/9–3/6	3/6–4/3	4/3–8/7	8/7–9/7	9/7–10/4	10/4–10/29
1997	3/23–4/16	4/16–5/10	5/10–6/4	6/4–6/28	6/28–7/23	7/23–8/17
1998	5/3–5/29	5/29–6/24	6/24–7/19	7/19–8/13	8/13–9/6	9/6–9/30
1999	2/21–3/18	3/18–4/12	4/12–5/8	5/8–6/5	6/5–7/12 8/15–10/7	7/12–8/15 10/7–11/9
2000	4/6–5/1	5/1–5/25	5/25–6/13	6/13–7/13	7/13–8/6	8/6–8/31
2001	2/2–6/6	6/6–7/5	7/5–8/1	8/1–8/26	8/26–9/20	9/20–10/15
2002	3/7–4/1	4/1–4/25	4/25–5/20	5/20–6/14	6/14–7/10	7/10–8/7
2003	4/21–5/16	5/16–6/9	6/9–7/4	7/4–7/29	7/29–8/22	8/22–9/15

Libra	Scorpio	Sagittarius	Capricorn	Aquarius	Pisces
9/1–9/26	9/26–10/20	1/1–1/26	1/26–2/19	2/19–3/15	3/15–4/8
		10/20–11/14	11/14–12/8	12/9–1/4	
10/17–11/10	11/10–12/4	12/4–12/27	12/27–1/20/78		1/4–2/2
8/6–9/7	9/7–1/7			1/20–2/13	2/13–3/9
9/17–10/11	10/11–11/4	1/7–2/5	2/5–3/3	3/3–3/29	3/29–4/23
		11/4–11/28	11/28–12/22	12/22–1/16/80	
10/30–11/24	11/24–12/18	12/18–1/11/81			1/16–2/9
8/18–9/12	9/12–10/9	10/9–11/5	1/11–2/4	2/4–2/28	2/28–3/24
			11/5–12/8	12/8–1/23/82	
10/2–10/26	10/26–11/18	11/18–12/12	1/23–3/2	3/2–4/6	4/6–5/4
			12/12–1/5/83		
11/9–12/6	12/6–1/1/84			1/5–1/29	1/29–2/22
9/1–9/25	9/25–10/20	1/1–1/25	1/25–2/19	2/19–3/14	3/14–4/7
		10/20–11/13	11/13–12/9	12/10–1/4	
10/16–11/9	11/9–12/3	12/3–12/27	12/28–1/19		1/4–2/2
8/7–9/7	9/7–1/7			1/20–2/13	2/13–3/9
9/16–10/10	10/10–11/3	1/7–2/5	2/5–3/3	3/3–3/28	3/28–4/22
		11/3–11/28	11/28–12/22	12/22–1/15	
10/29–11/23	11/23–12/17	12/17–1/10			1/15–2/9
8/18–9/12	9/12–10/8	10/8–11/5	1/10–2/3	2/3–2/27	2/27–3/23
			11/5–12/10	12/10–1/16/90	
10/1–10/25	10/25–11/18	11/18–12/12	1/16–3/3	3/3–4/6	4/6–5/4
			12/12–1/5		
11/9–12/6	12/6–12/31	12/31–1/25/92		1/5–1/29	1/29–2/22
8/31–9/25	9/25–10/19	10/19–11/13	1/25–2/18	2/18–3/13	3/13–4/7
			11/13–12/8	12/8–1/3/93	
10/16–11/9	11/9–12/2	12/2–12/26	12/26–1/19		1/3–2/2
8/7–9/7	9/7–1/7			1/19–2/12	2/12–3/8
9/16–10/10	10/10–11/13	1/7–2/4	2/4–3/2	3/2–3/28	3/28–4/22
		11/3–11/27	11/27–12/21	12/21–1/15	
10/29–11/23	11/23–12/17	12/17–1/10/97			1/15–2/9
8/17–9/12	9/12–10/8	10/8–11/5	1/10–2/3	2/3–2/27	2/27–3/23
			11/5–12/12	12/12–1/9	
9/30–10/24	10/24–11/17	11/17–12/11	1/9–3/4	3/4–4/6	4/6–5/3
11/9–12/5	12/5–12/31	12/31–1/24		1/4–1/28	1/28–2/21
8/31–9/24	9/24–10/19	10/19–11/13	1/24–2/18	2/18–3/12	3/13–4/6
			11/13–12/8	12/8	
10/15–11/8	11/8–12/2	12/2–12/26	12/26/01–1/18/02	12/8/00–1/3/01	1/3–2/2
8/7–9/7	9/7–1/7/03		12/26/01–1/18	1/18–2/11	2/11–3/7
9/15–10/9	10/9–11/2	1/7–2/4	2/4–3/2	3/2–3/27	3/27–4/21
		11/2–11/26	11/26–12/21	12/21–1/14/04	

How to Use the Mars, Jupiter, and Saturn Tables

Find the year of your birth on the left side of each column. The dates when the planet entered each sign are listed on the right side of each column. (Signs are abbreviated to three letters.) Your birthday should fall on or between each date listed, and your planetary placement should correspond to the earlier sign of that period.

MARS SIGNS 1901–2003

1901	MAR	1	Leo	1905	JAN	13	Scp
	MAY	11	Vir		AUG	21	Sag
	JUL	13	Lib		OCT	8	Cap
	AUG	31	Scp		NOV	18	Aqu
	OCT	14	Sag		DEC	27	Pic
	NOV	24	Cap	1906	FEB	4	Ari
1902	JAN	1	Aqu		MAR	17	Tau
	FEB	8	Pic		APR	28	Gem
	MAR	19	Ari		JUN	11	Can
	APR	27	Tau		JUL	27	Leo
	JUN	7	Gem		SEP	12	Vir
	JUL	20	Can		OCT	30	Lib
	SEP	4	Leo		DEC	17	Scp
	OCT	23	Vir	1907	FEB	5	Sag
	DEC	20	Lib		APR	1	Cap
1903	APR	19	Vir		OCT	13	Aqu
	MAY	30	Lib		NOV	29	Pic
	AUG	6	Scp	1908	JAN	11	Ari
	SEP	22	Sag		FEB	23	Tau
	NOV	3	Cap		APR	7	Gem
	DEC	12	Aqu		MAY	22	Can
1904	JAN	19	Pic		JUL	8	Leo
	FEB	27	Ari		AUG	24	Vir
	APR	6	Tau		OCT	10	Lib
	MAY	18	Gem		NOV	25	Scp
	JUN	30	Can	1909	JAN	10	Sag
	AUG	15	Leo		FEB	24	Cap
	OCT	1	Vir		APR	9	Aqu
	NOV	20	Lib		MAY	25	Pic

Year	Mon	Day	Sign		Year	Mon	Day	Sign
	JUL	21	Ari			AUG	19	Can
	SEP	26	Pic			OCT	7	Leo
	NOV	20	Ari		1916	MAY	28	Vir
1910	JAN	23	Tau			JUL	23	Lib
	MAR	14	Gem			SEP	8	Scp
	MAY	1	Can			OCT	22	Sag
	JUN	19	Leo			DEC	1	Cap
	AUG	6	Vir		1917	JAN	9	Aqu
	SEP	22	Lib			FEB	16	Pic
	NOV	6	Scp			MAR	26	Ari
	DEC	20	Sag			MAY	4	Tau
1911	JAN	31	Cap			JUN	14	Gem
	MAR	14	Aqu			JUL	28	Can
	APR	23	Pic			SEP	12	Leo
	JUN	2	Ari			NOV	2	Vir
	JUL	15	Tau		1918	JAN	11	Lib
	SEP	5	Gem			FEB	25	Vir
	NOV	30	Tau			JUN	23	Lib
1912	JAN	30	Gem			AUG	17	Scp
	APR	5	Can			OCT	1	Sag
	MAY	28	Leo			NOV	11	Cap
	JUL	17	Vir			DEC	20	Aqu
	SEP	2	Lib		1919	JAN	27	Pic
	OCT	18	Scp			MAR	6	Ari
	NOV	30	Sag			APR	15	Tau
1913	JAN	10	Cap			MAY	26	Gem
	FEB	19	Aqu			JUL	8	Can
	MAR	30	Pic			AUG	23	Leo
	MAY	8	Ari			OCT	10	Vir
	JUN	17	Tau			NOV	30	Lib
	JUL	29	Gem		1920	JAN	31	Scp
	SEP	15	Can			APR	23	Lib
1914	MAY	1	Leo			JUL	10	Scp
	JUN	26	Vir			SEP	4	Sag
	AUG	14	Lib			OCT	18	Cap
	SEP	29	Scp			NOV	27	Aqu
	NOV	11	Sag		1921	JAN	5	Pic
	DEC	22	Cap			FEB	13	Ari
1915	JAN	30	Aqu			MAR	25	Tau
	MAR	9	Pic			MAY	6	Gem
	APR	16	Ari			JUN	18	Can
	MAY	26	Tau			AUG	3	Leo
	JUL	6	Gem			SEP	19	Vir

	NOV	6	Lib		APR	7	Pic
	DEC	26	Scp		MAY	16	Ari
1922	FEB	18	Sag		JUN	26	Tau
	SEP	13	Cap		AUG	9	Gem
	OCT	30	Aqu		OCT	3	Can
	DEC	11	Pic		DEC	20	Gem
1923	JAN	21	Ari	1929	MAR	10	Can
	MAR	4	Tau		MAY	13	Leo
	APR	16	Gem		JUL	4	Vir
	MAY	30	Can		AUG	21	Lib
	JUL	16	Leo		OCT	6	Scp
	SEP	1	Vir		NOV	18	Sag
	OCT	18	Lib		DEC	29	Cap
	DEC	4	Scp	1930	FEB	6	Aqu
1924	JAN	19	Sag		MAR	17	Pic
	MAR	6	Cap		APR	24	Ari
	APR	24	Aqu		JUN	3	Tau
	JUN	24	Pic		JUL	14	Gem
	AUG	24	Aqu		AUG	28	Can
	OCT	19	Pic		OCT	20	Leo
	DEC	19	Ari	1931	FEB	16	Can
1925	FEB	5	Tau		MAR	30	Leo
	MAR	24	Gem		JUN	10	Vir
	MAY	9	Can		AUG	1	Lib
	JUN	26	Leo		SEP	17	Scp
	AUG	12	Vir		OCT	30	Sag
	SEP	28	Lib		DEC	10	Cap
	NOV	13	Scp	1932	JAN	18	Aqu
	DEC	28	Sag		FEB	25	Pic
1926	FEB	9	Cap		APR	3	Ari
	MAR	23	Aqu		MAY	12	Tau
	MAY	3	Pic		JUN	22	Gem
	JUN	15	Ari		AUG	4	Can
	AUG	1	Tau		SEP	20	Leo
1927	FEB	22	Gem		NOV	13	Vir
	APR	17	Can	1933	JUL	6	Lib
	JUN	6	Leo		AUG	26	Scp
	JUL	25	Vir		OCT	9	Sag
	SEP	10	Lib		NOV	19	Cap
	OCT	26	Scp		DEC	28	Aqu
	DEC	8	Sag	1934	FEB	4	Pic
1928	JAN	19	Cap		MAR	14	Ari
	FEB	28	Aqu		APR	22	Tau

	JUN	2	Gem		AUG	19	Vir
	JUL	15	Can		OCT	5	Lib
	AUG	30	Leo		NOV	20	Scp
	OCT	18	Vir	1941	JAN	4	Sag
	DEC	11	Lib		FEB	17	Cap
1935	JUL	29	Scp		APR	2	Aqu
	SEP	16	Sag		MAY	16	Pic
	OCT	28	Cap		JUL	2	Ari
	DEC	7	Aqu	1942	JAN	11	Tau
1936	JAN	14	Pic		MAR	7	Gem
	FEB	22	Ari		APR	26	Can
	APR	1	Tau		JUN	14	Leo
	MAY	13	Gem		AUG	1	Vir
	JUN	25	Can		SEP	17	Lib
	AUG	10	Leo		NOV	1	Scp
	SEP	26	Vir		DEC	15	Sag
	NOV	14	Lib	1943	JAN	26	Cap
1937	JAN	5	Scp		MAR	8	Aqu
	MAR	13	Sag		APR	17	Pic
	MAY	14	Scp		MAY	27	Ari
	AUG	8	Sag		JUL	7	Tau
	SEP	30	Cap		AUG	23	Gem
	NOV	11	Aqu	1944	MAR	28	Can
	DEC	21	Pic		MAY	22	Leo
1938	JAN	30	Ari		JUL	12	Vir
	MAR	12	Tau		AUG	29	Lib
	APR	23	Gem		OCT	13	Scp
	JUN	7	Can		NOV	25	Sag
	JUL	22	Leo	1945	JAN	5	Cap
	SEP	7	Vir		FEB	14	Aqu
	OCT	25	Lib		MAR	25	Pic
	DEC	11	Scp		MAY	2	Ari
1939	JAN	29	Sag		JUN	11	Tau
	MAR	21	Cap		JUL	23	Gem
	MAY	25	Aqu		SEP	7	Can
	JUL	21	Cap		NOV	11	Leo
	SEP	24	Aqu		DEC	26	Can
	NOV	19	Pic	1946	APR	22	Leo
1940	JAN	4	Ari		JUN	20	Vir
	FEB	17	Tau		AUG	9	Lib
	APR	1	Gem		SEP	24	Scp
	MAY	17	Can		NOV	6	Sag
	JUL	3	Leo		DEC	17	Cap

1947	JAN	25	Aqu		MAR	20	Tau
	MAR	4	Pic		MAY	1	Gem
	APR	11	Ari		JUN	14	Can
	MAY	21	Tau		JUL	29	Leo
	JUL	1	Gem		SEP	14	Vir
	AUG	13	Can		NOV	1	Lib
	OCT	1	Leo		DEC	20	Scp
	DEC	1	Vir	1954	FEB	9	Sag
1948	FEB	12	Leo		APR	12	Cap
	MAY	18	Vir		JUL	3	Sag
	JUL	17	Lib		AUG	24	Cap
	SEP	3	Scp		OCT	21	Aqu
	OCT	17	Sag		DEC	4	Pic
	NOV	26	Cap	1955	JAN	15	Ari
1949	JAN	4	Aqu		FEB	26	Tau
	FEB	11	Pic		APR	10	Gem
	MAR	21	Ari		MAY	26	Can
	APR	30	Tau		JUL	11	Leo
	JUN	10	Gem		AUG	27	Vir
	JUL	23	Can		OCT	13	Lib
	SEP	7	Leo		NOV	29	Scp
	OCT	27	Vir	1956	JAN	14	Sag
	DEC	26	Lib		FEB	28	Cap
1950	MAR	28	Vir		APR	14	Aqu
	JUN	11	Lib		JUN	3	Pic
	AUG	10	Scp		DEC	6	Ari
	SEP	25	Sag	1957	JAN	28	Tau
	NOV	6	Cap		MAR	17	Gem
	DEC	15	Aqu		MAY	4	Can
1951	JAN	22	Pic		JUN	21	Leo
	MAR	1	Ari		AUG	8	Vir
	APR	10	Tau		SEP	24	Lib
	MAY	21	Gem		NOV	8	Scp
	JUL	3	Can		DEC	23	Sag
	AUG	18	Leo	1958	FEB	3	Cap
	OCT	5	Vir		MAR	17	Aqu
	NOV	24	Lib		APR	27	Pic
1952	JAN	20	Scp		JUN	7	Ari
	AUG	27	Sag		JUL	21	Tau
	OCT	12	Cap		SEP	21	Gem
	NOV	21	Aqu		OCT	29	Tau
	DEC	30	Pic	1959	FEB	10	Gem
1953	FEB	8	Ari		APR	10	Can

	JUN	1	Leo		NOV	14	Cap
	JUL	20	Vir		DEC	23	Aqu
	SEP	5	Lib	1966	JAN	30	Pic
	OCT	21	Scp		MAR	9	Ari
	DEC	3	Sag		APR	17	Tau
1960	JAN	14	Cap		MAY	28	Gem
	FEB	23	Aqu		JUL	11	Can
	APR	2	Pic		AUG	25	Leo
	MAY	11	Ari		OCT	12	Vir
	JUN	20	Tau		DEC	4	Lib
	AUG	2	Gem	1967	FEB	12	Scp
	SEP	21	Can		MAR	31	Lib
1961	FEB	5	Gem		JUL	19	Scp
	FEB	7	Can		SEP	10	Sag
	MAY	6	Leo		OCT	23	Cap
	JUN	28	Vir		DEC	1	Aqu
	AUG	17	Lib	1968	JAN	9	Pic
	OCT	1	Scp		FEB	17	Ari
	NOV	13	Sag		MAR	27	Tau
	DEC	24	Cap		MAY	8	Gem
1962	FEB	1	Aqu		JUN	21	Can
	MAR	12	Pic		AUG	5	Leo
	APR	19	Ari		SEP	21	Vir
	MAY	28	Tau		NOV	9	Lib
	JUL	9	Gem		DEC	29	Scp
	AUG	22	Can	1969	FEB	25	Sag
	OCT	11	Leo		SEP	21	Cap
1963	JUN	3	Vir		NOV	4	Aqu
	JUL	27	Lib		DEC	15	Pic
	SEP	12	Scp	1970	JAN	24	Ari
	OCT	25	Sag		MAR	7	Tau
	DEC	5	Cap		APR	18	Gem
1964	JAN	13	Aqu		JUN	2	Can
	FEB	20	Pic		JUL	18	Leo
	MAR	29	Ari		SEP	3	Vir
	MAY	7	Tau		OCT	20	Lib
	JUN	17	Gem		DEC	6	Scp
	JUL	30	Can	1971	JAN	23	Sag
	SEP	15	Leo		MAR	12	Cap
	NOV	6	Vir		MAY	3	Aqu
1965	JUN	29	Lib		NOV	6	Pic
	AUG	20	Scp		DEC	26	Ari
	OCT	4	Sag	1972	FEB	10	Tau

	MAR	27	Gem	1978	JAN	26	Can
	MAY	12	Can		APR	10	Leo
	JUN	28	Leo		JUN	14	Vir
	AUG	15	Vir		AUG	4	Lib
	SEP	30	Lib		SEP	19	Scp
	NOV	15	Scp		NOV	2	Sag
	DEC	30	Sag		DEC	12	Cap
1973	FEB	12	Cap	1979	JAN	20	Aqu
	MAR	26	Aqu		FEB	27	Pic
	MAY	8	Pic		APR	7	Ari
	JUN	20	Ari		MAY	16	Tau
	AUG	12	Tau		JUN	26	Gem
	OCT	29	Ari		AUG	8	Can
	DEC	24	Tau		SEP	24	Leo
1974	FEB	27	Gem		NOV	19	Vir
	APR	20	Can	1980	MAR	11	Leo
	JUN	9	Leo		MAY	4	Vir
	JUL	27	Vir		JUL	10	Lib
	SEP	12	Lib		AUG	29	Scp
	OCT	28	Scp		OCT	12	Sag
	DEC	10	Sag		NOV	22	Cap
1975	JAN	21	Cap		DEC	30	Aqu
	MAR	3	Aqu	1981	FEB	6	Pic
	APR	11	Pic		MAR	17	Ari
	MAY	21	Ari		APR	25	Tau
	JUL	1	Tau		JUN	5	Gem
	AUG	14	Gem		JUL	18	Can
	OCT	17	Can		SEP	2	Leo
	NOV	25	Gem		OCT	21	Vir
1976	MAR	18	Can		DEC	16	Lib
	MAY	16	Leo	1982	AUG	3	Scp
	JUL	6	Vir		SEP	20	Sag
	AUG	24	Lib		OCT	31	Cap
	OCT	8	Scp		DEC	10	Aqu
	NOV	20	Sag	1983	JAN	17	Pic
1977	JAN	1	Cap		FEB	25	Ari
	FEB	9	Aqu		APR	5	Tau
	MAR	20	Pic		MAY	16	Gem
	APR	27	Ari		JUN	29	Can
	JUN	6	Tau		AUG	13	Leo
	JUL	17	Gem		SEP	30	Vir
	SEP	1	Can		NOV	18	Lib
	OCT	26	Leo	1984	JAN	11	Scp

	AUG	17	Sag		JUL	12	Tau
	OCT	5	Cap		AUG	31	Gem
	NOV	15	Aqu		DEC	14	Tau
	DEC	25	Pic	1991	JAN	21	Gem
1985	FEB	2	Ari		APR	3	Can
	MAR	15	Tau		MAY	26	Leo
	APR	26	Gem		JUL	15	Vir
	JUN	9	Can		SEP	1	Lib
	JUL	25	Leo		OCT	16	Scp
	SEP	10	Vir		NOV	29	Sag
	OCT	27	Lib	1992	JAN	9	Cap
	DEC	14	Scp		FEB	18	Aqu
1986	FEB	2	Sag		MAR	28	Pic
	MAR	28	Cap		MAY	5	Ari
	OCT	9	Aqu		JUN	14	Tau
	NOV	26	Pic		JUL	26	Gem
1987	JAN	8	Ari		SEP	12	Can
	FEB	20	Tau	1993	APR	27	Leo
	APR	5	Gem		JUN	23	Vir
	MAY	21	Can		AUG	12	Lib
	JUL	6	Leo		SEP	27	Scp
	AUG	22	Vir		NOV	9	Sag
	OCT	8	Lib		DEC	20	Cap
	NOV	24	Scp	1994	JAN	28	Aqu
1988	JAN	8	Sag		MAR	7	Pic
	FEB	22	Cap		APR	14	Ari
	APR	6	Aqu		MAY	23	Tau
	MAY	22	Pic		JUL	3	Gem
	JUL	13	Ari		AUG	16	Can
	OCT	23	Pic		OCT	4	Leo
	NOV	1	Ari		DEC	12	Vir
1989	JAN	19	Tau	1995	JAN	22	Leo
	MAR	11	Gem		MAY	25	Vir
	APR	29	Can		JUL	21	Lib
	JUN	16	Leo		SEP	7	Scp
	AUG	3	Vir		OCT	20	Sag
	SEP	19	Lib		NOV	30	Cap
	NOV	4	Scp	1996	JAN	8	Aqu
	DEC	18	Sag		FEB	15	Pic
1990	JAN	29	Cap		MAR	24	Ari
	MAR	11	Aqu		MAY	2	Tau
	APR	20	Pic		JUN	12	Gem
	MAY	31	Ari		JUL	25	Can

	SEP	9	Leo		MAR	23	Tau
	OCT	30	Vir		MAY	3	Gem
1997	JAN	3	Lib		JUN	16	Can
	MAR	8	Vir		AUG	1	Leo
	JUN	19	Lib		SEP	17	Vir
	AUG	14	Scp		NOV	4	Lib
	SEP	28	Sag		DEC	23	Scp
	NOV	9	Cap	2001	FEB	14	Sag
	DEC	18	Aqu		SEP	8	Cap
1998	JAN	25	Pic		OCT	27	Aqu
	MAR	4	Ari		DEC	8	Pic
	APR	13	Tau	2002	JAN	18	Ari
	MAY	24	Gem		MAR	1	Tau
	JUL	6	Can		APR	13	Gem
	AUG	20	Leo		MAY	28	Can
	OCT	7	Vir		JUL	13	Leo
	NOV	27	Lib		AUG	29	Vir
1999	JAN	26	Scp		OCT	15	Lib
	MAY	5	Lib		DEC	1	Scp
	JUL	5	Scp	2003	JAN	17	Sag
	SEP	2	Sag		MAR	4	Cap
	OCT	17	Cap		APR	21	Aqu
	NOV	26	Aqu		JUN	17	Pic
2000	JAN	4	Pic		DEC	16	Ari
	FEB	12	Ari				

JUPITER SIGNS 1901–2003

1901	JAN	19	Cap	1909	OCT	11	Lib
1902	FEB	6	Aqu	1910	NOV	11	Scp
1903	FEB	20	Pic	1911	DEC	10	Sag
1904	MAR	1	Ari	1913	JAN	2	Cap
	AUG	8	Tau	1914	JAN	21	Aqu
	AUG	31	Ari	1915	FEB	4	Pic
1905	MAR	7	Tau	1916	FEB	12	Ari
	JUL	21	Gem		JUN	26	Tau
	DEC	4	Tau		OCT	26	Ari
1906	MAR	9	Gem	1917	FEB	12	Tau
	JUL	30	Can		JUN	29	Gem
1907	AUG	18	Leo	1918	JUL	13	Can
1908	SEP	12	Vir	1919	AUG	2	Leo

1920	AUG	27	Vir		1951	APR	21	Ari
1921	SEP	25	Lib		1952	APR	28	Tau
1922	OCT	26	Scp		1953	MAY	9	Gem
1923	NOV	24	Sag		1954	MAY	24	Can
1924	DEC	18	Cap		1955	JUN	13	Leo
1926	JAN	6	Aqu			NOV	17	Vir
1927	JAN	18	Pic		1956	JAN	18	Leo
	JUN	6	Ari			JUL	7	Vir
	SEP	11	Pic			DEC	13	Lib
1928	JAN	23	Ari		1957	FEB	19	Vir
	JUN	4	Tau			AUG	7	Lib
1929	JUN	12	Gem		1958	JAN	13	Scp
1930	JUN	26	Can			MAR	20	Lib
1931	JUL	17	Leo			SEP	7	Scp
1932	AUG	11	Vir		1959	FEB	10	Sag
1933	SEP	10	Lib			APR	24	Scp
1934	OCT	11	Scp			OCT	5	Sag
1935	NOV	9	Sag		1960	MAR	1	Cap
1936	DEC	2	Cap			JUN	10	Sag
1937	DEC	20	Aqu			OCT	26	Cap
1938	MAY	14	Pic		1961	MAR	15	Aqu
	JUL	30	Aqu			AUG	12	Cap
	DEC	29	Pic			NOV	4	Aqu
1939	MAY	11	Ari		1962	MAR	25	Pic
	OCT	30	Pic		1963	APR	4	Ari
	DEC	20	Ari		1964	APR	12	Tau
1940	MAY	16	Tau		1965	APR	22	Gem
1941	MAY	26	Gem			SEP	21	Can
1942	JUN	10	Can			NOV	17	Gem
1943	JUN	30	Leo		1966	MAY	5	Can
1944	JUL	26	Vir			SEP	27	Leo
1945	AUG	25	Lib		1967	JAN	16	Can
1946	SEP	25	Scp			MAY	23	Leo
1947	OCT	24	Sag			OCT	19	Vir
1948	NOV	15	Cap		1968	FEB	27	Leo
1949	APR	12	Aqu			JUN	15	Vir
	JUN	27	Cap			NOV	15	Lib
	NOV	30	Aqu		1969	MAR	30	Vir
1950	APR	15	Pic			JUL	15	Lib
	SEP	15	Aqu			DEC	16	Scp
	DEC	1	Pic		1970	APR	30	Lib

	AUG	15	Scp	1985	FEB	6	Aqu
1971	JAN	14	Sag	1986	FEB	20	Pic
	JUN	5	Scp	1987	MAR	2	Ari
	SEP	11	Sag	1988	MAR	8	Tau
1972	FEB	6	Cap		JUL	22	Gem
	JUL	24	Sag		NOV	30	Tau
	SEP	25	Cap	1989	MAR	11	Gem
1973	FEB	23	Aqu		JUL	30	Can
1974	MAR	8	Pic	1990	AUG	18	Leo
1975	MAR	18	Ari	1991	SEP	12	Vir
1976	MAR	26	Tau	1992	OCT	10	Lib
	AUG	23	Gem	1993	NOV	10	Scp
	OCT	16	Tau	1994	DEC	9	Sag
1977	APR	3	Gem	1996	JAN	3	Cap
	AUG	20	Can	1997	JAN	21	Aqu
	DEC	30	Gem	1998	FEB	4	Pic
1978	APR	12	Can	1999	FEB	13	Ari
	SEP	5	Leo		JUN	28	Tau
1979	FEB	28	Can		OCT	23	Ari
	APR	20	Leo	2000	FEB	14	Tau
	SEP	29	Vir		JUN	30	Gem
1980	OCT	27	Lib	2001	JUL	14	Can
1981	NOV	27	Scp	2002	AUG	1	Leo
1982	DEC	26	Sag	2003	AUG	27	VIR
1984	JAN	19	Cap				

SATURN SIGNS 1903–2003

1903	JAN	19	Aqu		DEC	7	Gem
1905	APR	13	Pic	1915	MAY	11	Can
	AUG	17	Aqu	1916	OCT	17	Leo
1906	JAN	8	Pic		DEC	7	Can
1908	MAR	19	Ari	1917	JUN	24	Leo
1910	MAY	17	Tau	1919	AUG	12	Vir
	DEC	14	Ari	1921	OCT	7	Lib
1911	JAN	20	Tau	1923	DEC	20	Scp
1912	JUL	7	Gem	1924	APR	6	Lib
	NOV	30	Tau		SEP	13	Scp
1913	MAR	26	Gem	1926	DEC	2	Sag
1914	AUG	24	Can	1929	MAR	15	Cap

	MAY	5	Sag	1971	JUN	18	Gem
	NOV	30	Cap	1972	JAN	10	Tau
1932	FEB	24	Aqu		FEB	21	Gem
	AUG	13	Cap	1973	AUG	1	Can
	NOV	20	Aqu	1974	JAN	7	Gem
1935	FEB	14	Pic		APR	18	Can
1937	APR	25	Ari	1975	SEP	17	Leo
	OCT	18	Pic	1976	JAN	14	Can
1938	JAN	14	Ari		JUN	5	Leo
1939	JUL	6	Tau	1977	NOV	17	Vir
	SEP	22	Ari	1978	JAN	5	Leo
1940	MAR	20	Tau		JUL	26	Vir
1942	MAY	8	Gem	1980	SEP	21	Lib
1944	JUN	20	Can	1982	NOV	29	Scp
1946	AUG	2	Leo	1983	MAY	6	Lib
1948	SEP	19	Vir		AUG	24	Scp
1949	APR	3	Leo	1985	NOV	17	Sag
	MAY	29	Vir	1988	FEB	13	Cap
1950	NOV	20	Lib		JUN	10	Sag
1951	MAR	7	Vir		NOV	12	Cap
	AUG	13	Lib	1991	FEB	6	Aqu
1953	OCT	22	Scp	1993	MAY	21	Pic
1956	JAN	12	Sag		JUN	30	Aqu
	MAY	14	Scp	1994	JAN	28	Pic
	OCT	10	Sag	1996	APR	7	Ari
1959	JAN	5	Cap	1998	JUN	9	Tau
1962	JAN	3	Aqu		OCT	25	Ari
1964	MAR	24	Pic	1999	MAR	1	Tau
	SEP	16	Aqu	2000	AUG	10	Gem
	DEC	16	Pic		OCT	16	Tau
1967	MAR	3	Ari	2001	APR	21	Gem
1969	APR	29	Tau	2003	JUN	3	Can

CHAPTER 5

Astrology's Graphics: How to Read Those Fascinating Symbols on Your Chart

When you see an astrology chart for the first time, you'll be looking at a strange foreign language of pictographs, little symbols that look as ancient as cave drawings. These symbols or *glyphs,* as they are called, are used by astrologers worldwide and by computer astrology programs. So, if you want to read a horoscope chart or use one of the popular astrology programs on your PC, you must learn the glyphs.

Besides enabling you to read a horoscope chart, each glyph contains clues to the meaning of the signs and the planets. Since there are only twelve signs and ten planets (not counting a few asteroids and other space creatures some astrologers use), it's a lot easier than learning to read a foreign language.

Here's a code cracker for the glyphs, beginning with the glyphs for the planets. To those who already know their glyphs, don't just skim over the chapter. These familiar graphics have hidden meanings you will discover!

The Glyphs for the Planets

The glyphs for the planets are easy to learn. They're simple combinations of the most basic visual elements: the circle, the semicircle or arc, and the cross. However, each component of a glyph has a special meaning in relation to the other parts of the symbol.

The circle, which has no beginning or end, is one of the oldest symbols of spirit or spiritual forces. All of the early diagrams of the heavens—spiritual territory—are shown in circular form. The never-ending line of the circle is the perfect symbol for eternity. The semicircle or arc is an incomplete circle, symbolizing the receptive, finite soul, which contains spiritual potential in the curving line.

The vertical line of the cross symbolizes movement from heaven to earth. The horizontal line describes temporal movement, here and now, in time and space. Combined in a cross, the vertical and horizontal planes symbolize manifestation in the material world.

The Sun Glyph ☉

The sun is always shown by this powerful solar symbol, a circle with a point in the center. The center point is you, your spiritual center, and the symbol represents your infinite personality incarnating (the point) into the finite cycles of birth and death.

The sun has been represented by a circle or disk since ancient Egyptian times when the solar disk represented the Sun God, Ra. Some archaeologists believe the great stone circles found in England were centers of sun worship. This particular version of the symbol was brought into common use in the sixteenth century after German occultist and scholar Cornelius Agrippa (1486–1535) wrote a book called *Die Occulta Philosophia,* which became accepted as the authority in its field. Agrippa collected many medieval astrological and magical symbols in this book, which have been used by astrologers since then.

The Moon Glyph ☽

The moon glyph is the most recognizable symbol on a chart, a left-facing arc stylized into the crescent moon. As part of a circle, the arc symbolizes the potential fulfillment of the entire circle, the life force that is still incomplete. Therefore, it is the ideal representation of the reactive, receptive, emotional nature of the moon.

The Mercury Glyph ☿

Mercury contains all three elemental symbols: the crescent, the circle, and the cross in vertical order. This is the "Venus with a hat" glyph (compare with the symbol of Venus). With another stretch of the imagination, can't you see the winged cap of Mercury the messenger? Think of the up-turned crescent as antennae that tune in and transmit messages from the sun, reminding you that Mercury is the way you communicate, the way your mind works. The upturned arc is receiving energy into the spirit or solar circle, which will later be translated into action on the material plane, symbolized by the cross. All the elements are equally sized because Mercury is neutral; it doesn't play favorites! This planet symbolizes objective, detached, unemotional thinking.

The Venus Glyph ♀

Here the relationship is between two components: the circle of spirit and the cross of matter. Spirit is elevated over matter, pulling it upward. Venus asks, "What is beautiful? What do you like best? What do you love to have done to you?" Consequently, Venus determines both your ideal of beauty and what feels good sensually. It governs your own allure and power to attract, as well as what attracts and pleases you.

The Mars Glyph ♂

In this glyph, the cross of matter is stylized into an arrow-head pointed up and outward, propelled by the circle of spirit. With a little imagination, you can visualize it as the shield and spear of Mars, the ancient god of war. You can deduce that Mars embodies your spiritual energy projected into the outer world. It's your assertiveness, your initiative, your aggressive drive, what you like to do to others, your temper. If you know someone's Mars, you know whether they'll blow up when angry or do a slow burn. Your task is to use your outgoing Mars energy wisely and well.

The Jupiter Glyph ♃

Jupiter is the basic cross of matter, with a large stylized crescent perched on the left side of the horizontal, temporal plane. You might think of the crescent as an open hand, because one meaning of Jupiter is "luck," what's handed to you. You don't have to work for what you get from Jupiter; it comes to you, if you're open to it.

The Jupiter glyph might also remind you of a jumbo jet plane, with a huge tail fin, about to take off. This is the planet of travel, mental and spiritual, of expanding your horizons via new ideas, new spiritual dimensions, and new places. Jupiter embodies the optimism and enthusiasm of the traveler about to embark on an exciting adventure.

The Saturn Glyph ♄

Flip Jupiter over, and you've got Saturn. This might not be immediately apparent because Saturn is usually stylized into an "h" form like the one shown here. The principle it expresses is the opposite of Jupiter's expansive tendencies. Saturn pulls you back to earth: the receptive arc is pushed down underneath the cross of matter. Before there are any rewards or expansion, the duties and obligations of the material world must be considered. Saturn says, "Stop, wait, finish your chores before you take off!"

Saturn's glyph also resembles the sickle of old "Father Time." Saturn was first known as Chronos, the Greek god of time, for time brings all matter to an end. When it was the most distant planet (before the discovery of Uranus), Saturn was believed to be the place where time stopped. After the soul departed from earth, it journeyed back to the outer reaches of the universe and finally stopped at Saturn, or at "the end of time."

The Uranus Glyph ♅

The glyph for Uranus is often stylized to form a capital "H" after Sir William Herschel who discovered the planet. But the more esoteric version curves the two pillars of the

H into crescent antennae, or "ears," like satellite disks receiving signals from space. These are perched on the horizontal material line of the cross of matter and pushed from below by the circle of the spirit. To many sci-fi fans, Uranus looks like an orbiting satellite.

Uranus channels the highest energy of all, the white electrical light of the universal spiritual force that holds the cosmos together. This pure electrical energy is gathered from all over the universe. Because Uranian energy doesn't follow any ordinary celestial drumbeat, it can't be controlled or predicted (which is also true of those who are strongly influenced by this eccentric planet). In the symbol, this energy is manifested through the balance of polarities (the two opposite arms of the glyph) like the two polarized wires of a light bulb.

The Neptune Glyph Ψ

Neptune's glyph is usually stylized to look like a trident, the weapon of the Roman god Neptune. However, on a more esoteric level, it shows the large upturned crescent of the soul pierced through by the cross of matter. Neptune nails down, or materializes, soul energy, bringing impulses from the soul level into manifestation. That is why Neptune is associated with imagination or "imagining in," making an image of the soul. Neptune works through feeling, sensitivity, and mystical capacity to bring the divine into the earthly realm.

The Pluto Glyph ♀

Pluto is written two ways. One is a composite of the letters "PL," the first two letters of the word Pluto and coincidentally the initials of Percival Lowell, one of the planet's discoverers. The other, more esoteric symbol is a small circle above a large open crescent that surmounts the cross of matter. This depicts Pluto's power to regenerate. Imagine a new little spirit emerging from the sheltering cup of the soul. Pluto rules the forces of life and death. After this planet has passed a sensitive point in your chart, you are transformed, reborn in some way.

Sci-fi fans might visualize this glyph as a small satellite (the circle) being launched. It was shortly after Pluto's discovery that we learned how to harness the nuclear forces that made space exploration possible. Pluto rules the transformative power of atomic energy, which totally changed our lives and from which there is no turning back.

The Glyphs for the Signs

On an astrological chart, the glyph for the sign will appear after that of the planet. For example, when you see the moon glyph followed first by a number and then by another glyph representing the sign, this means that the moon was passing over a certain degree of that astrological sign at the time of the chart. On the dividing lines between the houses on your chart, you'll find the symbol for the sign that rules the house.

Because sun sign symbols do not contain the same basic geometric components of the planetary glyphs, we must look elsewhere for clues to their meanings. Many have been passed down from ancient Egyptian and Chaldean civilizations with few modifications. Others have been adapted over the centuries. In deciphering many of the glyphs, you'll often find that the symbols reveal a dual nature of the sign, which is not always apparent in the usual sun sign descriptions. For instance, the Gemini glyph is similar to the Roman numeral for two, and reveals this sign's longing to discover a twin soul. The Cancer glyph may be interpreted as resembling either the nurturing breasts or the self-protective claws of a crab, both symbols associated with the contrasting qualities of this sign. Libra's glyph embodies the duality of the spirit balanced with material reality. The Sagittarius glyph shows that the aspirant must also carry along the earthly animal nature in his quest. The Capricorn sea goat is another symbol with dual emphasis. The goat climbs high, yet is always pulled back by the deep waters of the unconscious. Aquarius embodies the double waves of mental detachment, balanced by the desire for connection with others in a friendly way. Finally, the two fishes of Pisces, which are forever tied together, show the duality of the soul and the spirit that must be reconciled.

The Aries Glyph ♈

Since the symbol for Aries is the Ram, this glyph is obviously associated with a ram's horns, which characterize one aspect of the Aries personality—an aggressive, me-first, leaping-headfirst attitude. But the symbol can be interpreted in other ways as well. Some astrologers liken it to a fountain of energy, which Aries people also embody. The first sign of the zodiac bursts on the scene eagerly, ready to go. Another analogy is to the eyebrows and nose of the human head, which Aries rules, and the thinking power that is initiated in the brain.

One theory of this symbol links it to the Egyptian god Amun, represented by a ram in ancient times. As Amun-Ra, this god was believed to embody the creator of the universe, the leader of all the other gods. This relates easily to the position of Aries as the leader (or first sign) of the zodiac, which begins at the spring equinox, a time of the year when nature is renewed.

The Taurus Glyph ♉

This is another easy glyph to draw and identify. It takes little imagination to decipher the bull's head with long curving horns. Like its symbol the Bull, the archetypal Taurus is slow to anger but ferocious when provoked, as well as stubborn, steady, and sensual. Another association is the larynx (and thyroid) of the throat area (ruled by Taurus) and the eustachian tubes running up to the ears, which coincides with the relationship of Taurus to the voice, song, and music. Many famous singers, musicians, and composers have prominent Taurus influences.

Many ancient religions involved a bull as the central figure in fertility rites or initiations, usually symbolizing the victory of man over his animal nature. Another possible origin is in the sacred bull of Egypt, who embodied the incarnate form of Osiris, god of death and resurrection. In early Christian imagery, the Taurus Bull represented St. Luke.

The Gemini Glyph ♊

The standard glyph immediately calls to mind the Roman numeral for two (II) and the Twins symbol, as it is called, for Gemini. In almost all drawings and images used for this sign, the relationship between two persons is emphasized. Usually one twin will be touching the other, which signifies communication, human contact, the desire to share.

The top line of the Gemini glyph indicates mental communication, while the bottom line indicates shared physical space.

The most famous Gemini legend is that of the twin sons, Castor and Pollux, one of whom had a mortal father while the other was the son of Zeus, king of the gods. When it came time for the mortal twin to die, his grief-stricken brother pleaded with Zeus, who agreed to let them spend half the year on earth in mortal form and half in immortal life, with the gods on Mt. Olympus. This reflects a basic duality of humankind, which possesses an immortal soul yet is also subject to the limits of mortality.

The Cancer Glyph ♋

Two convenient images relate to the Cancer glyph. It is easiest to decode the curving claws of the Cancer symbol, the Crab. Like the crab, Cancer's element is water. This sensitive sign also has a hard protective shell to protect its tender interior. The crab must be wily to escape predators, scampering sideways and hiding under rocks. The crab also responds to the cycles of the moon, as do all shellfish. The other image is that of two female breasts, which Cancer rules, showing that this is a sign that nurtures and protects others as well as itself.

In ancient Egypt, Cancer was also represented by the scarab beetle, a symbol of regeneration and eternal life.

The Leo Glyph ♌

Notice that the Leo glyph seems to be an extension of Cancer's glyph, with a significant difference. In the Cancer glyph, the lines curve inward protectively. The Leo glyph expresses energy outwardly. And there is no duality in the symbol, the Lion, or in Leo, the sign.

Lions have belonged to the sign of Leo since earliest times. It is not difficult to imagine the king of beasts with his sweeping mane and curling tail from this glyph. The upward sweep of the glyph easily describes the positive energy of Leo: the flourishing tail, their flamboyant qualities. Another analogy, perhaps a stretch of the imagination, is that of a heart leaping up with joy and enthusiasm, also very typical of Leo, which also rules the heart. In early Christian imagery, the Leo Lion represented St. Mark.

The Virgo Glyph ♍

You can read much into this mysterious glyph. For instance, it could represent the initials of "Mary Virgin," or a young woman holding a staff of wheat, or stylized female genitalia, all common interpretations. The "M" shape might also remind you that Virgo is ruled by Mercury. The cross beneath the symbol reveals the grounded, practical nature of this earth sign.

The earliest zodiacs link Virgo with the Egyptian goddess Isis who gave birth to the god Horus, after her husband Osiris had been killed, in the archetype of a miraculous conception. There are many ancient statues of Isis nursing her baby son, which are reminiscent of medieval Virgin and Child motifs. This sign has also been associated with the image of the Holy Grail, when the Virgo symbol was substituted with a chalice.

The Libra Glyph ♎

It is not difficult to read the standard image for Libra, the Scales, into this glyph. There is another meaning, however, that is equally relevant: the setting sun as it descends over the horizon. Libra's natural position on the zodiac wheel is the descendant, or sunset position (as the Aries natural position is the ascendant, or rising sign). Both images relate to Libra's personality. Libra is always weighing pros and cons for a balanced decision. In the sunset image, the sun (male) hovers over the horizontal earth (female) before setting. Libra is the space between these lines, harmonizing yin and yang, spiritual and material, male and female, ideal and real worlds. The glyph has also been linked to the kidneys, which are ruled by Libra.

The Scorpio Glyph ♏

With its barbed tail, this glyph is easy to identify as the Scorpion for the sign of Scorpio. It also represents the male sexual parts, over which the sign rules. From the arrowhead, you can draw the conclusion that Mars was once its ruler. Some earlier Egyptian glyphs for Scorpio represent it as an erect serpent, so the Serpent is an alternate symbol.

Another symbol for Scorpio, which is not identifiable in this glyph, is the Eagle. Scorpios can go to extremes, either soaring like the eagle or self-destructing like the scorpion. In early Christian imagery, which often used zodiacal symbols, the Scorpio Eagle was chosen to symbolize the intense apostle St. John the Evangelist.

The Sagittarius Glyph ♐

This glyph is one of the easiest to spot and draw: an upward pointing arrow lifting up a cross. The arrow is pointing skyward, while the cross represents the four elements of the material world, which the arrow must convey. Elevating materiality into spirituality is an important Sagittarius quality, which explains why this sign is associated with higher learning, religion, philosophy, travel—the aspiring professions. Sagittarius can also send barbed arrows of frankness in the pursuit of truth, so the Archer symbol for Sagittarius is apt. (Sagittarius is also the sign of the supersalesman.)

Sagittarius is symbolically represented by the centaur, a mythological creature who is half man, half horse, aiming his arrow toward the skies. Though Sagittarius is motivated by spiritual aspiration, it also must balance the powerful appetites of the animal nature. The centaur Chiron, a figure in Greek mythology, became a wise teacher who, after many adventures and world travels, was killed by a poisoned arrow.

The Capricorn Glyph ♑

One of the most difficult symbols to draw, this glyph may take some practice. It is a representation of the sea goat: a mythical animal that is a goat with a curving fish's tail. The goat part of Capricorn wants to leave the waters of the emotions and climb to the elevated areas of life. But the fish tail is the unconscious, the deep chaotic psychic level that draws the goat back. Capricorn is often trying to escape the deep, feeling part of life by submerging himself in work, steadily ascending to the top. To some people, the glyph represents a seated figure with a bent knee, a reminder that Capricorn governs the knee area of the body.

An interesting aspect of this glyph is the contrast of the sharp pointed horns—which represent the penetrating, shrewd, conscious side of Capricorn—with the swishing tail—which represents its serpentine, unconscious, emotional force. One Capricorn legend, which dates from Roman times, tells of the earthy fertility god, Pan, who tried to save himself from uncontrollable sexual desires by jumping into the Nile. His upper body then turned into a goat, while the lower part became a fish. Later, Jupiter gave him a safe haven in the skies, as a constellation.

The Aquarius Glyph ♒

This ancient water symbol can be traced back to an Egyptian hieroglyph representing streams of life force. Symbolized by the Water Bearer, Aquarius is distributor of the waters of life—the magic liquid of regeneration. The two waves can also be linked to the positive and negative charges of the electrical energy that Aquarius rules, a sort of universal wavelength. Aquarius is tuned in intuitively to higher forces via this electrical force. The duality of the glyph could also refer to the dual nature of Aquarius, a sign that runs hot and cold and that is friendly but also detached in the mental world of air signs.

In Greek legends, Aquarius is represented by Ganymede, who was carried to heaven by an eagle in order to become the cup bearer of Zeus and to supervise the annual flooding of the Nile. The sign later became associated with aviation and notions of flight.

The Pisces Glyph)(

Here is an abstraction of the familiar image of Pisces, two Fishes swimming in opposite directions yet bound together by a cord. The Fishes represent the spirit—which yearns for the freedom of heaven—and the soul—which remains attached to the desires of the temporal world. During life on earth, the spirit and the soul are bound together. When they complement each other, instead of pulling in opposite directions, they facilitate the Pisces creativity. The ancient version of this glyph, taken from the Egyptians, had no connecting line, which was added in the fourteenth century.

In another interpretation, it is said that the left fish indicates the direction of involution or the beginning of a cycle, while the right fish signifies the direction of evolution, the way to completion of a cycle. It's an appropriate grand finale for Pisces, the last sign of the zodiac.

CHAPTER 6

Astrology on the Internet

If you're online, you'll have no trouble finding astrology sites. Astrology is everywhere on the Internet, and a popular feature on most of the big websites. However, if you're curious to see a copy of your chart (or someone else's), want to study astrology in depth, or chat with another astrology fan then you'll need a guided tour!

There you'll find a whole new world of astrology waiting for a click of your mouse. Thousands of astrological sites offer you everything from chart services to chat rooms to individual readings. Even better, you'll find *free* software, *free* charts, *free* articles to download. You can virtually get an education in astrology from your computer screen, share your insights with new astrology-minded pals in a chat room or on a mailing list, then later meet them in person at one of the hundreds of conferences around the world.

The following sites were chosen for general interest from the vast number of astrology-oriented places on the net. Many have their own selection of links to other sites for further exploration. One caveat: Though these sites were selected with longevity in mind, the Internet is a volatile place where sites can disappear or change without notice. Therefore, some of our sites may have changed addresses, names, or content by the time this book is published.

Free Charts

Astrolabe Software at *http://www.alabe.com* distributes some of the most creative and user-friendly programs now available; Solar Fire is a favorite of top astrologers. Visitors to the site are greeted with a chart of the time you log on. You can get your chart calculated, with a free mini-interpretation e-mailed to you.

For an instant chart, surf to *http://www.astro.ch* and check into Astrodienst, an international site that has long been one of the best astrology sites on the Internet. Its world atlas will give you the accurate longitude and latitude of your birthplace for setting up your horoscope. Then you can print out your chart in a range of easy-to-read formats. One handy feature for beginners: The planetary placement is listed in words alongside the chart (a real help for those who haven't yet learned to read the astrology glyphs).

There are many other attractions at this site, such as a list of your astro-twins (famous people born on your birth-date). The site even sorts the "twins" to feature those who also have your identical rising sign. You can then click on their names and get an instant chart of your famous sign-mates.

Planning a vacation or relocation? First check an astro-map at Astro-click Travel, another clever feature on the Astrodienst site. On the interactive chart that appears, you can view your astrological chart projected on a map of the earth. The lines on the chart that track each of the planets indicate what type of experience you might expect at that location. Click on a line, and up pops an explanation. So click before you travel!

Free Software

Software manufacturers on the Web are generous with free downloads of demo versions of their software. You may then calculate charts using their data. Before you invest serious money in astrology software, you can see how the program works for your needs. You can preview Astrolabe Software programs favored by many professional astrolo-gers at *http://www.alabe.com*. Check out the latest demo of Solar Fire, one of the most user-friendly astrology programs available—you'll be impressed.

Matrix Software, another source of terrific astrology soft-

ware, also offers free demo disks. Address: *http:www.*
astrologysoftware.com

A Free Fully Functional Astrology Program

Walter Pullen's amazingly complete Astrolog program is
offered absolutely free at the site. Address: *http://www.mag-*
itech.com/~cruiser1/astrolog.htm

Astrolog is an ultrasophisticated program with all the
features of much more expensive programs. It comes in
versions for all formats—DOS, Windows, MAC, UNIX—
and has some cool features such as a revolving globe and
a constellation map. A "must" for those who want to get
involved with astrology without paying big bucks for a
professional-caliber program. Or for those who want to add
Astrolog's unique features to their astrology software library. This program has it all!

Another Free Program!

Surf to *http://www.astroscan.ca* for a free program called
Astroscan. Stunning graphics and ease of use make this a
winner. Astroscan has a fun list of celebrity charts you can
call up with a few clicks.

A Super Shareware Program

Check out Halloran Software's site at *http://www.hal-*
loran.com. There are several levels of Windows astrology
software from which to choose. The Astrology for Windows
shareware program is available in unregistered demo form
as a free download and in registered form for $26.50 (at
this writing). The calculations in this program may be all
that an astrology hobbyist needs. The price for the full-
service program is certainly reasonable.

Free Oracle Readings

There are many diversions at the Matrix site; you may consult the stars, the I Ching, the runes, and the tarot. Here's

where to connect with news groups and online discussions. Their almanac helps you schedule the best day to sign on the dotted line, ask for a raise, or plant your rosebush. Address: *http://thenewage.com*

Online Astrology Course

Schedule a long visit to *http://www.panplanet.com* where you will find the Canopus Academy of Astrology, a site loaded with goodies. For the experienced astrologer, there is a collection of articles from top astrologers. They've done the work for you when it comes to picking the best astrology links on the Web, so be sure to check out those bestowed with the Canopus Award of Excellence.

Astrologer Linda Reid, an accomplished astrology teacher and author, offers a complete online curriculum for all levels of astrology study plus individual tutoring. To get your feet wet, Linda is offering an excellent beginners' course at this site, a terrific way to get off and running in astrology.

Top Astrologers Comment on Current Events

The StarIQ site is home to many top astrologers, who comment on the latest news as well as submit articles. Visit this site for an astrological take on the headlines, and be sure to read the articles from some of the best minds in astrology. Address: *http://www.StarIQ.com*

Visit an Astro-Mall

For lighter entertainment, go to Astronet, *http://www.astrology.com/astronet*, for the Internet's equivalent of an astrology mall. Astronet offers interactive fun for everyone. At this writing, there's a special area for teenage astrology fans, advice to the lovelorn, plus a grab bag of horoscopes, a shopping area for books, reports, and software as well as links to all the popular fashion magazine astrology columns.

Swoon.com is another mall-like site aimed at dating, mating, and relating. It has fun features to spark up your love life and plenty of advice for lovers. Address: *http://www.swoon.com*

Find an Astrologer Here

The A.F.A. Website

This is the interesting website of the prestigious American Federation of Astrologers. The A.F.A. has a directory of astrologers restricted to those who meet their stringent requirements. Check out their correspondence course if you would like to study astrology in depth. Address: *http:// www.astrologers.com*

The NCGR Website

The website of the National Council for Geocosmic Research (NCGR), a leading astrology organization that places great emphasis on education, has a list of accredited astrologers nationwide on their site. Address: *http://www.geocosmic.org*

Tools Every Astrologer Needs Are Online

Internet Atlas

Find the geographic longitude and latitude and the correct time zone for any city worldwide. You'll need this information to calculate a chart. Address: *http:/www.astro.ch/atlas*

The Exact Time Anywhere in the World

A fun site with fascinating graphics that give you the exact time anywhere in the world. Click on the world map, and the correct time and zone for that place light up. Address: *http://www.timeticker.com*

Check the Weather Forecast

More accurate than your local TV forecast is the Weathersage, who uses astrology to predict snowstorms and hurricanes. Get your long-range forecast at this super site. Address: *http//www.weathersage.com*

Celebrate the Queen's Birthday

A great jumping off place for an astrology tour of the Internet, this site has a veritable Burke's Peerage of royal birthdays. There's a good selection of articles; tools such as a U.S. and World Atlas; information on conferences, software, tapes, and groups. The links at this site will send you off in the right direction. Information about the latest Palm Pilot astrology software is also available here. Adress: *http.//www.zodiacal.com*

Get a View of the Night Sky

Visit *http://www.skyviewzone.com* for a look at the evening's constellations. It is also an excellent place to preview and order the sophisticated Kepler astrology software.

Astrology Worldwide

Interested in astrology in Europe? Deborah Houlding, one of the U.K.'s top astrologers, has gathered some of the finest European talent on this super website, as well as a comprehensive list of links and conferences. Tour the world of astrology here. Address: *http://astrology-world.com*

Astrology Alive

Barbara Schermer has one of the most innovative and holistic approaches to astrology. She was one of the first astrologers to go online, so there's always a "cutting edge" to this site and a great list of links. Barbara is always on top of what's happening now in astrology. Address: *http://www.astrologyalive.com*

National Council for Geocosmic Research (NCGR)

A key stop on any astrological tour of the Net. Here's where you can find local chapters in your area, get information on the NCGR testing and certification programs, get a conference schedule. There is a list of certified astrologers for those who want readings. Order lecture tapes from their nationwide conferences, or get complete lists of conference topics to study at home. Good links to resources. Address: *http://www.geocosmic.org*

Where to Find Charts of the Famous

When the news is breaking, you can bet Lois Rodden will be the first to get accurate birthdays of the headline-makers, and put up their charts on her website: *http://www.astrodatabank.com*. Rodden's meticulous research is astrology's most reliable source for data of the famous and infamous. Her website specializes in birthdays and charts of current newsmakers, political figures, and international celebrities. You can also participate in an analysis of the charts and see what other astrologers have to say about them. The AstroDatabank program, which you can purchase at the site, provides thousands of birthdays sorted into categories. It's an excellent research tool.

Here is another site with birthdays and charts of famous and infamous people: *http://www.astropro.com*

Go to *http://www.imdb.com* for a comprehensive list of

film celebrities including bios, plus lists of famous couples from today and yesteryear. Look under "biographies."

Yet another good source for celebrity birthdates is the humorous Metamaze site: *http://www.metamaze.com/bdays*. You can find some interesting offbeat newsmakers here.

For Astrology Books

National Clearinghouse for Astrology Books

A wide selection of books on all aspects of astrology, from the basics to advanced, is available at this online bookstore. Also, many hard-to-find and recycled books. Address: *http://www.astroamerica.com*

The following addresses also have a good selection of astrology books for sale, some of which are unique to the site.

http://www.panplanet.com
http://thenewage.com
http://www.astrocom.com

Browse the huge astrology list of online bookstore Amazon.com at *http://www.amazon.com*.

Astrology Tapes for At-Home Study

You can study at home with world-famous astrologers via audiocassette recordings from Pegasus Tapes. There's an extensive selection taped from conferences, classes, lectures, and seminars. An especially good source for astrologers who emphasize psychological and mythological themes. Address: *http://www.pegasustape.com*

For History and Mythology Buffs

Be sure to visit the astrology section of this gorgeous site, dedicated to the history and mythology of many traditions.

One of the most beautifully designed sites we've seen. Address: *http://www.elore.com*

The leading authority on the history of astrology, Robert Hand, has an excellent site that features his cutting-edge research. See what one of astrology's great teachers has to offer. Address: *http://www.robhand.com*

The Project Hindsight group of scholarly astrologers is devoted to restoring the astrology of the Hellenistic period, the primary source for all later Western astrology. There are fascinating articles for astrology fans on this site. Address: *http://www.projecthindsight.com*

C.U.R.A. is a European site for historical researchers. Lots of information, especially if you speak French or Spanish. Address: *http://cura.free.fr*

Readers interested in mythology should also check out *http://pantheon.org/mythical* for stories of gods and goddesses.

Astrology Magazine

The Mountain Astrologer

A favorite magazine of astrology fans, *The Mountain Astrologer* has an interesting website featuring the latest news from an astrological point of view, plus feature articles from the magazine. Address: *http://www.mountainastrologer.com*

Financial Astrology

Find out how financial astrologers play the market. Here are hot picks, newsletters, specialized financial astrology software, and mutual funds run by astrology seers. Go to *www.afund.com* or *www.alphee.com* for tips and forecasts from two top financial astrologers.

CHAPTER 7

The Sydney Omarr Yellow Pages

If you've caught the "astrology bug," you'll want to expand your knowledge and connect with other astrology fans. Here are the resources you need to find the right astrology software for your computer, to meet other astrology fans, to study advanced techniques, or to buy books and tapes. You'll find the latest products and services available, as well as astrology organizations that hold meetings and conferences in your area.

Whether you'd like to know more about such specialties as financial astrology or techniques for timing events, or if you'd prefer the psychological or mythological approach, you'll meet the top astrologers at conferences sponsored by the National Council for Geocosmic Research. NCGR is dedicated to providing quality education, bringing astrologers and astrology fans together at conferences, and promoting fellowship. Their course structure provides a systematized study of the many facets of astrology.

You can explore astrology via your computer no matter what your level of expertise. Even if you are using an older model, there are still calculation and interpretation programs available. They may not have all the bells and whistles or the exciting graphics, but they'll get the job done!

Newcomers to astrology should learn some of the basics, including the glyphs, before you invest in a computer program. Use Chapter 5 in this book to help you learn the symbols easily; then you'll be able to read the charts without consulting the "help" section of your software every time. Several programs such as Astrolabe's Solar Fire have pop-up definitions to help you decipher the meanings of planets and aspects. Just click your mouse on a glyph or an icon on the screen, and a window with an instant definition appears.

You don't have to spend a fortune to get a perfectly adequate astrology program. In fact, if you are connected to the Internet, you can download one free. Astrology software is available at all price levels, from a sophisticated free application like Astrolog, which you can download from the website, to inexpensive programs for under $100 such as Winstar Express, to the more expensive astrology programs such as Winstar Plus, Solar Fire, or Io (for the MAC), which are used by serious students and professionals. Before you make an investment, it's a good idea to download a sample, which is usually available on the company's website, or to order a demo disk.

If you're baffled by the variety of software available, most of the companies on our list will be happy to help you find the right application for your needs.

Students of astrology who live in out-of-the-way places or are unable to fit classes into your schedule have several options. There are online courses offered at astrology websites, such as *www.panplanet.com*, the NCGR and A.F.A. websites. Some astrology teachers will send you a series of audiotapes, or you can order audiotaped seminars of recent conferences. Other teachers offer correspondence courses that use their workbooks or computer printouts.

Nationwide Astrology Organizations and Conferences

Contact these organizations for information on conferences, workshops, local meetings, conference tapes, referrals.

National Council for Geocosmic Research (NCGR)

Educational workshops, tapes, conferences, and a directory of professional astrologers are available from this nationwide organization devoted to promoting astrological education. For a $35 annual membership fee, you get their excellent publications and newsletters, plus the opportunity to network with other astrology buffs at local chapter events (there are chapters in 20 states).

For general information about NCGR, contact:

NCGR
P.O. Box 38866
Los Angeles, CA 90038
Website: http://www.geocosmic.org/

American Federation of Astrologers (A.F.A.)

This is one of the oldest astrological organizations in the United States, established 1938. They offer conferences, conventions, and a thorough correspondence course. If you are looking for a reading, the website will refer you to an accredited A.F.A. astrologer.

A.F.A.
P.O. Box 22040
Tempe, AZ 85285-2040
Phone: (888) 301-7630 or (480) 838-1751
Fax: (480) 838-8293
Website: http://www.astrologers.com

Association for Astrological Networking (A.F.A.N.)

Did you know that astrologers are still being harassed for practicing astrology? A.F.A.N. provides support and legal information, and works toward improving the public image of astrology. A.F.A.N.'s network of local astrologers links with the international astrological community. Here are the people who will go to bat for astrology when it is attacked in the media. Everyone who cares about astrology should join!

A.F.A.N.
8306 Wilshire Blvd.
PMB 537
Beverly Hills, CA 90211
Phone: (800) 578-2326
E-mail: info@afan.org
Website: http://www.afan.org

Astrology Conferences on Tape

Would you like to hear top astrology lectures on tape? Pegasus has a wonderful selection of tapes from conferences, featuring world-famous astrologers.

Pegasus Tapes
P.O. Box 419
Santa Ysabel, CA 92070

International Society for Astrology Research (ISAR)

For lectures, workshops, seminars. An international organization of professional astrologers dedicated to encouraging the highest standards of quality in the field of astrology with an emphasis on research.

ISAR
P.O. Box 38613
Los Angeles, CA 90038
Website: http://www.isarastrology.com
Phone: (800) 924-4747 or (510) 222-9436
Fax: (510) 222–2202

Astrology Software

Astrolabe

One of the top astrology software resources. Check out the latest version of their powerful Solar Fire software for

Windows. It's a breeze to use and will grow with your increasing knowledge of astrology to the most sophisticated levels. This company also markets a variety of programs for all levels of expertise and a wide selection of computer-generated astrology readings. A good resource for innovative software as well as applications for older computers.

Astrolabe
Box 1750-R
Brewster, MA 02631
Phone: (800) 843-6682
Website: http://www.alabe.com

Matrix Software

A wide variety of software in all price ranges, demo disks, student and advanced level, lots of interesting readings. Check out Winstar Express, a powerful but reasonably priced program suitable for all skill levels.

Matrix Software
407 N. State Street
Big Rapids, MI 49307
Phone: (800) 416-3924
Website: http://www.astrologysoftware.com

Astro Communications Services (ACS)

Books, software for MAC and IBM compatibles, individual charts, and telephone readings are offered by this California company. Find technical astrology materials here such as The American Ephemeris and PC atlases. ACS will calculate and send charts to you, a valuable service if you do not have a computer.

ACS Publications
5521 Ruffin Road
San Diego, CA 92123
Phone: (800) 888-9983

Fax: (858) 492-9917
Website: http://www.astrocom.com

Air Software

Here you'll find powerful, creative astrology software, like Star Trax 2000. For beginners, check out Father Time, which finds your best days. Check out Nostradamus, which answers all your questions. Financial astrology programs for stock market traders are a specialty.

Air Software
115 Caya Avenue
West Hartford, CT 06110
Phone: (800) 659-1247
Website: http://www.alphee.com

Time Cycles Research: For MAC Users

Here's where MAC users can find astrology software that's as sophisticated as it gets. If you have a MAC, you'll love their beautiful graphic IO Series programs.

Time Cycles Research
375 Willets Avenue
Waterford, CT 06385
Fax: (860) 442-0625
Website: http://www.timecycles.com

Astrology Magazines

In addition to articles by top astrologers, most have listings of astrology conferences, events, and local happenings.

American Astrology
Dept. 4
P.O. Box 2021
Marion, OH 43306-8121

Dell Horoscope
P.O. Box 54097
Boulder, CO 80322-4097

The Mountain Astrologer
P.O. Box 970
Cedar Ridge, CA 95924
Website: http://www.mountainastrologer.com

Astrology College

An accredited college dedicated to astrology is here at last!
Check out the Kepler College listed below.

Kepler College of Astrological Arts and Sciences

A degree-granting college, which is also a center of astrology, has long been the dream of the astrological community and is a giant step forward in providing credibility to the profession.

Therefore, the opening of Kepler College in 2000 was a historical event for astrology. It is the only college in the western hemisphere authorized to issue B.A. and M.A. degrees in Astrological Studies. The entire curriculum is based on astrology.

For more information, contact:

Kepler College of Astrological Arts and Sciences
4630 200th Street SW
Suite P
Lynnwood, WA 98036
Voice: (425) 673-4292
Fax: (425) 673-4983
Website: http://www.kepler.edu

CHAPTER 8

Consulting a Cosmic Counselor: What a Personal Reading Can Do for You

Could it be time for an astrology reading? An important date is coming up, perhaps a wedding or the start of a new business, and you're wondering if an astrologically picked date could influence the outcome. You've fallen in love and must know if it will last forever. Your partnership is not going well, and you're not sure if you can continue to work together. You're in a downslide when problems seem insurmountable. Or you simply want to have your chart interpreted by an expert. There are so many options for readings that sorting through them can be a daunting task. Besides individual one-on-one readings with a professional astrologer, there are telephone readings, Internet readings, tapes, computer-generated reports, and celebrity-sponsored readings. Here's what to look for and some cautionary notes.

Done by a qualified astrologer, the personal reading can be an empowering experience if you want to reach your full potential, size up a lover or business situation, or find out what the future has in store. There are astrologers who are specialists in certain areas such as finance or medical astrology. And, unfortunately, there are many questionable practitioners who range from streetwise gypsy fortunetellers to unscrupulous scam artists. The following basic guidelines can help you sort out your options to find the reading that's right for you.

What Information an Astrologer Needs

Nothing compares to a one-on-one consultation with a professional astrologer who has analyzed thousands of charts and can pinpoint the potential in yours. During your reading, you can get your specific questions answered. For instance, how to get along better with your mate or co-worker. There are many astrologers who now combine their skills with training in psychology and are well-suited to help you examine your alternatives.

To give you an accurate reading, an astrologer needs certain information from you: the date, time, and place where you were born. (A horoscope can be cast about anyone or anything that has a specific time and place.) Most astrologers will then enter this information into a computer, which will calculate a chart in seconds. From the resulting chart, the astrologer will do an interpretation.

If you don't know your exact birth time, you can usually locate it at the Bureau of Vital Statistics at the city hall or county seat of the state where you were born. If you still have no success in getting your time of birth, some astrologers can estimate an approximate birth time by using past events in your life to determine the chart. This technique is called *rectification*.

Choose an Astrologer with Care

Choose your astrologer with the same care as any trusted adviser such as a doctor, lawyer, or banker. Unfortunately, anyone can claim to be an astrologer—to date, there is no licensing of astrologers or universally established professional criteria. However, there are nationwide organizations of serious, committed astrologers that can help you in your search.

Good places to start your investigation are organizations such as the American Federation of Astrologers (A.F.A.) or the National Council for Geocosmic Research (NCGR), which offer a program of study and certification. If you live near a major city, there is sure to be an active NCGR chapter or astrology club in your area; many are listed in astrology magazines available at your local newsstand. In response to many requests for referrals, the NCGR has compiled a directory of professional astrologers, which includes a glossary of terms and an explanation of specialties within the astrological field. Contact the NCGR headquarters (see Chapter 6 and Chapter 7 in this book) for information.

Warning Signals

As a potentially lucrative freelance business, astrology has always attracted self-styled experts who may not have the knowledge or the counseling experience to give a helpful reading. These astrologers can range from the well-meaning amateur to the charlatan or street-corner gypsy who has for many years given astrology a bad name. Be very wary of astrologers who claim to have occult powers or who make pretentious claims of celebrated clients or miraculous achievements. You can often tell from the initial phone conversation if the astrologer is legitimate. He or she should ask for your birthday time and place, then conduct the conversation in a professional manner. Any astrologer who gives a reading based only on your sun sign is highly suspect.

When you arrive at the reading, the astrologer should be prepared. The consultation should be conducted in a private, quiet place. The astrologer should be interested in your problems of the moment. A good reading involves feedback on your part. So if the reading is not relating to your concerns, you should let the astrologer know. You should feel free to ask questions and get clarifications of technical terms. The more you actively participate, rather than expecting the astrologer to carry the reading or come forth with oracular predictions, the more meaningful your experience will be. An astrologer should help you validate your current experience and be frank about possible negative happenings, but also suggest a positive course of action.

In their approach to a reading, some astrologers may be more literal, others more intuitive. Those who have had counseling training may take a more psychological approach. Though some astrologers may seem to have an almost psychic ability, extrasensory perception or any other parapsychological talent is not essential. A very accurate picture can be drawn from the data in your horoscope chart.

An astrologer may do several charts for each client, including one for the time of birth and a "progressed chart," showing the evolution from birth to the present time. According to your individual needs, there are many other possibilities, such as a chart for a different location if you are contemplating a change of place. Relationships between any two people, things, or events can be interpreted with a chart that compares one partner's horoscope with the other's. A composite chart, which uses the midpoint between planets in two individual charts to describe the relationship, is another commonly used device.

An astrologer will be particularly interested in transits, those times when cycling planets activate the planets or sensitive points in your birth chart. These indicate important events in your life.

Many astrologers offer tape-recorded readings, another option to consider, especially if the astrologer you choose lives at a distance. In this case, you'll be mailed a taped reading based on your birth chart. This type of reading is more personal than a computer printout and can give you valuable insights, though it is not equivalent to a live dialogue with the astrologer when you can discuss your specific interests and issues of the moment.

What to Expect from a Telephone Reading

Telephone readings come in two varieties: a dial-in taped reading, usually recorded in advance by an astrologer, or a live consultation with an "astrologer" on the other end of the line. The taped readings are general daily or weekly forecasts, applied to all members of your sign and charged by the minute. The quality depends on the astrologer. One caution: Be aware that these readings can run up quite a telephone bill, especially if you get into the habit of calling every day. Be sure that you are aware of the per-minute cost of each call beforehand.

Live telephone readings also vary with the expertise of the astrologer. Ideally, the astrologer at the other end of the line enters your birth data into a computer, which then quickly calculates your chart. This chart will be referred to during the consultation. The advantage of a live telephone reading is that your individual chart is used and you can ask about a specific problem. However, before you invest in any reading, be sure that your astrologer is qualified and that you fully understand in advance how much you will be charged. There should be no unpleasant financial surprises later.

About Computer-Generated Reports

Companies that offer computer programs (such as ACS, Matrix, Astrolabe) also offer a variety of computer-generated horoscope readings. These can be quite comprehensive, offering a beautiful printout of the chart plus many pages of detailed information about each planet and aspect of the chart. You can then study it at your convenience. Of course, the interpretations will be general, since there is no personal input from you, and may not cover your immediate concerns. Since computer-generated horoscopes are much lower in cost than live consultations, you might consider them as either a supplement or a preparation for an eventual live reading. You'll then be more familiar with your chart and able to plan specific questions in advance. They also make a terrific gift for astrology fans. (There are several companies, listed in Chapters 6 and 7, that offer computerized readings prepared by reputable astrologers.)

Whichever option you decide to pursue, may your reading be an empowering one!

CHAPTER 9

What You Need to Know About Your Rising Sign

At the moment you were born, announcing your arrival in the world with a lusty cry, your horoscope was determined by the astrological sign passing over the eastern horizon. This sign is known as either your *rising sign* or your *ascendant*. What makes a horoscope "yours" is this rising sign. Other babies born later or earlier on the same day, in the same hospital, will have most planets in the same signs as you do. Most of your classmates in elementary school will have several planets in the same signs as your planets, especially the slow-moving planets (Uranus, Neptune, Pluto) and very possibly Jupiter and Saturn, which usually spend a year or more in each sign. But the moment you were born, in a specific place, is yours alone.

The degree of the sign on the horizon is important because it determines the signs that will influence the houses of your chart. As the earth turns on its axis every 24 hours, so does the horoscope change with the rotation. Every four minutes a new degree of the 360-degree zodiac passes over the horizon, and every two hours a new sign will rise. If you have read the description of the "houses" in Chapter 3 of this book, you'll know that the houses are twelve stationary divisions of the horoscope, which represent areas of life. The sign moving over the boundary (cusp) of each house describes that area of life. Sagittarius on the cusp of the second house, for instance, means you will deal with money in a Sagittarius way.

The rising sign marks the border of the first house, which represents your first presentation to the world, your physical body, how you come across to others. Once the rising

132

sign is established, it becomes possible to analyze a chart accurately because the astrologer knows in which house or area of life the planets will operate. For instance, if Mars is in Gemini and your rising sign is Taurus, then Mars will most likely be active in the second house, the house of finances, of your chart. If you were born later in the day and your rising sign is Virgo, then Mars will be positioned at the top of your chart, energizing your tenth house, the house of career.

Many astrologers insist on knowing the exact time of a client's birth before they will analyze a chart. The more exact your birth time, the more accurately an astrologer can position the planets in your chart. This is important because if you were born when the midportion of a sign was rotating over the horizon and a key planet, let's say Saturn, was in the early degrees of that sign, then it would already be over the horizon, located in the twelfth house rather than the first. So the interpretation of your horoscope would be quite different: You would not have the serious Saturn influence in the way you come across to others, which would be the case if you were born an hour earlier. If a planet is near the ascendant, sometimes even a few minutes can make a big difference.

Your rising sign has an important relationship with your sun sign. Some will complement the sun sign; others hide it under a totally different mask, as if playing an entirely different role, making it difficult to guess the person's sun sign from outer appearances. This may be the reason why you might not look or act like your sun sign's archetype. For example, a Leo with a conservative Capricorn ascendant would come across as much more serious than a Leo with a fiery Aries or Sagittarius ascendant. The exception is when the sun sign is reinforced by other planets. Then, with other planets on its side, the sun may assert its personality much more strongly, overcoming the image of a contradictory rising sign. As another example, a Leo with Venus and Jupiter also in Leo might counteract the conservative image of the Capricorn ascendant given in the first example. However, in most cases, the ascendant is the ingredient most strongly reflected in the first impression you make.

Rising signs change every two hours with the earth's rotation. Those born early in the morning when the sun was on the horizon will be most likely to project the image of their sun sign. These people are often called a "double Aries" or a "double Virgo" because the same sun sign and ascendant reinforce each other.

Look up your rising sign from the chart at the end of this chapter. Since rising signs change every two hours, it is important to know your birth time as close to the minute as possible. Even a few minutes' difference could change the rising sign and therefore the setup of your chart. If you are unsure about the exact time, but know within a few hours, check the following descriptions to see which is most like the personality you project.

Aries Rising: Fiery Emotions

You are the most aggressive version of your sun sign, with boundless energy that can be used productively if it's channeled in the right direction. Watch a tendency to overreact emotionally and blow your top. You come across as openly competitive, a positive asset in business or sports. Be on guard against impatience, which could lead to head injuries. Your walk and bearing could have the telltale head forward Aries posture. You may wear more bright colors, especially red, than others of your sign. You may also have a tendency to drive your car faster.

Taurus Rising: The Earth Mother

You'll exude a protective nurturing quality, even if you're male, which draws those in need of TLC and support. You're slow-moving, with a beautiful (or distinctive) speaking or singing voice that can be especially soothing or melodious. You probably surround yourself with comfort, good food, luxurious surroundings, and other sensual pleasures. You prefer welcoming others into your home to gadding about. You may have a talent for business, especially in trading, appraising, and real estate. A Taurus ascendant gives a well-padded or curvaceous physique that gains weight easily. Women with this ascendant are naturally sexy in a bodacious way.

Gemini Rising: Expressive Talents

You're naturally sociable, with lighter, more ethereal mannerisms than others of your sign, especially if you're female. You love to communicate with people, and express your ideas and feelings easily. You may have a talent for writing or public speaking. You may thrive on a constantly changing scenario with a varied cast of characters, though you may be far more sympathetic and caring than you project. You will probably travel widely, changing partners and jobs several times (or juggle two at once). Physically, you should cultivate a calm, tranquil atmosphere because your nerves are quite sensitive.

Cancer Rising: Sensitive Antennae

Like billionaire Bill Gates, you are naturally acquisitive, possessive, private, a moneymaker. You easily pick up others' needs and feelings—a great gift in business, the arts, and personal relationships. But you must guard against overreacting or taking things too personally, especially during full moon periods. Find creative outlets for your natural nurturing gifts, such as helping the less fortunate, particularly children. Your insights would be helpful in psychology. Your desire to feed and care for others would be useful in the restaurant, hotel, or child-care industries. You may be especially fond of wearing romantic old clothes, collecting antiques, and, of course, dining on exquisite food. Since your body may retain fluids, pay attention to your diet. To relax, escape to places near water.

Leo Rising: The Scene Player

You may come across as more poised than you really feel. However, you play it to the hilt, projecting a proud royal presence. A Leo ascendant gives you a natural flair for drama, like Marilyn Monroe. You'll also project a much more outgoing, optimistic, sunny personality than others of your sign. You take care to please your public by always projecting your best star quality, probably tossing a luxuriant mane of hair or sporting a striking hairstyle. Females often dazzle with spectacular jewelry. Since you may have a strong parental nature, you could well be the regal family matriarch or patriarch.

Virgo Rising: Cool and Calculating

Virgo rising masks your inner nature with a practical, analytical outer image. You seem neat, orderly, more particular than others of your sign. Others in your life may feel they must live up to your high standards. Though at times you may be openly critical, this masks a well-meaning desire to have only the best for loved ones. Your sharp eye for details could be used in the financial world, or your literary skills could draw you to teaching or publishing. The healing arts, health care, and service-oriented professions attract many with a Virgo ascendant. Like Madonna, you're likely to take good care of yourself, with great attention to health, diet, and exercise. Physically, you may have a very sensitive digestive system.

Libra Rising: The Charmer

Libra rising makes you appear as a charmer, more of a social, public person than others of your sign. Your private life will extend beyond your home and family to include an active social life. You may tend to avoid confrontations in relationships, preferring to smooth the way or negotiate diplomatically, rather than give in to an emotional reaction. Because you are interested in all aspects of a situation, you may be slow to reach decisions. Physically, you'll have good proportions and pleasing symmetry. You're likely to have pleasing, if not beautiful, facial features. You move gracefully, and you have a winning smile and good taste in your clothes and home decor. Legal, diplomatic, or public relations professions could draw your interest. Men with Libra rising, like Bill Clinton and John F. Kennedy, have charming smiles and an easy social manner that charms the ladies.

Scorpio Rising: Magnetic Power

Even when you're in the public eye, like Jacqueline Onassis, you never lose your intriguing air of mystery and sense of underlying power. You can be a master manipulator, always in control and moving comfortably in the world of power. Your physical impression comes across as intense. Many of you have remarkable eyes, with a direct, penetrating gaze. But you'll never reveal your private agenda, and you tend to keep your true feelings under wraps (watch a tendency toward paranoia). You may have an interesting romantic history with secret love affairs. Many of you heighten your air of mystery by wearing black. You're happiest near water and should provide yourself with a seaside retreat.

Sagittarius Rising: The Wanderer

You travel with this ascendant. You may also be a more outdoor, sportive type, with an athletic, casual, outgoing air. Your moods are camouflaged with cheerful optimism or a philosophical attitude. Though you don't hesitate to speak your mind, you can also laugh at your troubles or crack a joke more easily than others of your sign, like Candice Bergen who is best known for her comedy role as the outspoken "Murphy Brown." A Sagittarius ascendant can also draw you to the field of higher education or to spiritual life. You'll seem to have less attachment to things and people, and may travel widely. Your strong, fast legs are a physical bonus.

Capricorn Rising: Serious Business

This rising sign makes you come across as serious, goal-oriented, disciplined, and careful with cash. You are not one of the zodiac's big spenders, though you might splurge occasionally on items with good investment value. You're the traditional, conservative type in dress and environment, and you might come across as quite formal and business-like. You'll function well in a structured or corporate environment where you can climb to the top. (You are always aware of who's the boss.) In your personal life, you could be a loner or a single parent who is "father and mother" to your children. Like Paul Newman, you're likely to prefer a quiet private life to living in the spotlight.

Aquarius Rising: One of a Kind

You come across as less concerned about what others think and could even be a bit eccentric. Your appearance is sure to be unique and memorable. You're more at ease with groups of people than others in your sign, and you may be attracted to public life. Your appearance may be unique, either unconventional or unimportant to you. Those of you whose sun is in a water sign (Cancer, Scorpio, Pisces) may exercise your nurturing qualities with a large group, an extended family, or a day-care or community center. Audrey Hepburn and Princess Diana, who had this rising sign, were known for their unique charisma and work on behalf of worthy causes.

Pisces Rising: Romantic Roles

Your creative, nurturing talents are heightened and so is your ability to project emotional drama. And your dreamy eyes and poetic air bring out the protective instinct in others. You could be attracted to the arts, especially theater, dance, film, and photography, or to psychology, spiritual practice, and charity work. You are happiest when you are using your creative ability to help others, like Robert Redford has done. Since you are vulnerable to mood swings, it is especially important for you to find interesting, creative work where you can express your talents and boost your self-esteem. Accentuate the positive. Be wary of escapist tendencies, particularly involving alcohol or drugs to which you are supersensitive.

RISING SIGNS—A.M. BIRTHS

	1 AM	2 AM	3 AM	4 AM	5 AM	6 AM	7 AM	8 AM	9 AM	10 AM	11 AM	12 NOON
Jan 1	Lib	Sc	Sc	Sc	Sag	Sag	Cap	Cap	Aq	Aq	Pis	Ar
Jan 9	Lib	Sc	Sc	Sag	Sag	Sag	Cap	Cap	Aq	Pis	Ar	Tau
Jan 17	Sc	Sc	Sc	Sag	Sag	Cap	Cap	Aq	Aq	Pis	Ar	Tau
Jan 25	Sc	Sc	Sag	Sag	Sag	Cap	Cap	Aq	Pis	Ar	Tau	Tau
Feb 2	Sc	Sc	Sag	Sag	Cap	Cap	Aq	Pis	Pis	Ar	Tau	Gem
Feb 10	Sc	Sag	Sag	Sag	Cap	Cap	Aq	Pis	Ar	Tau	Tau	Gem
Feb 18	Sc	Sag	Sag	Cap	Cap	Aq	Pis	Pis	Ar	Tau	Gem	Gem
Feb 26	Sag	Sag	Sag	Cap	Aq	Aq	Pis	Ar	Tau	Tau	Gem	Gem
Mar 6	Sag	Sag	Cap	Cap	Aq	Pis	Pis	Ar	Tau	Gem	Gem	Can
Mar 14	Sag	Cap	Cap	Aq	Aq	Pis	Ar	Tau	Tau	Gem	Gem	Can
Mar 22	Sag	Cap	Cap	Aq	Pis	Ar	Ar	Tau	Gem	Gem	Can	Can
Mar 30	Cap	Cap	Aq	Pis	Pis	Ar	Tau	Tau	Gem	Can	Can	Can
Apr 7	Cap	Cap	Aq	Pis	Ar	Ar	Tau	Gem	Gem	Can	Can	Leo
Apr 14	Cap	Aq	Aq	Pis	Ar	Tau	Tau	Gem	Gem	Can	Can	Leo
Apr 22	Cap	Aq	Pis	Ar	Ar	Tau	Gem	Gem	Gem	Can	Leo	Leo
Apr 30	Aq	Aq	Pis	Ar	Tau	Tau	Gem	Can	Can	Can	Leo	Leo
May 8	Aq	Pis	Ar	Ar	Tau	Gem	Gem	Can	Can	Leo	Leo	Leo
May 16	Aq	Pis	Ar	Tau	Gem	Gem	Can	Can	Can	Leo	Leo	Vir
May 24	Pis	Ar	Ar	Tau	Gem	Gem	Can	Can	Leo	Leo	Leo	Vir
June 1	Pis	Ar	Tau	Gem	Gem	Can	Can	Can	Leo	Leo	Vir	Vir
June 9	Ar	Ar	Tau	Gem	Gem	Can	Can	Leo	Leo	Leo	Vir	Vir
June 17	Ar	Tau	Gem	Gem	Can	Can	Can	Leo	Leo	Vir	Vir	Vir
June 25	Tau	Tau	Gem	Gem	Can	Can	Leo	Leo	Leo	Vir	Vir	Lib
July 3	Tau	Gem	Gem	Can	Can	Can	Leo	Leo	Vir	Vir	Vir	Lib
July 11	Tau	Gem	Gem	Can	Can	Leo	Leo	Leo	Vir	Vir	Lib	Lib
July 18	Gem	Gem	Can	Can	Can	Leo	Leo	Vir	Vir	Vir	Lib	Lib
July 26	Gem	Gem	Can	Can	Leo	Leo	Vir	Vir	Vir	Lib	Lib	Lib
Aug 3	Gem	Can	Can	Can	Leo	Leo	Vir	Vir	Vir	Lib	Lib	Sc
Aug 11	Gem	Can	Can	Leo	Leo	Leo	Vir	Vir	Lib	Lib	Lib	Sc
Aug 18	Can	Can	Can	Leo	Leo	Vir	Vir	Vir	Lib	Lib	Sc	Sc
Aug 27	Can	Can	Leo	Leo	Leo	Vir	Vir	Lib	Lib	Lib	Sc	Sc
Sept 4	Can	Can	Leo	Leo	Leo	Vir	Vir	Vir	Lib	Lib	Sc	Sc
Sept 12	Can	Leo	Leo	Leo	Vir	Vir	Lib	Lib	Lib	Sc	Sc	Sag
Sept 20	Leo	Leo	Leo	Vir	Vir	Vir	Lib	Lib	Sc	Sc	Sc	Sag
Sept 28	Leo	Leo	Leo	Vir	Vir	Lib	Lib	Lib	Sc	Sc	Sag	Sag
Oct 6	Leo	Leo	Vir	Vir	Vir	Lib	Lib	Sc	Sc	Sc	Sag	Sag
Oct 14	Leo	Vir	Vir	Vir	Lib	Lib	Lib	Sc	Sc	Sag	Sag	Cap
Oct 22	Leo	Vir	Vir	Lib	Lib	Lib	Sc	Sc	Sc	Sag	Sag	Cap
Oct 30	Vir	Vir	Vir	Lib	Lib	Sc	Sc	Sc	Sag	Sag	Cap	Cap
Nov 7	Vir	Vir	Lib	Lib	Lib	Sc	Sc	Sc	Sag	Sag	Cap	Cap
Nov 15	Vir	Vir	Lib	Lib	Sc	Sc	Sc	Sag	Sag	Cap	Cap	Aq
Nov 23	Vir	Lib	Lib	Lib	Sc	Sc	Sag	Sag	Sag	Cap	Cap	Aq
Dec 1	Vir	Lib	Lib	Sc	Sc	Sc	Sag	Sag	Cap	Cap	Aq	Aq
Dec 9	Lib	Lib	Lib	Sc	Sc	Sag	Sag	Sag	Cap	Cap	Aq	Pis
Dec 18	Lib	Lib	Sc	Sc	Sc	Sag	Sag	Cap	Cap	Aq	Aq	Pis
Dec 28	Lib	Lib	Sc	Sc	Sag	Sag	Sag	Cap	Aq	Aq	Pis	Ar

RISING SIGNS—P.M. BIRTHS

	1 PM	2 PM	3 PM	4 PM	5 PM	6 PM	7 PM	8 PM	9 PM	10 PM	11 PM	12 MIDNIGHT
Jan 1	Tau	Gem	Gem	Can	Can	Can	Leo	Leo	Vir	Vir	Vir	Lib
Jan 9	Tau	Gem	Gem	Can	Can	Can	Leo	Leo	Vir	Vir	Vir	Lib
Jan 17	Gem	Gem	Can	Can	Can	Leo	Leo	Vir	Vir	Vir	Lib	Lib
Jan 25	Gem	Gem	Can	Can	Leo	Leo	Leo	Vir	Vir	Lib	Lib	Lib
Feb 2	Gem	Can	Can	Can	Leo	Leo	Vir	Vir	Vir	Lib	Lib	Sc
Feb 10	Gem	Can	Can	Leo	Leo	Leo	Vir	Vir	Lib	Lib	Lib	Sc
Feb 18	Can	Can	Can	Leo	Leo	Vir	Vir	Vir	Lib	Lib	Sc	Sc
Feb 26	Can	Can	Leo	Leo	Leo	Vir	Vir	Lib	Lib	Lib	Sc	Sc
Mar 6	Can	Leo	Leo	Leo	Vir	Vir	Vir	Lib	Lib	Sc	Sc	Sc
Mar 14	Can	Leo	Leo	Vir	Vir	Vir	Lib	Lib	Lib	Sc	Sc	Sag
Mar 22	Leo	Leo	Leo	Vir	Vir	Lib	Lib	Lib	Sc	Sc	Sc	Sag
Mar 30	Leo	Leo	Vir	Vir	Vir	Lib	Lib	Sc	Sc	Sc	Sag	Sag
Apr 7	Leo	Leo	Vir	Vir	Lib	Lib	Lib	Sc	Sc	Sc	Sag	Sag
Apr 14	Leo	Vir	Vir	Vir	Lib	Lib	Sc	Sc	Sc	Sag	Sag	Cap
Apr 22	Leo	Vir	Vir	Lib	Lib	Lib	Sc	Sc	Sc	Sag	Sag	Cap
Apr 30	Vir	Vir	Vir	Lib	Lib	Sc	Sc	Sc	Sag	Sag	Cap	Cap
May 8	Vir	Vir	Lib	Lib	Lib	Sc	Sc	Sag	Sag	Sag	Cap	Cap
May 16	Vir	Vir	Lib	Lib	Sc	Sc	Sc	Sag	Sag	Cap	Cap	Aq
May 24	Vir	Lib	Lib	Lib	Sc	Sc	Sag	Sag	Sag	Cap	Cap	Aq
June 1	Vir	Lib	Lib	Sc	Sc	Sc	Sag	Sag	Cap	Cap	Aq	Aq
June 9	Lib	Lib	Lib	Sc	Sc	Sag	Sag	Sag	Cap	Cap	Aq	Pis
June 17	Lib	Lib	Sc	Sc	Sc	Sag	Sag	Cap	Cap	Aq	Aq	Pis
June 25	Lib	Lib	Sc	Sc	Sag	Sag	Sag	Cap	Cap	Aq	Pis	Ar
July 3	Lib	Sc	Sc	Sc	Sag	Sag	Cap	Cap	Aq	Aq	Pis	Ar
July 11	Lib	Sc	Sc	Sag	Sag	Sag	Cap	Cap	Aq	Pis	Ar	Tau
July 18	Sc	Sc	Sc	Sag	Sag	Cap	Cap	Cap	Aq	Pis	Ar	Tau
July 26	Sc	Sc	Sag	Sag	Sag	Cap	Cap	Aq	Pis	Ar	Tau	Tau
Aug 3	Sc	Sc	Sag	Sag	Cap	Cap	Aq	Aq	Pis	Ar	Tau	Gem
Aug 11	Sc	Sag	Sag	Sag	Cap	Cap	Aq	Pis	Ar	Tau	Tau	Gem
Aug 18	Sc	Sag	Sag	Cap	Cap	Aq	Pis	Pis	Ar	Tau	Gem	Gem
Aug 27	Sag	Sag	Sag	Cap	Cap	Aq	Pis	Ar	Tau	Tau	Gem	Gem
Sept 4	Sag	Sag	Cap	Cap	Aq	Pis	Pis	Ar	Tau	Gem	Gem	Can
Sept 12	Sag	Sag	Cap	Aq	Aq	Pis	Ar	Tau	Tau	Gem	Gem	Can
Sept 20	Sag	Cap	Cap	Aq	Pis	Pis	Ar	Tau	Gem	Gem	Can	Can
Sept 28	Cap	Cap	Aq	Aq	Pis	Ar	Tau	Tau	Gem	Gem	Can	Can
Oct 6	Cap	Cap	Aq	Pis	Ar	Ar	Tau	Gem	Gem	Can	Can	Leo
Oct 14	Cap	Aq	Aq	Pis	Ar	Tau	Tau	Gem	Gem	Can	Can	Leo
Oct 22	Cap	Aq	Pis	Ar	Ar	Tau	Gem	Gem	Can	Can	Leo	Leo
Oct 30	Aq	Aq	Pis	Ar	Tau	Tau	Gem	Can	Can	Can	Leo	Leo
Nov 7	Aq	Aq	Pis	Ar	Tau	Tau	Gem	Can	Can	Can	Leo	Leo
Nov 15	Aq	Pis	Ar	Tau	Gem	Gem	Can	Can	Can	Leo	Leo	Vir
Nov 23	Pis	Ar	Ar	Tau	Gem	Gem	Can	Can	Leo	Leo	Leo	Vir
Dec 1	Pis	Ar	Tau	Tau	Gem	Can	Can	Can	Leo	Leo	Vir	Vir
Dec 9	Ar	Tau	Tau	Gem	Gem	Can	Can	Leo	Leo	Vir	Vir	Vir
Dec 18	Ar	Tau	Gem	Gem	Can	Can	Can	Leo	Leo	Vir	Vir	Vir
Dec 28	Tau	Tau	Gem	Gem	Can	Can	Leo	Leo	Vir	Vir	Vir	Lib

CHAPTER 10

Parenting by the Stars

During 2003, the lucky and expansive planet Jupiter travels through Leo, the sign of children, then moves into Virgo, the sign of caregiving. It's the ideal time to look at what astrology has to say about parenting. By illuminating your child's basic nature, astrology can help you decide which kind of care will develop positive attributes and fulfill the individual needs of each sun sign.

If you are planning a family, you might be considering timing the birth of your child to complement the other family sun signs. However, there is also the theory that each child will come at a time that will be right for what he or she is meant to accomplish. In other words, if you were hoping for a Libra child and he or she arrives during Virgo, that Virgo energy may be just what is needed to stimulate or complement your family. Remember, there are many astrological elements besides the sun sign that indicate strong family ties. Usually each child will share a particular planetary placement, an emphasis on a particular sign or house, or a certain chart configuration with the parents and other family members. Often there is a significant planetary angle that will define the parent–child relationship, such as family sun signs that form a T-square or a triangle.

One important thing you can do is to be sure the exact moment of birth is recorded. (There are many jokes about the astrologer–mother who goes into labor with a stopwatch!) This will be essential in calculating an accurate astrological chart, if you should wish to have one drawn up in the future.

The following descriptions can be applied to the sun or moon sign (if known) of a child. The sun sign will describe basic personality, and the moon sign indicates the child's emotional needs. It wouldn't hurt to read Pisces as well, with Mars and Uranus in Pisces for much of this year, since many children born in 2003 will have a strong Pisces emphasis.

The Aries Child

Baby Aries is quite a handful! This energetic child will walk—and run—as soon as possible, and perform daring feats of exploration. Caregivers should be vigilant. Little Aries seems to know no fear, and is especially vulnerable to head injuries. Many Aries children, in their rush to get on with life, seem hyperactive; they are easily frustrated when they can't get their own way. Violent temper tantrums and dramatic physical displays are par for the course with this child.

The very young Aries should be monitored carefully, since they are prone to take risks and may injure themselves. Aries love to take things apart and may break toys easily. But with encouragement, the child will develop formidable coordination. Aries bossy tendencies should be molded into leadership qualities rather than bullying techniques. Otherwise, the "me-first" Aries will have many clashes with other strong-willed youngsters. Encourage this child to take out aggressions and frustrations in active, competitive sports, where they usually excel. When young Aries learns to focus energies long enough to master a subject and learns consideration for others, the indomitable Aries spirit will rise to the head of the class.

The Caregiver for Aries

Since this child is usually vocal in expressing needs, you'll have little guesswork. Your key emphasis is to help this child control his or her temper, develop self-discipline, and respect authority. You may find yourself breaking up quite a few arguments. Be vigilant, but give this child plenty of space. Encourage young Aries to express overflowing energy in constructive physical activity and to develop leadership skills. It is important to emphasize manners and consideration for others, which will help willful Aries get along socially with playmates.

The Taurus Child

This is a cuddly, affectionate child who eagerly explores the world of the senses, especially the sense of taste and touch. The Taurus child can be a big eater and will put on weight easily if not encouraged to exercise. Since this child likes comfort and gravitates to beauty, try coaxing little Taurus to exercise to music. Or take him or her outdoors on hikes or long walks in a local park or woodland. Though Taurus may be a slow learner, this sign has an excellent retentive memory and generally masters a subject thoroughly. Taurus is interested in results and will see each project patiently through to completion, continuing long after others have given up.

Choose Taurus toys carefully to help develop innate talents. Construction toys, such as blocks or erector sets, appeal to their love of building. Paints or crayons develop their sense of color. Many Taurus have musical talent and love to sing, which is apparent at a young age. Little Taurus will usually want a pet or two, and a few plants of his or her own. Give little Taurus a mini-garden and watch the natural green thumb develop. This child has a strong sense of acquisition and an early grasp of material value. After filling a piggy bank, Taurus graduates to a savings account—before other children have even started to learn the value of money.

The Caregiver for Taurus

Be affectionate, demonstrative, and generous with hugs and cuddles. Teach little Taurus to share possessions and to give as well as to accumulate. Be patient. Any pushing will bring out the Taurus stubborn side, and Taurus has a will that won't be budged. Introduce changes and new things gradually, for Taurus adapts best when well prepared.

The Gemini Child

Little Gemini will talk as soon as possible, filling the air with questions and chatter. This is a friendly child who enjoys social contact, seems to require company, and adapts quickly to different surroundings. Geminis have quick minds that easily grasp the use of words, books, and telephones, and will probably learn to talk and read at an earlier age than most.

Though they are fast learners, Gemini may have a short attention span, darting from subject to subject. Projects and games that help focus the mind could be used to help them concentrate. Musical instruments, typewriters, and computers help older Gemini children combine mental with manual dexterity. Geminis should be encouraged to finish what they start before they go on to another project. Otherwise, they can become jack-of-all trade types who have trouble completing anything they do. Their disposition is usually cheerful and witty, making these children popular with their peers and delightful company at home.

The Caregiver for Gemini

Gemini needs good communication, discussion, and sharing. This is a verbal child who enjoys talking things over and who grasps ideas easily. Avoid isolation or too much solitude. Give this child a variety of toys to suit the need for diversity. Alternate different kinds of activity. Teach little Gemini to follow projects through to completion.

The Cancer Child

This emotional, sensitive child is especially influenced by patterns set in early life. Young Cancers cling to their first memories as well as their childhood possessions. They thrive in calm emotional waters, with a loving, protective mother, and usually remain close to her (even if their relationship with her was difficult) throughout their lives. Divorce, death—anything that disturbs the safe family unit—is devastating to Cancers, who may need extra support and reassurance during a family crisis.

They sometimes need a firm hand to push the positive, creative side of their personality and to discourage them from getting swept away by emotional moods or resorting to emotional manipulation to get their way. If this child is praised and encouraged to find creative expression, Cancers will be able to express their positive side consistently on a firm, secure foundation.

The Caregiver for Cancer

Pour on praise and encouragement, and tone down criticism. The calmer the home atmosphere, the better. This child may need more time with Mother than other children, so be sure that the primary caregiver is warm, motherly, and supportive.

The Leo Child

Leo children love the limelight and will plot to get the lion's share of attention. These children assert themselves with flair and drama, and can behave like tiny tyrants to get their way. But in general they have a sunny, positive disposition, and are rarely subject to blue moods. At school, they're the type that is voted most popular, head cheerleader, homecoming queen. Leo is sure to be noticed for personality, if not for stunning looks or academic work; the homely Leo will be a class clown; the unhappy Leo can be the class bully.

Above all, a Leo child cannot tolerate being ignored for long. Drama or performing arts classes, sports, and school politics are healthy ways for Leo to be a star. But Leos must learn to take lesser roles occasionally, or they will have some painful put-downs in store. Usually, Leo popularity is well earned; they are hard workers who try to measure up to their own high standards—and usually succeed.

The Caregiver for Leo

Warmth, affection, praise, and attention are key words for Leo's parents and caregivers. Choose an open, warm, positive person to care for Leo, rather than a strict disciplinarian. Give Leo plenty of playmates, a fun atmosphere. Lonely Leos will resort to dramatic scenes to capture center stage. Encourage their natural leadership ability. Cheer on their outside activities. Develop their performing talents. It is important to teach them to channel their "show-off" tendencies in creative ways so they learn to share the spotlight.

The Virgo Child

The young Virgo can be a quiet, serious child, with a quick, intelligent mind. Early on, little Virgo shows far more attention to detail and concern with small things than other children. Little Virgo has a built-in sense of order and a fascination of how things work. It is important for these children to have a place of their own, which they can order as they wish and where they can read or busy themselves with crafts and hobbies.

This child's personality can be very sensitive. Little Virgo may get "hyper" and overreact to seemingly small irritations, which can take the form of stomach upsets or delicate digestive systems. But this child will flourish where there is mental stimulation and a sense of order. Virgos thrive in school, especially in writing or language skills, and seem truly happy when buried in books. Chances are, young Virgo will learn to read ahead of classmates. Hobbies that involve detail work or that develop fine craftsmanship are especially suited to young Virgos.

The Caregiver for Virgo

Though they might not show it, Virgo children need dem-
onstrations of affection and support to shore up sensitive
self-esteem. Coach the shy child in social and athletic skills.
Perfecting a sport or dance routine can engross young
Virgos and give them healthy exercise. (It is often difficult
to get these children to exercise.) Young Virgos may be
quite demanding of themselves and others, so encourage
them to lighten up and to be more accepting of imperfec-
tions.

The Libra Child

The Libra child learns early about the power of charm and
good looks. This is often a very physically appealing child
with an enchanting dimpled smile, who is naturally sociable
and enjoys the company of both children and adults. It is
a rare Libra child who is a discipline problem. But when
their behavior is unacceptable, they respond better to calm
discussion than displays of emotion, especially if the discussion revolves around fairness. Because young Libras without a strong direction tend to drift with the mood of the
group, these children should be encouraged to develop
their unique talents and powers of discrimination so they
can later stand on their own.

In school, this child is usually popular and will often have
to choose between social invitations and studies. In the teen
years, social pressures mount as the young Libra begins to
look for a partner. This is the sign of "best friends," so
Libra's choice of companions can have a strong effect on
his or her future direction. Beautiful Libra girls may be
tempted to go steady or have an unwise early marriage.
Chances are, both sexes will fall in and out of love several
times in their search for the ideal partner.

The Caregiver for Libra

Naturally cooperative, Libras are usually quite easy to supervise. These children relate well to others and usually

enjoy playing with other children. Or they'll share activities with a companion or special friend. Develop their creative talents and artistic hobbies. Give them an attractive harmonious atmosphere to live in, letting them choose the colors and decor of their room.

The Scorpio Child

The Scorpio child may seem quiet and shy on the surface, but will surprise others with intensity of feelings and force of willpower. Scorpio children are single-minded when they want something and intensely passionate about whatever they do. One of a caregiver's tasks is to teach this child to balance activities and emotions, yet at the same time to make the most of their great concentration and intense commitment.

Since young Scorpios do not show their depth of feelings easily, parents will have to learn to read almost imperceptible signs that troubles are brewing beneath the surface. Both Scorpio boys and girls enjoy games of power and control on or off the playground. She may take an early interest in the opposite sex, masquerading as a tomboy, while he may be intensely competitive and something of a loner. When their powerful energies are directed into work, sports, or challenging studies, Scorpio is a superachiever thoroughly focused on a goal. With trusted friends, young Scorpio is devoted and caring—the proverbial friend "through thick and thin," loyal for life.

The Caregiver for Scorpio

Scorpio children need a great deal of affection and guidance in expressing their sensitive feelings. It is especially important not to violate their trust (these children can instantly detect what's going on behind closed doors), invade their privacy (allow them secret places to stash special belongings), or read their diary. A creative caregiver can help channel one of this child's greatest assets—the intense Scorpio drive—into constructive areas that will assure approval and success.

The Sagittarius Child

This restless, athletic child will be out of the playpen and off on explorative adventures as soon as possible. Little Sagittarius is remarkably well coordinated, attempting daredevil feats on any wheeled vehicle from scooters to skateboards. These natural athletes need little encouragement to channel their energies into sports. Their cheerful friendly dispositions earn them popularity in school. Once they have found a subject where their talent and imagination can soar, they will do well academically. They love animals, especially horses, and will be sure to have a pet or two, if not a home zoo. When they are old enough to take care of themselves, they'll clamor to be off on adventures of their own, away from home if possible.

This is a child who loves to travel, will not get homesick at summer camp, and may sign up to be a foreign exchange student or spend summers abroad. Outdoor adventure appeals to little Sagittarius, especially if it involves an active sport, such as skiing, cycling, or mountain climbing. Give them enough space and encouragement, and their fiery spirit will propel them to achieve high goals.

The Caregiver for Sagittarius

This independent child needs plenty of room to move around—no fenced-in playpens. Take the young Sagittarius on your travels, letting him or her explore new places. This is a great game player, full of laughs and fun. Be enthusiastic. Encourage Sagittarius to aim high and follow through, to take responsibility for their actions.

The Capricorn Child

This purposeful goal-oriented child will work to capacity if he or she feels this will bring results. They're not ones who enjoy work for its own sake—there must be an end in sight. Authority figures can do much to motivate this child. But once set on an upward path, young Capricorn will mobilize his or her energy and talent and will work harder, and with more perseverance, than any other sign. Capricorn has built-in self-discipline that can achieve remarkable results, even if lacking the flashy personality, quick brainpower, or penetrating insight of others. Once involved, young Capricorn will stick to a task until it is mastered. This child also knows how to use others to advantage, and may well become the team captain or class president.

A wise parent will set realistic goals for the Capricorn child, paving the way for the early thrill of achievement. Youngsters should be encouraged to express their caring, feeling side to others, as well as their natural aptitude for leadership. Capricorn children may be especially fond of grandparents and older relatives, and will enjoy spending time with them and learning from them. It is not uncommon for young Capricorns to have an older mentor or teacher who guides them. With their great respect for authority, Capricorn children will take this influence very much to heart.

The Caregiver for Capricorn

Capricorn responds well to a structured environment with clear boundaries and rules. Reward early achievements, helping young Capricorn aim high and set realistic goals. Give them small responsibilities early (they can handle it) and much praise. Teach them generosity with their siblings and playmates. Encourage Capricorn to nurture younger friends and pets. Help them relate to their peer group in a noncompetitive way.

The Aquarius Child

The Aquarius child has an innovative, well-focused mind that often streaks so far ahead of peers that this child seems like an "oddball." Routine studies never hold the restless youngster for long; he or she will look for another, more experimental place to try out their ideas and to develop their inventions. Life is a laboratory to the inquiring Aquarius mind.

School politics, sports, science, and the arts offer scope for this child's talents. But if there is no room for expression within approved social limits, Aquarius is sure to rebel. Questioning institutions and religions comes naturally, so these children may find an outlet elsewhere, becoming "rebels with a cause." It is better not to force this child to conform. Instead, channel forward-thinking young minds into constructive group activities.

The Caregiver for Aquarius

Play up whatever is unique about Aquarius children; never criticize them for being nonconformists. Encourage independence, originality, and inventiveness. Give them a safe place to explore and experiment. When disciplining Aquarius, appeal to reason and concern for the good of the group, rather than enforcing rigid rules.

The Pisces Child

Give young Pisces praise, applause, and a gentle but firm push in the right direction. Lovable Pisces children may be abundantly talented. But they may be hesitant to express themselves because they are quite sensitive and easily hurt. It is a parent's challenge to help them gain self-esteem and self-confidence. However, this same sensitivity makes them trusted friends who'll have many confidants as they develop socially. It also endows many Pisces with spectacular creative talent.

Pisces adores drama and theatrics of all sorts. Encourage them to channel their creativity into art forms rather than indulging in emotional dramas. As they develop their creative ideas, they may need more solitude than other children. But though daydreaming can be creative, it is important that these natural dreamers not dwell too long in the world of fantasy. Teach them practical coping skills for the real world. Since Pisces are sensitive physically, parents should help them build strong bodies with proper diet and regular exercise. Young Pisces may gravitate to individual sports, such as swimming, sailing, and skiing, rather than to team sports. Or they may prefer artistic physical activities like dance or ice skating.

Born "givers," these children are often drawn to the underdog (they fall quickly for sob stories) and attract those who might take advantage of their empathic nature. Teach them to choose friends wisely and to set boundaries in relationships, to protect their emotional vulnerability—invaluable lessons in later life.

The Caregiver for Pisces

Since Pisces children react strongly to their emotional and physical environment, give them a harmonious, rational atmosphere to balance their sensitive feelings. Establish clear emotional boundaries to give Pisces secure footing. Build up their confidence by praising their natural creative talent. Because Pisces children need to integrate their world of fantasy with the realities of life, emphasize the need to develop order, clarity, and discrimination.

CHAPTER 11

Let Astrology Point the Way to Financial Opportunity

Coming up is a year of changes, the logical time to revamp your finances. Like many tyrants, kings, and tycoons, you, too, can benefit from astrology's insights in predicting current growth trends. (The legendary tycoon J. P. Morgan is rumored to have consulted an astrologer.) So find out where your best opportunities lie and what stage of the wheel of success you'll be passing through this year, then make savvy decisions to play the market or stay on the sidelines. Using the trends in this chapter, you can formulate your strategy for building wealth in any kind of market during 2003.

Think Out of the Box

When the planet Uranus changes signs, as it does in 2003, it's time to think out of the box and tune your antennae to the future. As Uranus moves into Pisces, all things relating to Pisces will become major issues for the next seven years. While Uranus was in Aquarius, the sign of high technology, it sent the stocks of dot coms and Internet start-ups soaring. Now watch what it does for Pisces businesses. Scientific medicine should have spectacular success. Look for new advances in pharmaceuticals, especially antibiotics (inspired by bioterrorism), in embryonic research, and in genetics. Hospitals should become more focused on treating each person as an individual, perhaps based on a personal genetic profile. There should be terrific investment opportunities in these areas.

Our huge appetite for oil (petroleum is associated with Pisces) has caused international crises and conflicts, and may remain one of America's most vulnerable points. This year, expect major changes in our energy policy and consumption. Redesigned fuel-efficient or electrical cars are possibilities. Offshore oil exploration and development of oceanic energy reserves may be accelerated, as well as development of hydroelectric power companies, as we tap oceans and rivers for power sources. Look for investment opportunities in power-saving devices of all kinds.

Pisces is associated with all things aquatic, of course. Fish farms, water purifying systems, swimming pools, ocean studies, shipping, sea plants as food, ocean exploration, submarine travel, and naval supplies are investment possibilities.

Creative areas have historically done well, as Uranus in Pisces stimulates avant-garde artists. New music, computer-generated art and entertainment, and the dance world (especially ballet) should thrive. Other Pisces areas include film, footwear, cosmetics, podiatry, fountains, gases, dance, alcohol and other intoxicants, any business involving fantasy and creativity, religion-oriented businesses, yoga and other spiritual practices, retreats, charities, and any institutions that help the underdog.

The Jupiter Factor

Good fortune and big money are always associated with Jupiter, which embodies the principle of expansion. Jupiter has a twelve-year cycle, staying in each sign for approximately one year. When Jupiter enters a sign, the fields influenced by that sign seem new and profitable, and they usually provide excellent investment opportunities. Areas of speculation governed by the sign Jupiter is passing through will have the hottest market potential—they're the ones that currently arouse excitement and enthusiasm.

During 2003, Jupiter transits two signs. It completes its

trip through Leo on August 27, then enters Virgo. The areas each sign influences should have expansive opportunities. Readers with strong fire sign (Leo, Aries, Sagittarius) influences in their horoscope should have many growth opportunities during the first half of the year. Those born in earth signs (Virgo, Capricorn, Taurus) should take advantage of Jupiter's beneficial rays starting in September.

On the downside, Aquarius may feel out of sync and need to focus on relationships rather than a personal agenda until Jupiter changes signs in September.

Jupiter-Favored Growth Areas

Look to areas favored by Leo until August 27: games, places of amusement, show business, theater, entertainers, jewelry, showy floral arrangements, gold and the gold coin business, golf, loan companies, oranges, the Pacific Ocean area, all pleasurable and luxurious things, high fashion, sporting events and arenas, gambling casinos, the Sun Belt.

Starting in September, watch these efficient Virgo-related areas: organizers, accountants, administrators, haute cuisine, public health, the medical and health industry, medicinal herbs, grain production, education, the service business, sanitation, sewing and tailoring, personal trainers, health clubs. All that is health-promoting, detail-oriented, and educational gets a big boost from Virgo.

In Your Personal Life

Find the house where Jupiter in Leo and Jupiter in Virgo will fall in your chart to indicate where you'll have the most expansive potential this year. Just look up your rising sign from the chart in this book (pp. 140–141) and check the following list. (Those who know their exact birth time and place, and who have access to the Internet, can get an accurate chart online from one of the sources recommended in the Internet chapter in this book.)

ARIES RISING: A CREATIVE BONANZA
For anyone involved in creative fields, this is bonanza time—the inspiration flows! Put some fun into your life and

help others to do so for profit. Your best ideas will come when you play at your job (don't they always?), finding more creative ways to get the work done. The only danger here is too much fun—you may be more interested in pleasure than profit. Love affairs, fun times, and recreation can impose on work time. You may find it difficult to stick to any routines. Since this placement also rules children, you may find yourself involved with them in some way—or you may become a parent.

TAURUS RISING: LUCK BEGINS AT HOME

Your success potential is tied to your domestic life. This is often a time of moving or relocating, as you try to arrange your personal lifestyle for the next twelve years. This is the time to establish your personal space, strengthen family ties, and give yourself a solid base of operations. You can now create the much-needed balance between your private life and the outside world that will shore you up for the next twelve years. Aim for greater family harmony and inner strength. Opportunities to invest in real estate could be winners.

GEMINI RISING: COMMUNICATIONS

You will overflow with ideas, so record them for future reference. Write up a storm! Sign up for a course that interests you—it could pay off in the future. Your social life is buzzing, as the phone rings off the hook. Make new business contacts in your local area. You may also find a lucky financial venture that involves your friends or siblings. In the fall, home life takes priority. This is the time to redecorate, renovate, expand, or buy a new home.

CANCER RISING: INCREASE YOUR SECURITY

Be a saver, not a spender, this year. Now is the time to use those contacts you made last year to consolidate your financial security. You may find that your cash flow increases, as there is generally more money available for big splurges. Watch this tendency! It might be a better idea to use this time of opportunity to protect yourself with backup funds for a more secure future. This is a time to develop good money management habits!

LEO RISING: THE IMAGE THAT SELLS

For most of the year, you hold the luckiest cards. With Jupiter energizing your ascendant, you look like a winner without even trying. Use this time to kick off the next twelve-year cycle in the most advantageous way. Circulate among influential people, make personal contacts, sell yourself. Push yourself out in the public eye, even if you're the shy type. This is the time to be your most social self! One cautionary note: Jupiter means expansion—and this position rules your physical body—so watch your diet. You'll tend to put on weight easily. The latter half of the year, focus on making a budget and savings plan that you can live with. If you've been caught up in an extravagant lifestyle, do a reality check.

VIRGO RISING: WARM-UP FOR THE BIG TIME

You've come to the end of a twelve-year Jupiter cycle, and in September will start another cycle. Use the first half of the year to review what you've learned in the last twelve years, to experiment with new ventures. Proceed slowly, as you will be bringing many matters that have occupied you over the past dozen years to a close. It's also a good time to get centered spiritually, to line up your ducks in a row, so you'll be ready to seize the moment when opportunities arise in September with Jupiter in Virgo. Then go for it in October when you'll hold the best cards in the deck.

LIBRA RISING: THE BIG LEAGUE

Jupiter brings you group connections this year. Others will be looking to you for inspiration. Since you can now win the support of the movers and shakers in your field and are ready to lead the pack, put some of the ideas formulated in previous cycles into action. This is the time when you make the team, come to the aid of your party, or find a new audience for your talents. In the fall, you may be ready for some solitude! This is a good time to rest, regroup, do some solitary creative work, or fund-raise for your favorite hospital or charity.

SCORPIO RISING: BUILD YOUR PRESTIGE
It's a great time to promote yourself, be highly visible, and build up your professional image. This cycle favors public activities rather than domestic life. It's a great time to deal with VIPs and top brass. You should be feeling superconfident, and it will show. You may be starting a new career or making a stronger commitment to the one you're in. Follow up with social contacts, and exercise your leadership skill in the fall.

SAGITTARIUS RISING: AIM HIGH
This is the ideal time to get higher education, develop your philosophy of life, and formulate new directions for the future. Aim high, look at the big overall picture. Publish your book, get a college or graduate degree, travel abroad. Expand your mind and horizons. Take a calculated risk. You may feel like changing your life around and trying something completely new. The ideas you get early in the year and the interesting people you meet will enhance your reputation and career.

CAPRICORN RISING: WATCH THE CASH FLOW
You'll have opportunities to use credit and to deal with banks, loan companies, and the IRS. Be very careful with your credit cards during this period. There could be a strong temptation to overextend. You may find others more than willing to lend you money at high interest. If you're a risk taker, you may have to keep a strict eye on expenditures—Jupiter encourages gambling! You might also find yourself managing money for others and getting involved in joint ventures.

AQUARIUS RISING: MAKING COMMITMENTS
Commitments can be fortunate for you this year. Many people marry at this time. However, this is not a good time for solo ventures. You are best off working in tandem and letting your partner share the spotlight. You may have to

submerge your own agenda for a while in order to take full advantage of this period. So think "togetherness." You can use others to your advantage, but don't try to take over. Since this is the area of open enemies, you could learn much about your adversaries and gain the advantage in the future.

PISCES RISING: DETAILS, DETAILS

This is the time when you may seem bogged down in details, in learning the operation of the company from the ground up, or in taking care of the mundane aspects that make a business operate efficiently. But remember, it is only through creating a smooth working operation that fortunes can be made in the long haul. You have only to read the financial section of your newspaper to see how many promising companies get swept away by poor management. This is also an excellent time to take care of yourself. Set up a diet and exercise regime. Get your body in good shape.

CHAPTER 12

The Astro-Dating Game

Be a love magnet by using the secrets of astrological seduction.

Do you know the turn-on color for Aries? Would you take a Cancer to a family dinner? Would playing hard to get make a Taurus pursue you? If you're looking for love, you'll want to make the best first impression possible to get your romance off to the right start. So what do you wear?

Look no further than astrology to give you the stellar secrets to attracting, pleasing, and pampering potential partners. In your sun sign chapters in this book you can evaluate your compatibility with every other sign. Then it's time to cast your bait in the right direction. Here's how to play the Astro-Dating game with every sign: where to meet one, where to go, and what to do.

Aries

WHERE TO MEET ONE:
Aries are impulsive, action-ready types who love the newest, hottest places. Keep up on the latest happenings in your town, the hip restaurants, sports events, competitions. You'll find Aries where the action is. When you get together, keep an upbeat, enthusiastic, positive attitude. No complaining, heavy emotions, or talk about previous relationships, please! Don't be too easy to get—this is one sign that enjoys pursuit.

WHERE TO GO:
Your Ram is an activist, so don't plan a cozy evening at home unless Aries is doing the cooking or watching the

tennis matches. Think adventure, excitement, fast action. Keep Aries moving. The newest dance club, a sports event, games of all kinds are good. Try races, adventure sports, spicy foods, the newest "scene," a live music event, a hike together, a workout, a bike trip, the wildest rides at your local amusement park. Be a doer!

WHAT TO WEAR:
Light Aries fires with red—if not a whole outfit, just a touch somewhere interesting. Wear one of the newest trends (if it looks good on you). Wear a hat to attract Aries attention. By all means, be up-to-date fashionwise. Be sure whatever shoes you wear can take lots of action, since you'll be on the go! Nothing turns a Ram off more than a date with sore feet!

Taurus

WHERE TO MEET ONE:
Meet Taurus where there's money to be made or handled: a stock broker's office, a bank, an investment adviser, a real estate office, a store. Scout the local real estate for sales in your area. A pet shop, dog run, zoo, or animal training school could lure animal lovers. Gardening stores, home improvement stores, art galleries, music stores, concerts, food emporiums, restaurants, and parks are other Taurus hangouts. Warning: This is a possessive sign, so if Taurus likes you, playing hard to get could be a signal that you're not interested.

WHERE TO GO:
Think rich and delicious. Taurus loves luxury, comfort, beauty, so let that be your clue. Pick a sensual environment. If you're inviting Taurus home, be sure to stock your refrigerator and be sure the place looks good and smells good. If you're wining and dining, scope out your Bull's food preferences and head for the poshest restaurant in town. If you're a super chef, then do a culinary tour de force for

Taurus, and be sure there are plenty of seconds. Finish with the richest dessert you can find, or have some delicious ice cream on hand. If you can't afford to wine and dine, then find the cafe with the best desserts and go after dinner. You can't go wrong with music, but find out what Taurus likes first. Other earthy attractions: picnics at a beautiful country setting, Shakespeare plays (he was a Taurus). Taurus is touchy-feely, so a dual massage could set the stage for seduction.

WHAT TO WEAR:

Most Taurus prefer classic, elegant, conservative clothes in beautiful sensual fabrics. There is the odd Taurus who wants you to look like a "babe" and goes for heavy-handed sex appeal. But if you're thinking long term, wear something soft and feminine (if you're female) in a fabric that begs to be touched, like cashmere. Taurus women like the rich look, so, if you're a man, dress like a tycoon or like you're about to become one.

Gemini

WHERE TO MEET ONE:

Keep up with the latest news and hit the hot spots. Geminis are on a constant search for mental stimulation, so they're sure to be at the most interesting place in town. A bookstore, a lecture by a famous person, the opening of a restaurant, the local newspaper office, the newest movie. A party, wedding, or other social event draws sociable Geminis. Don't be possessive with Gemini—this sign loves to flirt and will interpret jealousy as insecurity, a real downer.

WHERE TO GO:

Choose a place that appeals to Gemini mental interests and love of variety. Have several alternatives if Gemini gets bored or restless with your first choice. Pick a venue that promotes good conversation and has stimulating people nearby. Gemini is curious about other people. So if there are different cultures living in your town, unusual places, even if a bit oddball, plan an evening of exploration. Variety is spice to Gemini. So expect to share your dinner, or opt for a buffet or a cuisine where dishes are shared by everybody. A party followed by a lecture followed by a buffet dinner would be perfect. Gemini enjoys scenes with a constant flow of attractive people. A museum, a hot cafe or coffee bar, an exercise class, or a walk in an unexplored neighborhood would be fun. Be spontaneous. Don't hesitate to scrap your plans and try something else if the place you choose doesn't live up to expectations.

WHAT TO WEAR:
Gemini has an eye for style and will appreciate anything unique or unusual you wear. You can be as high fashion as you want with this sign. Just don't look boring. Since Gemini is attracted to beautiful hands, be sure your nails are manicured and wear a lovely ring.

Cancer

WHERE TO MEET ONE:
Food, family, shelter, and water are your key words for Cancer. Head for the shore, take boating or sailing lessons. Vacation at a resort with sailing or a fabulous beach. A gourmet restaurant or food store, a cooking class, a family reunion, an art or music venue, the local Home Depot, a housewarming party, a cookout at the beach are all places you might meet a Cancer. Take a course in photography or interior design (Cancers are talented at both).

WHERE TO GO:
Cancers are born romantics, highly emotional and sensitive. Usually, they're domestic and love to cook, so a terrific restaurant or an evening at home cooking together would go over well. Pull out your best dishes, candles, wine, and music for this home-loving sign. If you're going out, seafood is sure to be a hit. Rent a romantic movie, attend a

concert, go sailing or swimming—anything near water will be appreciated. Cancers are family-oriented, so don't be afraid to include them in your family celebrations. Encourage their creativity by taking a course together in cooking, photography, interior design, or home maintenance.

WHAT TO WEAR:
If you're a woman, wear something soft and clingy that shows off your curvaceous bosom; a nice chest is a big plus with Cancer. Classy couture looks are also winners (many top designers and fashion icons are Cancer). Cancers are sensitive to color coordination, so you're better off wearing subtle blues, greens, or neutrals that blend together. Think Armani. Jarring brights or oddball styles are a no-no.

Leo

WHERE TO MEET ONE:
Head for the Leo lairs: public life, politics, show business, big business, major social events, prestige restaurants, country clubs, gambling casinos, sporting events. Your Leo enjoys the spotlight. Join an amateur theater group or acting class. Canvass for your local political club. Shop at the priciest clothing and jewelry stores. Polish up your dancing technique, and shine with Leo on the dance floor. Parties are Leo magnets, so dress to the nines and socialize. Your attitude should be upbeat, positive, and adoring. Leo loves compliments—in quantity!

WHERE TO GO:
Show off your Leo—this is not a sign that prefers quiet evenings at home. Invite Leo to a local charity ball, a top sporting event, a big party. Take Leo out on the town, but make sure to go first-class. Leos love dressing up to the nines and consorting with local celebrities. Throw a party of your own and ask Leo to be cohost or hostess. Then invite the most attractive people you know. Cultural events, the theater, rock concerts, opera, nightclubs are Leo terri-

tory. Give Leo the royal treatment, and they'll return the favor. Theater is always a Leo favorite. Make it an upbeat show, such as a musical, with beautiful costumes.

WHAT TO WEAR:
Male or female, be sure your hair is looking its best—the Lion is always aware of manes. Wear your best designer duds, and Leo will love to show you off. But be sure you don't outshine your mate (difficult to do, with Leo).

Virgo

WHERE TO MEET ONE:
No-nonsense Virgo is discriminating and enjoys high-quality events, places with a purpose, educational or health-oriented activities. Health-oriented Virgos can be found doing volunteer work at hospitals, serving in health food stores, taking notes at nutritional lectures. Virgos like detailed crafts and can often be found perfecting their skills in crafts workshops. Bookstores and literary events appeal to bookish Virgos.

WHERE TO GO:
Put some thought into planning your Virgo date. Virgos are not especially spur-of-the-moment types. Aim for quality and mental stimulation rather than showmanship. Virgo is discriminating, so go somewhere that's the best in its class (not necessarily the most expensive). A picnic or hike in a beautiful outdoor setting, a cultural or literary event, a seminar or lecture with a notable speaker, an exhibit, a museum or a walking tour of a favorite neighborhood, a wine- or food-tasting event are appealing possibilities. Virgo is interested in health, so take a yoga class together. Be sure to tidy up your home if you're inviting Virgo over. Serve healthful food that is not too complicated but well prepared.

WHAT TO WEAR:
Clean, neat, and elegant are Virgo rules. Whatever your style, be it tailored or avant-garde, be sure it's clean and well pressed. Your grooming should be faultless. White is a special Virgo color, and what could give you a cleaner look! Remember Ingrid Bergman's white suit in *Casablanca* or Garbo's white evening gown.

Libra

WHERE TO MEET ONE:
Beauty-loving Libras are fond of all the arts and are one of the most social signs. Parties, gatherings, anywhere people meet and greet are where to find Libra. Fashion shows, art openings, charity events are likely Libra meeting places. Take a course in interior design or fashion design. Haunts of the legal profession might also turn up some Libras, lovers of fairness and justice. When you've met your Libra, keep it light and lively. Libras do not want to know about any heavy emotional baggage.

WHERE TO GO:
You're in luck. Libra likes to do things with a partner, and will be happy to accompany you shopping, hanging out, traveling, socializing. Libra adores fine dining in an elegant atmosphere. Let Libra revamp your wardrobe or give your home a makeover. Libra adores frequent, thoughtful gifts like flowers or the latest novel. Cultural events, art films, dual sports like tennis, kayaking, a bicycle built for two, dancing would be fun with Libra. Take a cooking or art course together.

WHAT TO WEAR:
Libra is the most fashion-conscious of all signs, so be sure to look your best. Pay particular attention to color harmony—clashing colors are a Libra turnoff. Choose pale, subtle shades, nothing glaring, with an interesting accessory or two. Wear a touch of pink, a favorite Libra color.

Scorpio

WHERE TO MEET ONE:

Scorpio, one of the zodiac's great water lovers, will often be found biking, hiking, or just hanging out by the shore or riverside. Scorpio is fascinated by power and the mysteries of life, so look for Scorpios in places where powerful, charismatic types gather. Dynamic sports, powerful racing machines, military or police hangouts, edgy musical venues are their ticket. A bookstore that specializes in murder mysteries could be a Scorpio lair. Ancient history or archaeology has great appeal to Scorpio, so investigate the local digs or fine antiques stores. A lecture by the latest guru or preacher with hypnotic appeal is sure to attract the more spiritual Scorpios. Keep your air of mystery around Scorpio—don't tell all or be too available. Let them try to figure you out.

WHERE TO GO:

Take Scorpio to a mystery play or thriller movie. A seafood restaurant is usually a winner. They may prefer to spend time alone with you, so choose a beautiful, secluded place where you can focus on each other. And don't bring your cell phone! A more casual date could be stargazing, a midnight walk along the beach, an afternoon sail, exploring the hidden places in your city. Sporting events with lots of intense action attract Scorpio, so get tickets to your local tournament.

WHAT TO WEAR:

Scorpio loves sexy black, especially black leather, whether it's buttery soft or biker tough. Touchy-feely fabrics like cashmere appeal. Show off your sexuality in a subtle way, unless you want Scorpio to take action immediately.

Sagittarius

WHERE TO MEET ONE:

Sporting events and tournaments attract Sagittarius. Gambling casinos and comedy clubs are also meccas for this fun-loving sign. Join the hottest sports club, and wear bright, sharp workout wear. Learn a new sport, especially one that uses the legs like hiking, climbing, skiing. Tours to interesting and often remote places attract wandering Sagittarius. Keep your disposition sunny-side up with this sign. Brush up on a few good jokes. Be healthy, happy, and ready for adventure.

WHERE TO GO:
Make your date an active one: kayaking or canoeing on your local river or lake, playing tennis or golf, exploring a local park, training for a marathon together, biking your local hills. Sagittarius likes to laugh, so go to a comedy club, play silly games, go to a fair or carnival with wild rides. Sagittarius loves horses, so go to the local racetrack or go horseback riding. Any event involving animals is sure to be a hit: the zoo, the circus, a horse show or dog show.

WHAT TO WEAR:
Wear great-looking sportswear, especially if it shows off your legs. Sagittarius has lots of fashion flair, so go all out with designer duds if you're going out on the town. You can run wild with fashion—Sagittarius will love your adventurous spirit.

Capricorn

WHERE TO MEET ONE:
You're most likely to meet Capricorn on the job or where business people hang out. Join an investment club. Conservative environments attract Capricorns: country clubs, golf or tennis clubs, traditional resorts. Capricorns are strivers, so find them at stores where fine clothing is sold, at upper-range real estate offices (selling or buying property), auctions, or charity benefits. Mountain-climbing clubs or ski resorts are good bets for meeting a Mountain Goat (as the Goat is the symbol for Capricorn). Behave yourself with this sign—no outrageous behavior, please.

WHERE TO GO:
Think classic, all-American fun, nothing too unconventional. Capricorns appreciate quality, but not extravagance, so take them to a traditional restaurant rather than a flashy one. Don't swamp them with totally unfamiliar food. Capricorns enjoy outdoor activity: hiking in your local park, a round of golf, or a set of tennis together. Good seats at the theater, opera, or a rock concert would impress this sign. Capricorn takes romance seriously, so proceed in a slow, stately, and proper way. Observe all the formalities, and brush up on your manners.

WHAT TO WEAR:
Capricorn has an eye for quality, so wear that elegant vintage dress. Well-cut classic clothes appeal to most Capricorns. A few designer labels wouldn't hurt. Go for the ladylike look rather than overtly sexy. In other words, look like someone who could be introduced to Mother.

Aquarius

WHERE TO MEET ONE:
Aquarius can turn up anywhere there's something new, original, or political happening. A computer expo, a far-out rock concert, a political rally, a fund-raiser for an offbeat cause, a political protest, a radical lecture, a team sport, a lecture by a far-out new guru, a cutting-edge clothing store are possibilities. Aquarius likes groups and is sure to have plenty of buddies, so join the party! When you meet your dreamboat, don't be possessive. Although this sign is loaded with charisma and a magnet to the opposite sex, once they're interested in you, they tend to keep it platonic with others.

WHERE TO GO:
Think out of the box and try something offbeat. Don't be too romantic, too fast. Aquarius likes to be friends first. Aquarius loves doing things that are unconventional, new,

cutting edge. They love surprises, doing things spontane-
ously, so nothing should seem too "planned." Include a
group of like-minded friends, people Aquarius might like
to meet. Raise funds for a worthy cause together. Attend
a lecture at your local New Age center. Meditate together.
Canvass your neighborhood together for your favorite
candidate.

WHAT TO WEAR:
Wear something original and memorable that sets you apart
from the crowd. Try wearing electric blue, an Aquarius
color. You don't have to be conventional with this sign.
Just wear what is appropriate to the event, with a slight
personal twist.

Pisces

WHERE TO MEET ONE:
Waterside places are the Pisces habitat. Try the local beach,
marina, yacht club, surfer store, fish market, trout stream.
Pisces rules illusion. Therefore, any place that has to do with
show business, such as a drama or filmmaking course, should
have a quota of this sign. In sports, find Pisces on the ice:
skating and hockey are favorites. You'll find this sign at spiritual places such as yoga retreats or church socials. Charity
work and hospital volunteering could net you one of the
Fishes.

WHERE TO GO ON A DATE:
A film or play is the obvious choice. Choose a restaurant
that has a definite mood. Pisces loves exotic food in a dramatic setting. Seafood restaurants, those with harbor or
river views, are sure winners. A wine tasting, poetry reading, sunset sail, afternoon at the aquarium, picnic by the
lake, dancing, ice skating, ice fishing are all good bets.
Pisces loves fantasy, romance, mood-inducing settings with
a touch of magic. Let your imagination roam free—the
more theatrical the setting, the better.

WHAT TO WEAR:
To please the Pisces male, appeal to his fantasy. Chances are, it will be a touch exotic, soft, feminine, flowing. Show off your mermaid curves. Men of this sign, like Fabio, can be colorful and flamboyant like the heroes of a romance novel, so dress like a heroine.

The Gemini Orbit—
Your Personality, Love
Connections, Family, Work,
and Style!

Are You True to Your Cosmic Calling?

What is a Gemini like? The recipe for the Gemini personality is derived from several ingredients. Your sign's *element:* air. The way Gemini *operates:* mutable—constantly changing. Your sign's *polarity:* positive, masculine, yang. Your *planetary ruler:* Mercury, the planet of communication. Your sign's *place* in the zodiac: third. Your *symbol:* the Twins, which indicates the dual nature of your sign. Put 'em all together, and you've got Gemini.

Everything we say about Gemini is extrapolated from the above recipe. Could an air sign with a Mercury ruler have a facility with words? And is Gemini the type to sit around the house? Only if there are a few telephones ringing and a party going on! Do you like to do two things at once? Are you ever searching for your "twin soul." If you're a typical social Gemini, a desert island would not be your favorite vacation spot.

Some of you may say, "I'm not like that at all!" There are many solitary unsocial Geminis. Lots of planets in earth or water signs, for instance, could mute your personality a bit. The more Gemini planets you have, the more you'll fit the typical Gemini descriptions in the following chapters.

CHAPTER 13

Gemini Profiles

The Gemini Man: The Restless Spirit

The Gemini man is on a perpetual journey in search of the extraordinary, the startling, the intrigue of life. You can't bear boredom, and will seek out activity to avoid being stuck in a rut. You seem to be forever in motion. Even when you're sitting still, your mind is racing. You are a lover of games on every level who can make a game of the most complicated situations. On the negative side, it is difficult for you to take anything or anyone too seriously. Weighty matters tend to drag you down, unless your mind is challenged by a crisis situation. You'd rather dabble in lots of different projects, then fly off when things get sticky.

In childhood, Gemini is the bright funny little boy who gets bored in school and could devise some jolly pranks to amuse yourself. You'll have many interests, which keep changing constantly. In your early years you should learn self-discipline as well as the satisfaction of setting goals and reaching them. Otherwise, you'll have a tendency to skim the surface of life, with much activity but few real accomplishments.

Young adulthood is an experimental time, and you're not about to deny yourself any adventures. A born flirt and charming chameleon who can't resist an exciting affair of the heart, you usually opt for several romantic experiences at once. This could result in becoming a perennial playboy, even to leading a double life, both hazards of the ever-curious and charming Gemini man.

In a Relationship

The woman who succeeds in tying Gemini down would be well advised to give him lots of rope and keep an open mind. This is likely to be a nontraditional marriage—exciting but not particularly stable. Though Gemini is not naturally inclined to be monogamous, he will stick with a woman who is bright, entertaining, sociable, interesting, and companionable. It would help if she is involved in his professional life, too, as well as having strong interests of her own. His hot-cold temperament and roving eye could cause his mate a great deal of insecurity, unless she is an independent person as well.

The Gemini Woman: The Power Talker

It's no surprise that the comedienne whose signature line is "Can we talk?" is a Gemini—Joan Rivers. Your verbal skills are legendary, giving you the ability to talk yourself into or out of any situation. The written and spoken word is your means of seduction, sales, and self-defense. You'll talk with your expressive hands (the Gemini part of the body), and use body language to add extra emphasis.

You're highly charged with nervous energy, seeming to be everywhere at once. And you have enough sides to your personality to dazzle even those close to you. One moment you are a capable executive, the next a little girl filled with wonder, the next an earthy sensualist, the next an expert in verbal karate, the next a comedienne. It's no wonder there are so many actresses under this sign. And, best of all, you do everything with a light, quicksilver touch, so the effort never shows.

While your brain is busily skipping about, juggling many people and projects at once, you manage to skip away from heavy emotional involvements. You're not one to be tied down in any way. However, though variety may be the spice of your life, it can also be hard to digest. You need a substantial anchor and truly caring relationships to get you through the tough times. If you learn to live with a few normal human flaws and foibles (you can't laugh everything off!) instead of constantly changing your mind, you'll find your twin sides working together more smoothly. And you will have a much better idea of what you're really looking for.

The little Gemini girl is the bright precocious one who learns to read and write ahead of everyone. She is very well-coordinated, moves quickly, and talks even more rapidly. She bores easily with her toys, and may even invent new games to play with them.

Gemini's problem is making up her mind. There is always something more interesting to do, a more exciting place to go, people who might be more fun. You must learn early to stick to one thing until you have mastered it—or you'll end up being the proverbial "jill-of-all-trades."

Propelled by your great reservoir of nervous energy the young Gemini is likely to have more than one job, more than one boyfriend, and a full schedule of social activities. Juggling is second nature to you. The more balls in the air, the less likely you are to get bored. One challenge is to find situations that give you a chance to grow. Otherwise, you'll skip from job to job, love affair to love affair, at a great strain on your nerves. When you find a man who stimulates you mentally as well as emotionally and physically, you may be tempted to take a chance on love. It is important that you separate dream from reality here—and not confuse surface attraction with true communication. Otherwise, you may marry on impulse, quickly tire of the situation, and search for excitement elsewhere. Since you often retain your looks and youthful outlook, it is not unusual for you to finally settle with a much younger man.

In a Relationship

Keeping your foothold in the working world after marriage provides you with the outside stimulation you need and also the financial means to delegate the more boring routine tasks of housekeeping to someone else. If you apply your creativity to making the marriage special, you can keep the union lively, with no need to look for greener pastures. You're sure to promote a social life, entertain frequently, and decorate with flair and originality. Your relationship may also benefit if you take an active part in your husband's business. But too much togetherness can seem confining for your restless sign. If your husband is too progressive and demanding, you may be tempted to take flight. However, if you can negotiate enough room for personal freedom, you'll provide a life of sparkle and variety.

Gemini in the Family

The Gemini Parent

Geminis take a great interest in their child's different stages, watching the young personality unfold. You may find the early babyhood years most difficult, when the child is dependent and needs steady, routine care. After the child learns to communicate, you'll take on the role of teacher, introducing the child to the world of ideas and mental pursuits, helping with homework, and making difficult subjects easier to understand. One of your greatest assets as a parent is your own insatiable curiosity about the world, which you can communicate to the children by introducing them early to the world of ideas and books. You are also an excellent coach, teaching your child social abilities and the art of handling others at an early age. As your child matures, your youthful, ever-fresh outlook makes you a wonderful friend and companion through the years.

The Gemini Stepparent

Your verbal skills and sense of humor will often come to the rescue in the initial stages of starting up a new family. You're a communicator who can quickly get shy youngsters to open up and difficult personalities to communicate. Your natural sociability and flair for entertainment encourage everyone to have fun, making family get-togethers seem like parties. Since you have many outside activities and interests, the children will be able to have as much time as they need alone with their parent. Soon your new family will find that you are a fun-loving addition to their lives, a wise adviser, and an excellent noncompetitive companion.

The Gemini Grandparent

You're an upbeat grandparent who still finds life an interesting adventure. You're always the life of the party, up on all the latest family gossip, as well as what's happening with the rest of the world. Visits with you are full of laughter and good stories! You'll take a special interest in your grandchildren's education and support them in whatever career path they choose. Like Barbara Bush, you may have a large extended family that reaches out to the children of your community. You'll give your own children plenty of space to rear the grandchildren as they please, never interfering with Mother's rules or taking over the grandchildren's upbringing.

"Never complain" was the motto of the Duchess of Windsor (a Gemini), and it could be yours, too. You accentuate the positive and keep a cheerful attitude. Your mentor should be the famous Gemini pastor Norman Vincent Peale, author of *The Power of Positive Thinking,* one of the most influential self-help books of all time. Dr. Peale lived a productive life well into his nineties, still writing and preaching. You, too, realize how the right mental attitude can influence any situation for the better, and you'll be sure to pass on your wisdom to your grandchildren.

CHAPTER 14

Gemini Flair: Your Key to Looking and Living Well

Why do you look better in certain colors? Find lazy vacations at the beach a big yawn? Own two of everything? Collect rings or gloves? It could be you're responding to the call of Gemini! Each sun sign resonates to certain colors, styles, places, and these are sure to be your favorites. Use the following guide to steer your style in the right direction. The advice on where-to-go, what-to-wear, and how to create your happiest place to live is based on the specific colors, surroundings, and attitudes that best suit your Gemini personality type. You can't go wrong!

Gemini Living Space

You need a place that accommodates all your different interests, with plenty of storage space, so you can sweep your projects quickly out of sight when friends drop in. A light, neutral background allows you to change color accents and accessories with your mood. Lots of bookcases, a telephone or three, and furniture you can rearrange in many different combinations would provide you with enough variety. You're the sign with a telephone on both sides of the bed and alongside the bathtub. Have a separate room or corner with a desk where you can organize all your lists, fax machine, Palm Pilot, Rolodexes, and appointment books, so you won't waste time looking for them. Many Geminis enjoy having houses in more than one place (you're often bicoastal). You may keep a country house or residences in different cities so you can switch environments when bored.

Gemini's Sounds

Your music tastes are usually eclectic. You pay attention to the words as well as the melody, so the witty lyrics of Cole Porter and the poetry of Bob Dylan appeal, as do the hottest rap artist and the latest experiment of Paul McCartney. You like abstract classical music, but nothing too heavy or loud that might distract from conversation or bring on the blues. You're a natural disk jockey, so customize your own mix of musical moods on tapes or CDs. Paula Abdul, Miles Davis, Alanis Morrisette, rap music, Cole Porter, Prince, Judy Garland, and continental tunes from Charles Aznavour would give you the full range of Gemini sounds.

The Gemini Palette

The Gemini palette—soft silvery gray, pale yellow, airy Wallis Windsor blue—consists of great background colors, elegant ones you can live with over a period of time. They adapt to different seasons and climates; they won't compete with your personality or distract from your total image. You can change the look of these colors at will, accenting them with bright touches or blending with other pastels. And these colors tolerate a frequent change of accessories, according to your mood of the moment.

Gemini in Style

Gemini always likes to do something interesting with your clothes. You have fun with fashion and never take your fashion image too seriously. Nicole Kidman dresses with great Gemini flair in clothes that get people talking. Annette Bening opts for simple elegant clothes that set off her delicate beauty. Other Gemini beauties—like Elizabeth Hurley (who once attended the Academy Awards in a gown held together with safety pins) and Angelina Jolie—enjoy being downright outrageous, keeping their fans guessing! Some Geminis, like the late Marilyn Monroe, love to flaunt their sex appeal, making a game of it. Play up your expressive hands with a perfect manicure and beautiful rings. A hairstyle you can wear several different ways would satisfy your need for variety.

Double-duty clothes that can work all day and then dash to a party at night are perfect for busy Geminis. Add a witty, scene-stealing jewel or two, a dramatic scarf, or trendy shoes and handbag to quick-change your outfit's personality—and you're ready to go!

Some great fashion icons, like the Duchess of Windsor, were born under your sign, and you couldn't find better inspiration than this legendary fashion devotee. We remember Wallis Simpson for her witty way with accessories, like those fabulous jewels she wore with casual aplomb (some engraved with secret messages from the Duke). Yet she never varied her signature swept-back hairdo or her elegantly simple style of dressing.

Since you have such a changeable personality, you'll probably experiment with every kind of look before you settle on the style that has your name on it. Usually you're up to the minute with a touch of the newest trend coming down the runway. The fashion duo Dolce and Grabbana, the with-it looks of Anna Sui, or the newest androgynous menswear styles would be fun for you to try on for size. Gemini models who express your flair, like Naiomi Campbell, Elizabeth Hurley, and Brooke Shields, have the ability to change their image with their hairstyle—being a vamp one moment, then the innocent girl next door the next.

The Healing Arts of Gemini

Too much coffee? Too little sleep? Are people getting on your nerves? Gemini's fast-paced action-packed life can be stressful, so here are some ways to unwind and put the spring back into your step.

One of the most social signs, Gemini is associated with the nervous system, our body's lines of communication. If your nerves are on edge, you may be trying to do too many things at once, leaving no time for fun and laughter. When you've overloaded your circuits, it's time to get together with friends, go out to parties, do things in groups to release tension and bring perspective into your life. Investigate natural tension relievers such as yoga or meditation. Doing things with your hands—playing the piano, typing, craftwork—is also helpful.

Gemini is also associated with the lungs, and they are especially sensitive. If you smoke, please consider quitting. Yoga, which incorporates deep breathing into physical exercise, brings oxygen into your lungs. Among its many benefits are the deep relaxation and tranquillity so needed by your sign.

Your active social life can easily sabotage your diet. Party buffets and restaurant meals can pile on the pounds, especially because you love to sample a bit of everything. Your challenge is to find an eating system that provides enough variety so you won't get bored. Develop a strategy for eating in restaurants and coping with buffets (pile the plate with salad and veggies to fill up before you sample the desserts).

Combine healthful activities with social get-togethers for fun and plenty of fringe benefits for everyone. Include friends in your exercise routines; join an exercise class or jogging club. Gemini excels at sports that require good timing and manual dexterity as well as communication with others, like tennis (Steffi Graf) or golf. Those of you who jog may want to add hand weights or upper-body exercises, which will benefit the Gemini-ruled arms and hands. If you spend long hours at the computer, try an ergonomic keyboard for comfort and protection against carpal tunnel syndrome.

Gemini Hip Hideaways and Hangouts

Sometimes you just have to get away from it all! But Gemini never likes to get too far away from civilization. Stay away from desert islands, unless you need some peace and quiet to write your novel. Stick to places where there's a lively social scene, some interesting scenery, local characters who provide good conversation, and an Internet cafe to keep up with your email.

Improve your language skills by visiting a foreign country; you'll have no trouble communicating in sign language, if necessary. Consider a language school in the south of France or in Switzerland, where you'll mix with fellow students of many nationalities while you perfect your accent.

Lightness is the key to Gemini travel. Don't weigh yourself down with luggage. Dare to travel with an empty suitcase, then acquire clothes and supplies at your destination. Imagine how fast you'll speed through the airport!

Keep a separate tiny address book for each city, so the right numbers are always handy. Invest in beautifully designed travel cases and briefcases, since you're on the go so much. Spend some time looking for the perfect luggage, portable notebook computer (with a modem), and cellular telephone to keep you in touch at all times.

CHAPTER 15

Gemini Survival Skills on the Job

Gemini has many winning cards to play in the career game. Your quick mind works best in a career where there is enough mental stimulation to keep you from getting bored. High-pressure situations that would be stressful to others are stimulating to you. Many things happening simultaneously—phones ringing off the hook, daily client meetings, constant changes—create a situation in which you thrive, getting to use all your communications skills. Consider the way the Gemini mayor of New York City, Rudolph Giuliani, masterfully handled the World Trade Center crisis, for the prime example of Gemini grace under pressure.

Your ability to communicate with a variety of people works well in sales, journalism, public relations, politics, agent or broker work, personnel or consulting—literally any job that requires verbal or writing skills. You who learn languages easily could be a language teacher or interpreter. Manual dexterity is another Gemini gift that can find craft, musical, or medical expression (especially surgery or chiropractic work).

What to avoid: a job that is too isolated, routine, detail-oriented, or confining. Stay away from companies that are hidebound, with rigid rules. Instead, look for a place that gives you strong backup as well as free rein. Gemini often succeeds in a freelance position, provided you have a solid support system to help with the details and routine chores.

For inspiration: the ups and downs of master dealmaker and real estate tycoon Donald Trump should make fascinating reading for ambitious Geminis. Here's a tycoon who changed the skyline of New York and who has a colorful life in a variety of venues.

The Gemini in Charge

You operate best as a dealmaker or an entrepreneur rather than a designer or producer. You often change your mind, so you should hire assistants who are adaptable enough to keep up with you yet who can provide organization, direction, and structure. Sometimes you have so many projects going on at once that others are dizzy, yet you are known for innovative ideas and cool analysis of problems. You are especially gifted in making a deal, coordinating the diverse aspects of a project.

Gemini is fun to work for—sociable, witty, and clever. Your office will be a beehive of activity, with telephone lines buzzing and clients coming and going. What is lacking in job security you make up in opportunities for others to experiment, to develop flexibility and a sense of gamesmanship.

Gemini Teamwork

You work beautifully on a team, where your light sense of humor, friendliness, and ability to express yourself clearly are appreciated. Your position should be dealing with the public in a sales or communications position. You are also skilled at office politics. It's all part of the game to you. You rarely get emotionally involved. Let someone else do the record keeping, financial management, or accounting. As a Gemini you can handle a position where you report to several different people or juggle several different assignments, though you may do less well if the job requires intense concentration, patience, and perseverance.

To Get Ahead Fast

To get ahead fast, pick a job with variety and mental stimulation. Play up your best attributes, especially the following:

- Verbal and written communication skills
- Ability to handle several tasks at once
- Charm and sociability
- Manual dexterity
- Ability to learn quickly
- Analytical ability

CHAPTER 16

Gemini Rich and Famous: And How They Got There!

There's no better way to learn about the pitfalls and prizes of your sign than to study the lives of your rich and famous sign-mates. For sure you'll find the Gemini traits of wit, brilliance, charm, and communication skills in John F. Kennedy, Mario Cuomo, Sir Paul McCartney. You recognize the famous Gemini sense of humor in Joan Rivers, Dr. Ruth Westheimer, Mike Myers, Bob Hope, and John Goodman. And there's the quirky Gemini beauty in Nicole Kidman, Angelina Jolie, Anne Heche, Helen Hunt, Kristin Scott-Thomas, and Brooke Shields.

Astrology can tell you more about your sun sign heroes and heroines than tabloids or magazine articles. Like what really turns them on (check their Venus). Or what makes them rattled (scope their Saturn). Compare similarities and differences between the celebrities who embody the typical Gemini sun sign traits and those who seem untypical. Then look up the influence of other planets in the horoscope of your favorites, using the charts in this book. It's a fun way to further your education in astrology.

Gemini Celebrities

Raymond Burr (5/21/17)
Laurence Olivier (5/22/1907)
Richard Benjamin (5/22/38)
Naiomi Campbell (5/22/70)
Douglas Fairbanks (5/23/1883)

Drew Carey (5/23/58)
Bob Dylan (5/24/41)
Priscilla Presley (5/24/45)
Roseanne Cash (5/24/50)
Kristin Scott-Thomas (5/24/60)
Miles Davis (5/25/26)
Dixie Carter (5/25/39)
Ian Mackellen (5/25/39)
Connie Selleca (5/25/55)
Mike Myers (5/25/63)
Anne Heche (5/25/69)
John Wayne (5/26/1907)
Peggy Lee (5/26/20)
Stevie Nicks (5/26/48)
Philip Michael Thomas (5/26/49)
Helena Bonham-Carter (5/26/66)
Vincent Price (5/27/11)
Henry Kissinger (5/27/23)
Tony Hillerman (5/27/25)
Louis Gossett, Jr. (5/27/36)
Siouxie Sioux (5/27/57)
Gladys Knight (5/28/44)
Rudolph Giuliani (5/28/44)
Sondra Locke (5/28/47)
Bob Hope (5/29/1903)
John F. Kennedy (5/29/17)
Kevin Conway (5/29/42)
Anthony Geary (5/29/47)
Annette Bening (5/29/58)
Rupert Everett (5/29/59)
Benny Goodman (5/30/1909)
Prince Ranier (5/31/23)
Clint Eastwood (5/31/30)
Peter Yarrow (5/31/38)
Sharon Gless (5/31/43)
Tom Berenger (5/31/50)
Joe Namath (5/31/50)
Lea Thompson (5/31/61)
Brooke Shields (5/31/65)
Andy Griffith (6/1/26)
Marilyn Monroe (6/1/26)

Edward Woodward (6/1/30)
Pat Boone (6/1/34)
Morgan Freeman (6/1/37)
Rene Auberjonois (6/1/40)
Jonathan Pryce (6/1/47)
Ron Wood (6/1/47)
Alanis Morrisette (6/1/74)
Hedda Hopper (6/2/1890)
Sally Kellerman (6/2/37)
Stacey Keach (6/2/41)
Marvin Hamlisch (6/2/44)
Tony Curtis (6/3/25)
Curtis Mayfield (6/3/42)
Deniece Williams (6/3/51)
Dr. Ruth Westheimer (6/4/28)
Bruce Dern (6/4/36)
Michelle Phillips (6/4/44)
Parker Stevenson (6/4/52)
Angelina Jolie (6/4/75)
Bill Moyers (6/5/34)
Mark Wahlberg (6/5/71)
Sandra Bernhard (6/6/55)
Jessica Tandy (6/7/1909)
James Ivory (6/7/28)
Tom Jones (6/7/40)
Liam Neeson (6/7/52)
Prince (6/7/58)
Barbara Bush (6/8/25)
Joan Rivers (6/8/33)
Kathy Baker (6/8/50)
Michael J. Fox (6/9/61)
Johnny Depp (6/9/63)
Prince Philip (6/10/21)
Lionel Jeffries (6/10/26)
Grace Mirabella (6/10/30)
Liz Hurley (6/10/65)
Gene Wilder (6/11/35)
Chad Everett (6/11/37)
Adrienne Barbeau (6/11/45)
George Bush (6/12/24)
Timothy Busfield (6/12/57)

Basil Rathbone (6/13/1892)
Christo (6/13/35)
Tim Allen (6/13/53)
Ally Sheedy (6/13/62)
Donald Trump (6/14/46)
Boy George (6/14/61)
Steffi Graf (6/14/69)
Mario Cuomo (6/15/32)
Waylon Jennings (6/15/37)
Helen Hunt (6/15/63)
Courteney Cox (6/15/64)
Corin Redgrave (6/16/39)
Joan van Ark (6/16/43)
Yasmine Bleeth (6/16/68)
Dean Martin (6/17/17)
Joe Piscopo (6/17/51)
Jason Patric (6/17/66)
E. G. Marshall (6/18/10)
Roger Ebert (6/18/42)
Paul McCartney (6/18/42)
Isabella Rossellini (6/18/52)
Gena Rowlands (6/19/34)
Phylicia Rashad (6/19/48)
Kathleen Turner (6/19/54)
Paula Abdul (6/19/63)
Danny Aiello (6/20/33)
Lionel Richie (6/20/50)
John Goodman (6/20/52)
Cyndi Lauper (6/20/53)

CHAPTER 17

Gemini Connections: How You Get Along with Every Sign

Whether you're looking for a business partner or a life companion, this compatibility "cheat sheet" will help you understand each other's basic needs. Once you understand how your partner's sun sign is likely to view commitment and what each of you wants from a relationship, you'll be in a much better position to judge whether your cosmic combination has lasting potential.

Gemini/Aries

WHAT WORKS:
There is fast-paced action here. Gemini gets a charge of excitement. Aries gets constant changes to keep up with. Both are spontaneous, optimistic, energetic. Differences of opinion only keep the atmosphere stimulating.

WHAT DOESN'T:
Juggling life with you could have Aries seeing double. Aries is direct and to the point, but Gemini can't or won't be pinned down. This hyperactive combination could get on both your nerves unless you give each other plenty of space. Gemini, tone down the flirting—Aries must be number one!

Gemini/Taurus

WHAT WORKS:
The sign next door can be your best friend as well as lover. In this case, you drag Taurus out of the house and into social life, adding laughter to love. Taurus has a soothing, stabilizing quality that supports your restlessness and allows you to be more creative than ever.

WHAT DOESN'T:
Homebody Taurus usually wants one-on-one relations, while social Gemini loves to flirt with a crowd. You will have to curb roving eyes and bodies and plan to spend more time at home, which might cramp your style and leave you gasping for air. Infidelity can be serious business with Taurus, but taken lightly by Gemini. The line between freedom and license swings and sways here. You could feel Taurus is holding you back.

Gemini/Gemini

WHAT WORKS:
When Gemini Twins find each other, you know you'll never be bored. There is enough multifaceted mental activity, games, and delightful social life to double your pleasure. Your partner will understand the complexities of your sign as only a fellow Gemini can.

WHAT DOESN'T:
When the realities of life hit, you may go off in four directions at once. This combination lacks focus. It functions best in a light, creative atmosphere where there are no financial concerns. Serious practical problems could split your personalities and send you running elsewhere for protection and guidance.

Gemini/Cancer

WHAT WORKS:
This is a very public pair with charisma to spare. Your sparkling wit sets off Cancer poise with the perfect light touch. Cancer adds warmth and caring to Gemini. This sign's shrewd insight can make your ideas happen. You can go places together!

WHAT DOESN'T:
It's not easy for Gemini to deliver the kind of devotion Cancer needs. There are too many other exciting options. Nor do you react well to the Cancer need to mother you or to Cancer pleas for sympathy. Their up-and-down moods get on your nerves. Why can't they learn to laugh away their troubles or to find new interests? When Cancer clings, Gemini does a vanishing act. You need to have strong mutual interests or projects to hold this combo together. But it has been done!

Gemini/Leo

WHAT WORKS:
Gemini good humor, ready wit, and social skills delight and complement Leo. Here is someone who can share the spotlight without trying to steal the show from the regal Lion. This is one of the most entertaining combinations. Steady Leo provides the focus Gemini often lacks, and directs the Twins toward achieving goals and status.

WHAT DOESN'T:
Gemini loves to flirt and flit among many interests, romantic and otherwise. This is sure to irritate the Lion, who does one thing at a time and does it well. Gemini might be a bit bored with Leo self-promotion, and might poke fun at this sign's notorious vanity. The resulting feline roar will be no laughing matter!

Gemini/Virgo

WHAT WORKS:
Both Mercury-ruled, your deepest bond will be mental communication and appreciation of each other's intelligence. The Virgo Mercury is earthbound and analytical, while the Gemini Mercury is a jack-of-all-trades. Gemini shows Virgo the big picture; Virgo takes care of the details. Your combined talents make a stimulating partnership. Virgo becomes the administrator here, Gemini the "idea" person.

WHAT DOESN'T:
Your different priorities can be irritating to each other. Virgo needs a sense of order. Gemini needs to experiment and is forever the gadabout. An older Gemini who has slowed down somewhat makes the best partner here.

Gemini/Libra

WHAT WORKS:
Air signs Gemini and Libra have both mental and physical rapport. This is an outgoing combination, full of good talk. You'll never be bored. Libra good looks and charm, as well as fine mind, could keep restless Gemini close to home.

WHAT DOESN'T:
Both of you have a low tolerance for boredom and practical chores. The question of who will provide, do the dirty work, and clean up can be the subject of many a debate. There could be more talk than action here, leaving you turning elsewhere for substance.

Gemini/Scorpio

WHAT WORKS:
You're a fascinating mystery to each other. Gemini is immune from Scorpio paranoia, laughs away dark moods, and

matches wits in power games. Scorpio intensity, focus, and sexual magnetism draw Gemini like a moth to a flame. You're intrigued by Scorpio secrets . . . here's a puzzle that would be fun to solve! And steamy Scorpio brings intensity and a new level of thrills to your sex life.

WHAT DOESN'T:
Scorpio gets "heavy," possessive, and jealous, which Gemini doesn't take seriously. To make this one last, Gemini needs to treat Scorpio like the one and only, while Scorpio must use a light touch, and learn not to take Gemini flirtations to heart.

Gemini/Sagittarius

WHAT WORKS:
These polar opposites shake each other up—happily. Sagittarius helps Gemini see higher truths, to look beyond the life of the party and the art of the deal. Gemini adds mental challenge and flexibility to Sagittarius.

WHAT DOESN'T:
Gemini pokes holes in Sagittarius theories. Sagittarius can brand Gemini as a superficial party animal. Work toward developing nonthreatening, nonjudgmental communication. However, you can't talk away practical financial realities. You need a well-thought-out program to make things happen.

Gemini/Capricorn

WHAT WORKS:
Capricorn benefits from the Gemini abstract point of view and lighthearted sense of fun. Gemini shows Capricorn how to enjoy the rewards of hard work. Support and structure are Capricorn gifts to Gemini. (Taking that literally, Capri-

corn Howard Hughes designed the famous bra that supported Gemini Jane Russell's physical assets!)

WHAT DOESN'T:
Capricorn can be ultraconservative and tightfisted with money, which Gemini will not appreciate. The Gemini free-spirited, fun-loving attitude could grate against the Capricorn driving ambition. Gemini will have to learn to take responsibility and to produce solid results.

Gemini/Aquarius

WHAT WORKS:
In this open and spontaneous relationship, the pressure's off. You two air signs have room to breathe freely. At the same time, you can count on each other for friendship, understanding, and mental stimulation—plus highly original romantic ideas. You'll keep each other entertained, and your love life will be fresh and stimulating.

WHAT DOESN'T:
Be sure to leave time in your busy schedule for each other. If there is no commitment, you could both fly off. A sharing of causes, projects, or careers could hold you together.

Gemini/Pisces

WHAT WORKS:
You are both dual personalities in mutable, freedom-loving signs. You fascinate each other with ever-changing facets. You keep each other from straying by providing constant variety and new experiments to try together.

WHAT DOESN'T:
At some point, you'll need a frame of reference for this relationship to hold together. Since neither likes structure,

this could be a problem. Overstimulation is another monster that can rise to the surface. Pisces sensitive feelings and Gemini hyperactive nerves could send each other searching for more soothing, stabilizing alternatives.

CHAPTER 18

Astrological Outlook for Gemini in 2003

You have been undergoing "hazardous conditions." Saturn in your sign is no plaything. The pressure has been on, but you have been up to it. Saturn leaves Gemini in early June.

Focus this year on promotion, production, and more effective ways of distribution. Uranus enters Pisces in March, and that planet will be going back and forth from Aquarius to Pisces. Conditions surrounding business and career will be exciting yet unorthodox. You will find yourself in charge of public relations and public image—ways to increase visibility all around.

Lucky numbers: 8, 9, 4.

Attention revolves around relationships that include partnership and marriage. You may change your living quarters to make room for an addition to your family in the not-too-distant future.

Capricorn and Cancer individuals will play memorable roles in your life throughout the year. Pluto will be in your seventh house, affecting legal contracts, public relations, and your marital status. You can expect some upsets in those areas.

With Capricorn, you might feel restrained, lacking necessary freedom for some time. Still, you learn more about percentages involved in borrowing and lending money. Also, with Capricorn, you enter areas previously prohibited.

With Cancer, money is involved, including payments and collections. You locate lost valuables. It is important to protect your possessions. Refuse to give up something of value for nothing. The relationship with a Cancer will be a "learning experience," possibly involving travel. This relationship will be serious, and could lead to marriage.

Regard the following pages as your diary in advance. There will be lucky lottery numbers, racetrack selections, times to take the initiative, and other times to lie low.

Highlights of the year will be an appreciation of your efforts, possibly leading to promotion. You will prove that you can be serious when need be. Turn the page, and let us start now.

CHAPTER 19

Eighteen Months of Day-by-Day Predictions—July 2002 to December 2003

All times are calculated for EST and EDT.

JULY 2002

Monday, July 1 (Moon in Pisces to Aries 3:48 p.m.)
Obtain a family agreement on how to celebrate the holiday. The "Fourth" this year will be of vital importance. Find out whom you want to be with, and where. Take notes, especially of your dreams. Properly interpreted, dreams could be the guideposts to the future.

Tuesday, July 2 (Moon in Aries) Be realistic in making plans for the upcoming holiday. People who make grandiose promises may not be capable of fulfilling them. Be self-reliant; don't disappoint young persons who look up to you. Pisces and Virgo play extraordinary roles.

Wednesday, July 3 (Moon in Aries) Be positive of material, food, and beverages. Become familiar with historical facts relating to the holiday. Do not be shy about being patriotic! Capricorn and Cancer figure in this scenario. An older family member deserves special consideration.

Thursday, July 4 (Moon in Aries to Taurus 4:15 a.m.)
Happy Fourth! Maintain a universal outlook. Absorb information concerning Independence Day. This could be a memorable time, if you are determined to make it so. Open

lines of communication. Someone in another city wants to tell you something.

Friday, July 5 (Moon in Taurus)   The holiday is over and you did well! This is a new day and could feature creative projects, love, romance, and style. Emphasize originality, derring-do. Others follow you, and rely upon your leadership. Leo and Aquarius figure in this exciting scenario.

Saturday, July 6 (Moon in Taurus to Gemini 2:59 p.m.) On this Saturday, you make discoveries about "certain people." You may not be completely happy, but you will be informed. Questions will be asked about commitments and marriage. An individual behind the scenes wants to know too much, too soon.

Sunday, July 7 (Moon in Gemini)   What a Sunday! The moon is in your sign. You will be at the right place at a special moment. Your vitality returns; optimism replaces gloom. As you read these lines, circumstances are turning in your favor. Be selective and critical; insist on quality.

Monday, July 8 (Moon in Gemini to Cancer 10:34 p.m.) Your cycle remains high, despite slight impediments. Scorpio attempts to bully, but will not succeed in shaking your beliefs. Many rely upon you; don't let them down! Proofreading is necessary, along with some research. You'll be engaged in a debate.

Tuesday, July 9 (Moon in Cancer)   Your financial picture is bright, despite a minor setback. A flirtation could get more involved than you originally anticipated. A trip out of town may be necessary. Know when to say, "Enough is enough!" Virgo and Sagittarius figure prominently in this scenario.

Wednesday, July 10 (Moon in Cancer to Leo 3:06 a.m.)   A new outlook on profits and losses is necessary. You could be more affluent than you originally estimated. Taurus, Libra, and Scorpio are in this picture, and could have these letters or initials in their names: F, O, X. Lucky lottery: 6, 13, 16, 18, 19, 24.

Thursday, July 11 (Moon in Leo)   On this Thursday, "lie low," if possible. Someone wants something for nothing. You could be the prime target. A Cancer is persuasive, flatters you, and does have a motive. Define terms; do not fall victim to self-deception.

Friday, July 12 (Moon in Leo)   On this Friday, you feel vigorous, creative, and sexy. The Leo moon coincides with sociability, popularity, and the renewal of a relationship with a sibling. Capricorn and Cancer will play surprising roles, and can help cut through red tape.

Saturday, July 13 (Moon in Leo to Virgo 5:39 a.m.) On this Saturday, you complete a project. Communication from someone overseas elevates your morale. Maintain a universal outlook. Avoid narrow-minded people. Your sense of prophesy is heightened—predict the future; make it come true. Have luck with number 9.

Sunday, July 14 (Moon in Virgo)   Avoid a wild-goose chase. Do not be a passenger in an automobile driven by a heavy drinker. Make a fresh start; don't become enthralled by one who talks big but does not have two nickels to rub together. This message will become crystal clear by tonight.

Monday, July 15 (Moon in Virgo to Libra 7:38 a.m.) The spotlight is on cooperative efforts, public appearances, and dealings with city officials. People are willing to listen, if you actually have something important to say. Where you live and marriage—these things figure prominently.

Tuesday, July 16 (Moon in Libra)   Highlight versatility, be selective, make inquiries, and realize you are influential, perhaps in your own way. Favors are returned. This means those you helped in the past will return the kindness. Your popularity is on the rise. Participate in political and charitable campaigns.

***Wednesday, July 17 (Moon in Libra to Scorpio 10:12
a.m.)***   On this Wednesday, do some rewriting and research, and attend to basic issues. The Libra moon relates
to the "stirring of your creative juices." You have plenty
of sex appeal, and could be involved in a relationship that
provides pleasure but nothing else. Scorpio is involved.

Thursday, July 18 (Moon in Scorpio)   The focus is on
the area of your chart relating to work and health—reports
in all areas are favorable, if not extraordinary. A friendship
ensues with someone you previously felt was dull or incon-
sequential. An excellent day for reading, writing, and learning by teaching others.

***Friday, July 19 (Moon in Scorpio to Sagittarius 2:01
p.m.)***   A low-key approach brings the desired results.
Don't reveal your ace-in-the-hole. Be confident within; let
others know you will fight if the cause is right. Taurus,
Libra, and Scorpio play "amazing" roles. Decorate, re-
model, and beautify your home—domestic issues dominate
this scenario.

Saturday, July 20 (Moon in Sagittarius)   Define terms;
locate missing legal papers. See people, places, and relationships as they really are, not merely as you wish they
could be. A temporary delay works in your favor—time is
on your side, and becomes your tremendous ally. A Pisces
is in the picture.

***Sunday, July 21 (Moon in Sagittarius to Capricorn 7:27
p.m.)***   Spiritual values surface. Questions arise concerning morality, character, honor, partnership, and marriage.
Do your own thing; don't follow others. Do things your
way, whether or not it makes you popular. Leo and Aquarius will figure in this scenario.

Monday, July 22 (Moon in Capricorn)   A universal outlook proves beneficial. Avoid anything that is "narrow-
minded." Communicate with someone from another land.
Find out how your talent or product would "fit." A reunion

tonight proves dramatic, romantic, and satisfying. Aries plays a role.

Tuesday, July 23 (Moon in Capricorn)   You've waited for this day—it is here now, so make the most of it by taking the lead, and displaying your pioneering spirit. Someone who claims, "I love you," should be asked to "prove it." Leo and Aquarius will be a major part of your scenario.

Wednesday, July 24 (Moon in Capricorn to Aquarius 2:39 a.m.)   Accent cooperative efforts. Investigate travel plans. Look beyond the immediate. Peer into the future, where answers reside. Attention during part of this day will revolve around food, recipes, and restaurant management. Lucky lottery: 2, 3, 5, 18, 20, 21.

Thursday, July 25 (Moon in Aquarius)   At the track: post position special—number 5 p.p. in the seventh race. Your popularity is on the rise. More people want to be with you, to read what you write. The focus is on publishing, advertising, showmanship, and design. A Sagittarius plays a fantastic role.

Friday, July 26 (Moon in Aquarius to Pisces 12:04 p.m.)   Be methodical and thorough. Check accounting and computer figures. Within 24 hours, you will have more responsibility and authority. You'll earn more money, and at times during the day, you wish for peace and quiet as in the past. Scorpio plays a top role.

Saturday, July 27 (Moon in Pisces)   Be ready for a change of scene. Realize that today you exude personal magnetism and sex appeal. Be aware, daring, and confident, but don't break too many hearts. You will be approached by a Virgo who has something of value to relate—listen, but avoid being naive.

Sunday, July 28 (Moon in Pisces to Aries 11:38 p.m.)
A relative who has been "in hiding" will make an appear-

ance. All in all, this will prove to be a pleasant experience. You will obtain cooperation in making your surroundings more beautiful, especially at home. Focus on emotional security, financial advantages, and a decision regarding where you will live.

Monday, July 29 (Moon in Aries) Get your second wind! Your cycle moves up. Within 24 hours, a major wish will be fulfilled. In matters of speculation, stick with number 8. Define terms, play the waiting game, but know when to say, "Enough is enough!" Pisces and Virgo play exciting roles.

Tuesday, July 30 (Moon in Aries) Following an initial delay, a promise made to you by an executive will be fulfilled. Exude confidence; state your case and then leave matters as they are. Focus on promotion, production, and extra responsibility. You'll be up to it, no matter what the pressure.

Wednesday, July 31 (Moon in Aries to Taurus 12:15 p.m.) Lucky lottery: 1, 9, 10, 12, 39, 44. Look beyond the immediate. Let go of a burden not your own in the first place. Someone you helped in the recent past will return the favor, albeit reluctantly. Be creatively selfish; let others know your time and efforts are valuable.

AUGUST 2002

Thursday, August 1 (Moon in Taurus) A blend of practicality and imagination is featured. Time is on your side; you can afford to play the "waiting game." Wait for the right offer. Don't force issues. Pisces and Virgo will be featured. At least one will ask, "What am I doing here?"

Friday, August 2 (Moon in Taurus to Gemini 11:44 p.m.) As you prepare for the weekend, remember obligations to someone who was there when you needed him. Focus on business and career pressure. You will be up to it. You get the green light from a legal counselor. Capricorn and Cancer will play sensational roles.

Saturday, August 3 (Moon in Gemini)   Your cycle is moving up. You could receive a "stunning" offer. Circumstances are turning in your favor, so be selective and choose quality. Wear brighter colors; make personal appearances. A Libra helps you gain recognition. Lucky lottery: 7, 12, 18, 22, 30, 50.

Sunday, August 4 (Moon in Gemini)   Make a fresh start. Take the initiative. Realize that you are exuding personal magnetism and sex appeal. Don't break too many hearts—at the very least, offer tea and sympathy. Within 24 hours, one of your original concepts "catches on."

Monday, August 5 (Moon in Gemini to Cancer 8:00 a.m.)   The focus is on cooperative efforts, public relations, legal affairs, and your marital status. A Cancer will be bold enough to tell you, "You are so attractive, I would like to know you better!" Home economics are discussed.

Tuesday, August 6 (Moon in Cancer)   Show off your sense of humor. You are on the verge of earning more money. Collect and research data—those who think you could be a "pushover" will suffer a rude awakening. Know your subjects. Plunge into a debate. You can win big!

Wednesday, August 7 (Moon in Cancer to Leo 12:25 p.m.) The feeling of entrapment is temporary. People want to be with you, and have questions to ask. Be pleasant, but know when to announce, "Enough is enough!" Taurus, Leo, and Scorpio will play major roles. Revise, review, line up your schedule, and set priorities.

Thursday, August 8 (Moon in Leo)   The new moon in Leo coincides with different friends and an unusual course of action. Don't start anything that you cannot finish, including a love relationship. A relative is restless and needs you to buoy confidence. Virgo plays an "interesting" role.

Friday, August 9 (Moon in Leo to Virgo 2:02 p.m.) Attention revolves around your family and home. A visitor from another state says, "I knew you wouldn't mind my coming unannounced." Be pleasant, but state, "I am always happy to see you but please no more unannounced visits!" Taurus, Libra, and Scorpio figure in this scenario.

Saturday, August 10 (Moon in Virgo) Your key words should be, "Wait and see!" You do not have the necessary facts. They will be forthcoming within 3 days. Meanwhile, deal gingerly with Pisces and Virgo. A mystical experience last night could be interpreted as a "prophetic dream."

Sunday, August 11 (Moon in Virgo to Libra 2:37 p.m.) Evaluate your property. Decide what you want to do in connection with sales and purchases. You hold the trump card. Legal authorities are on your side. Move ahead in a confident, direct way. Capricorn and Cancer will play outstanding roles.

Monday, August 12 (Moon in Libra) On this Monday, look beyond previous experiences. Focus on imagination, prophesy, and the ability to look past the obvious. Aries and Libra will play major roles and they want to be helpful. Let go of an obligation you had no right to carry in the first place.

Tuesday, August 13 (Moon in Libra to Scorpio 4:00 p.m.) Get off to a fresh start. Replace gloom with optimism. The lunar position emphasizes the "stirring of creative juices." There have been self-doubts, but put them aside. You are doing the right thing at the right time. A love relationship prospers.

Wednesday, August 14 (Moon in Scorpio) Work methods are reviewed. A passionate Scorpio says, "You can do this much better if you do it my way!" Maintain your emotional equilibrium and then "do things" your way. You'll be dealing intensely with persons born under Cancer and Capricorn.

Thursday, August 15 (Moon in Scorpio to Sagittarius 7:25 p.m.)   Your sense of humor is your ally. Laugh at your own foibles. Focus on versatility, diversity, intellectual curiosity, and the determination to select quality. Sagittarius and another Gemini figure in today's exciting scenario. Your lucky number is 3.

Friday, August 16 (Moon in Sagittarius)   Focus on reviewing, rewriting, and rebuilding—you can renew a friendship with a temperamental Scorpio. Be willing to tear down in order to rebuild—make intelligent concessions without abandoning your basic principles. Taurus is also in this picture.

Saturday, August 17 (Moon in Sagittarius)   Focus on public appearances, legal affairs, your reputation, and marital status. Do what you know must be done, then "be done with it." Examine various aspects of a project without scattering your forces. You possess "winning ways," and tonight you'll know this is a fact.

Sunday, August 18 (Moon in Sagittarius to Capricorn 1:15 a.m.)   Some of your legal questions and problems will be answered in a positive way. Focus on home ownership, romantic issues, and the ability to beautify your surroundings. Someone who is knowledgeable about art, music, and literature could come into your life. Be receptive, but not naive.

Monday, August 19 (Moon in Capricorn)   An aura of deception exists, deliberate or otherwise. Accounting procedures require revision. A computer error is not unlikely. Pisces and Virgo will play outstanding roles, and could have these letters or initials in their names: G, P, Y.

Tuesday, August 20 (Moon in Capricorn to Aquarius 9:16 a.m.)   You can have things "your way"—the rub is, "What *is* your way?" Tonight will be time for greater self-discovery. Are you taking too much for granted? Capricorn and Cancer play leading roles, and have these letters or initials in their names: H, Q, Z.

Wednesday, August 21 (Moon in Aquarius)   Look beyond the immediate. Plan ahead for a journey that could take you overseas. You actually require representation in another nation. Know it, and do something about it. Aries and Libra play fascinating roles, and have these letters in their names: I and R. Your lucky number is 9.

Thursday, August 22 (Moon in Aquarius to Pisces 7:10 p.m.)   The full moon in your ninth house, in Aquarius, indicates clearly that through an innovative process you will create a profitable enterprise. Emphasize originality, daring, adventure, and new fields to conquer. On a personal level, you could fall madly in love with a Leo.

Friday, August 23 (Moon in Pisces)   Focus on cooperative efforts and activities connected with City Hall. You'll receive proposals that include career and marriage. If married, the spark that brought you together in the first place reignites. Accent direction, motivation, where you are going and why.

Saturday, August 24 (Moon in Pisces)   Focus on your ability to accept more leadership responsibility. The emphasis is on social activities, and political and charitable campaigns. A Sagittarius and another Gemini will figure prominently, and have these letters in their names: C, L, U. Your lucky number is 3.

Sunday, August 25 (Moon in Pisces to Aries 6:47 a.m.) Solve a mathematical problem. By doing this, you display skill and knowledge. A Pisces helps you overcome difficulties in reaching the top. You know inwardly that you belong in an elevated position—the key now is to act as if you are aware of it.

Monday, August 26 (Moon in Aries)   The moon in Aries relates to your eleventh house—your popularity is on the rise. You win friends and influence people. This will be one of your most exciting, creative days. The number 5 numerical cycle relates to change, a variety of sensations, and a display of writing skills.

Tuesday, August 27 (Moon in Aries to Taurus 7:30 p.m.)
Attention revolves around your home, family, domesticity, and the ability to beautify surroundings. Music will be in your life, as you strive for harmony. You will be complimented on your appearance and voice. A gift is received from a Libra who genuinely does care for you.

Wednesday, August 28 (Moon in Taurus)   The Taurus moon relates to your twelfth house—you've been keeping a secret, and now you can come out in the open. Define terms; state who you are and why you are here. Pisces and Virgo will play outstanding roles, and have these letters or initials in their names: G, P, Y.

Thursday, August 29 (Moon in Taurus)   A power play day. You begin to "feel your oats" as August winds down. Focus on investments, production, and dealings with executives. Before this day is finished, you will have "revealed" much of your itinerary: why you are here and how you intend to accomplish goals.

Friday, August 30 (Moon in Taurus to Gemini 7:44 a.m.)
Questions and pressures relating to marriage will be much in evidence in the next 24 hours. Check travel plans. Look beyond the immediate. Let go of a burden not really your own in the first place. Aries and Libra will play "sensational" roles.

Saturday, August 31 (Moon in Gemini)   On this last day of August, your inventive capabilities surge forward. The moon in your sign relates to your high cycle—this means you will be at the right place at a special moment. Leo and Aquarius play outstanding roles. Have luck with number 1.

SEPTEMBER 2002

Sunday, September 1 (Moon in Gemini to Cancer 5:13 p.m.)   On this Sunday, you will surprise many with a display of confidence. The moon in your sign, plus the number 8 numerical cycle, coincides with important contacts, projects, and accomplishments. Capricorn and Cancer will play outstanding roles.

Monday, September 2 (Moon in Cancer)   Look beyond the immediate. Check with a travel agent about a possible journey overseas. A love relationship is at a standstill—but only temporarily. Refuse to be taken for granted, and almost before you know it, you'll be regarded in a different, more positive way.

Tuesday, September 3 (Moon in Cancer to Leo 10:34 p.m.)   The money situation will show much improvement. Stress independence; show off your pioneering spirit. What had been held back from you will be released. Do your own thing; do not follow others. Leo and Aquarius will play dramatic roles.

Wednesday, September 4 (Moon in Leo)   Within 24 hours, you could be embarking upon a "short journey" in connection with a relative. Stick to a sensible pace. Let it be known you do not intend to become part of a wild-goose chase. A Cancer has your best interests at heart and will prove it.

Thursday, September 5 (Moon in Leo)   Social activities accelerate. Forces tend to be scattered. Questions arise, "Which invitations to accept?" You will be consulted about color coordination, design, entertainment, and showmanship. Have luck with number 3.

Friday, September 6 (Moon in Leo to Virgo 12:14 a.m.) You have a definite path to follow, despite minor obstacles. This is your "makeover" day. Revise, review, rewrite—and remember that hard writing makes easy reading. Tear down in order to rebuild. You will be rewarded for extra time spent in the "rebuilding process."

Saturday, September 7 (Moon in Virgo to Libra 11:56 p.m.)   Your possessions, including property, turn out to be worth more than you originally estimated. Check the facts and figures. Do your own investigating. A Pisces means well, but lacks well-researched conclusions. Virgo will also play a role. Have luck with number 5.

Sunday, September 8 (Moon in Libra)   On this Sunday, if possible, remain on familiar ground and reestablish connections with your family. Beautify your surroundings. Make a decision about design and architecture associated with where you live. Taurus, Libra, and Scorpio play outstanding roles.

Monday, September 9 (Moon in Libra to Scorpio 11:48 p.m.)   Define terms, outline boundaries, and do not drive with a heavy drinker. Avoid self-deception. See people, places, and relationships in a realistic light. Pisces and Virgo play major roles, could have these letters or initials in their names: G, P, Y.

Tuesday, September 10 (Moon in Scorpio)   This could be your power play day! The moon position relates to the stirring of creative juices. The number 8 numerical cycle coincides with added responsibility, a leadership role, production, promotion, and a greater degree of financial security.

Wednesday, September 11 (Moon in Scorpio)   Finish what you start. Realize that your original idea is ready to "take off." Emphasize universal appeal. Open lines of communication. Aries and Libra will play constructive roles. One relationship is running its course—another is on the way. Be receptive.

Thursday, September 12 (Moon in Scorpio to Sagittarius 1:44 a.m.)   Make a fresh start. Exercise independence of thought and action. The numerical cycle number 1 equates to the sun. This combines with your Mercury—your ideas, formats, and other contributions will be appreciated and will pay you handsomely. Leo is in this picture.

Friday, September 13 (Moon in Sagittarius)   Not an unlucky day for you! Separate superstition from fact. Focus on your family, partnership, cooperative efforts, and your marital status. You might be wondering, "Why are things happening so fast?" People you associate with could be temperamental and lack patience.

Saturday, September 14 (Moon in Sagittarius to Capricorn 6:47 a.m.) Questions about partnership, legal affairs, and marriage loom large. Lie low. Don't start a debate or a fight, but don't run away either. Social activities accelerate. Somehow people feel it is their duty to introduce you to someone who could play an important role in your life.

Sunday, September 15 (Moon in Capricorn) Be receptive, not naive. Keep both feet on the ground; find out what you are getting into before progressing too far. People, especially Sagittarius, will compliment and flatter you. Taurus, Leo, and Scorpio also play roles and have these initials in their names: D, M, V.

Monday, September 16 (Moon in Capricorn to Aquarius 2:54 p.m.) On this Monday, investigate where angels fear to tread. A computer error is likely; accounting procedures require review. You exude personal magnetism, and an aura of sensuality and sex appeal. At least one member of the opposite sex confides, "I can hardly keep my hands off you!"

Tuesday, September 17 (Moon in Aquarius) A short trip involves a relative. Make crystal clear, "I don't want to be involved in any wild-goose chase!" Taurus, Libra, and Scorpio figure prominently, and could have these initials in their names: F, O, X. The Aquarius moon relates to travel, spirituality, and gaining self-recognition.

Wednesday, September 18 (Moon in Aquarius) Lie low; play the waiting game. Travel is involved, as well as advertising, publishing, and showmanship. Use your Gemini wit and wisdom. You are going places. You are in charge of your own destiny. Pisces and Virgo will play major roles.

Thursday, September 19 (Moon in Aquarius to Pisces 1:17 a.m.)   Within 24 hours, you receive news that a project, long delayed, is given the green light. Deal with people in other cities and lands. Don't wait to be told—take the initiative, and contact higher-ups. Capricorn and Cancer will figure in this scenario.

Friday, September 20 (Moon in Pisces)   The Pisces moon relates to your career, promotion, production, and a work assignment that includes a sea resort. You have proven yourself; there's no need to keep an appointment hat in hand. Speak up, and assert your views. Do not back down from your principles. Aries is in this picture.

Saturday, September 21 (Moon in Pisces to Aries 1:10 p.m.)   A love relationship fills you with magnetic appeal. Maintain your self-esteem. Begin a project. Let love lead the way in many areas. Leo and Aquarius figure prominently, and could have these initials in their names: A, S, J. Have luck with number 1.

Sunday, September 22 (Moon in Aries)   A family member makes a surprise announcement, and it's very favorable. You can hardly believe your "good luck." The moon in Aries, your eleventh house, coincides with your ability to win friends and influence people. Excellent for obtaining funding, and for displaying Gemini wit and wisdom.

Monday, September 23 (Moon in Aries)   Racing luck—all tracks: post position special—number 3 p.p. in the fifth race. People question you about participation in political charitable campaigns. Be pleasant, but avoid definite commitments. Sagittarius plays a role.

Tuesday, September 24 (Moon in Aries to Taurus 1:53 a.m.)   On this day, attend to details. Realize that within 24 hours, secrets will be exposed—to your advantage. You could be in the midst of a winning streak. Deal with facts and figures; research subjects which you might be called upon to debate.

Wednesday, September 25 (Moon in Taurus)   Lucky lottery: 2, 5, 12, 13, 18, 25. Read, write, and learn by teaching. What you once took for granted will require additional study. A flirtation is more serious than you originally anticipated—know when to say, "Enough is enough!"

Thursday, September 26 (Moon in Taurus to Gemini 2:25 p.m.)   Focus on "backstage." The answers will be found, if you look in areas previously covered. What you discover will have a "stunning effect." Don't make a federal case out of minor infidelity. Voice, sound, design, and a domestic relationship all figure prominently.

Friday, September 27 (Moon in Gemini)   In your high cycle, you can put across ideas and concepts previously rejected. You get the proverbial "second chance." Pisces and Virgo will play major roles, and could have these letters or initials in their names: G, P, Y. Maintain an aura of intrigue and mystery.

Saturday, September 28 (Moon in Gemini)   What you have been waiting for is here. A powerful individual announces, "I will back you!" Focus on production and a financial transaction that definitely is not minor league. Capricorn and Cancer will play dynamic roles, and have these letters in their names: H, Q, Z.

Sunday, September 29 (Moon in Gemini to Cancer 12:59 a.m.)   Spiritual values surface. More money will become available. You will wonder, "What did I do that was right? I would like to find out and do it again!" The best answer is: It was in your stars, planets, and numbers. Libra plays a sensational role.

Monday, September 30 (Moon in Cancer)   On this last day of September, with the moon in its own sign, Cancer, your concentration will be on locating lost articles and increasing your earning power. Your prestige moves up. You are due to gain recognition. Leo and Aquarius figure in this dramatic scenario.

Tuesday, October 1 (Moon in Cancer to Leo 7:56 a.m.)
On this Tuesday, you learn where you stand and how far you can go. The moon position accents your earning power and ability to locate lost articles and to improve your income potential. You'll be asked questions about a foreign land, possible investment.

Wednesday, October 2 (Moon in Leo)   You'll conclude, "October could be my lucky month!" It could be, especially if you make a fresh start in a new direction—details are forthcoming by tonight. Leo and Aquarius play top roles, and sincerely want to be your valuable allies. Your fortunate number is 1.

Thursday, October 3 (Moon in Leo to Virgo 10:50 a.m.)
Focus on cooperative efforts, partnership, and marriage. A Leo relative who seems to have all the answers is himself in a quandary. Be cooperative to a certain point and then say, "Thanks but no thanks!" Cancer and Capricorn will not bow out of the picture.

Friday, October 4 (Moon in Virgo)   Highlight diversity and versatility, and become knowledgeable about the value of your property. Sagittarius and another Gemini will play fascinating roles, and have these letters or initials in their names: C, L, U. Have luck with number 3, tonight!

Saturday, October 5 (Moon in Virgo to Libra 10:50 a.m.)   You'll be tested and challenged. Many people ask questions in the hope that you will be embarrassed. Maintain your emotional equilibrium. Answer truthfully; that is all anyone can ask of you. Taurus, Leo, and Scorpio play memorable roles, and have these initials in their names: D, M, V.

Sunday, October 6 (Moon in Libra)   The new moon in Libra in your fifth house relates to children, challenge, variety, and a stirring of creative juices. An upstart Leo attempts to goad you into losing your temper. Have none of it! In matters of speculation, stick with number 5.

Monday, October 7 (Moon in Libra to Scorpio 9:57 a.m.)
Attention revolves around your home, family, security, and property values. You look different and your voice is unusual—people comment; accept this as a compliment. If there is music in your life tonight, dance to your own tune. Libra is represented.

Tuesday, October 8 (Moon in Scorpio)   Time is on your side—wait and see. Focus on work methods, and winning the friendship of someone who shares your basic interests. You'll be asked to participate in an enterprise that is due to become profitable. Pisces and Virgo play outstanding roles.

Wednesday, October 9 (Moon in Scorpio to Sagittarius 10:21 a.m.)   You missed an opportunity 24 hours ago—today you get the proverbial second chance. You'll be on the inside of a proposition that has been built to acquire a profit. Consult familiar friends, including a Cancer and a Capricorn. Your lucky number is 8.

Thursday, October 10 (Moon in Sagittarius)   On this Thursday, questions loom large, such as, "What are you going to do about cooperative efforts, partnership, and marriage?" Have the answers at hand. Be sure others realize you could at any moment take off for a trip overseas.

Friday, October 11 (Moon in Sagittarius to Capricorn 1:45 p.m.)   The moon in Sagittarius, your seventh house, relates to long-term commitments, including marriage. You meet new people, and emphasize originality, entertainment, and romance. Shake off lethargy. Refuse to be a prisoner of preconceived notions.

Saturday, October 12 (Moon in Capricorn)   Financial questions are answered. A review is agreed upon. Focus on direction, motivation, and a decision relating to your partnership and martial status. Cancer and Capricorn play outstanding roles, and could have these letters or initials in their names: B, K, T.

Sunday, October 13 (Moon in Capricorn to Aquarius 8:51 p.m.)   The lunar position coincides with an interest in the occult. There are some mysteries you want to solve—it won't matter if you try, so go ahead. To repeat a line from Shakespeare, "There are more things in heaven and earth . . . than are dreamt of in your philosophy, Horatio!"

Monday, October 14 (Moon in Aquarius)   Before this day is finished, you'll have the feeling of more freedom. Plan ahead in connection with a possible journey. Financial pressures are due to be relieved within 24 hours. Taurus, Leo, and Scorpio will play outstanding roles.

Tuesday, October 15 (Moon in Aquarius)   The moon in Aquarius relates to advertising, travel, publishing, and a recognition of spiritual values. People who previously took you for granted will now take a "second look." A Virgo member of the opposite sex confides, "I find you so attractive that at times I can hardly keep my hands off you!"

Wednesday, October 16 (Moon in Aquarius to Pisces 7:08 a.m.)   Look beyond the immediate. Take advantage of a "publishing opportunity." The highlight is also on your home, loved ones, insurance, and protection of your property. Taurus and Libra will play outstanding roles. A family member compliments you on your voice. Be happy about it!

Thursday, October 17 (Moon in Pisces)   Transform a tendency to brood into a positive meditation. Bring forth your psychic abilities. Trust your inner feelings. Do not equate delay with defeat. What you are waiting for will arrive within 3 days. Pisces and Virgo will be active in your scenario and helpful, too.

Friday, October 18 (Moon in Pisces to Aries 7:12 p.m.) Be ready for a "powerful" weekend. The emphasis is on promotion, production, and added recognition and prestige.

Some people ask, "To what do you attribute your success?" Take time to smile and modestly state, "I didn't figure I had that much success!"

Saturday, October 19 (Moon in Aries)   Your wishes will be fulfilled! The Aries moon represents your eleventh house—that section of your horoscope represents your hopes, wishes, and ability to win friends and influence people. Look to the future. Design a product so that it will meet the requirements of the future. Your lucky number is 9.

Sunday, October 20 (Moon in Aries)   Spiritual values surface in a dramatic way. Spirited discussion revolves around Charles Darwin and Alfred Russell Wallace. It will be stated that Wallace and Darwin were on the same wavelength, except that Wallace claimed a man had spiritual values. Leo dominates this scenario.

Monday, October 21 (Moon in Aries to Taurus 7:55 a.m.)   The full moon in your eleventh house coincides with romance, speculation, and personal magnetism. In continuation of a debate, you point out that Alfred Russell Wallace stunned colleagues by publishing his book *Scientific Developments in Modern Spiritualism.*

Tuesday, October 22 (Moon in Taurus)   You gain followers today by exhibiting your charm, personality, and sense of humor. Those you once sought guidance from will now return the compliment. Give full play to your intellectual curiosity, and investigate the practicality of travel in connection with a unique project.

Wednesday, October 23 (Moon in Taurus to Gemini 8:16 p.m.)   Lucky lottery: 2, 13, 20, 22, 24, 42. A secret meeting takes place. You might not be invited, but don't make a federal case of it. You are needed more than you need others. Maintain your emotional equilibrium. Laugh at those who take themselves too seriously.

Thursday, October 24 (Moon in Gemini) Your cycle moves up. Within 24 hours, you'll name your own ticket and price. A voluble Taurus talks sense and you must listen carefully to understand. Read, write, teach, and go slow on that flirtation—it could be getting out of hand.

Friday, October 25 (Moon in Gemini) The moon in your sign equates to your "high cycle." Accent your personality. Be with people who are bright and at times controversial. Take the initiative. You will be at the right place at the right time. It is possible that you might change your residence and marital status.

Saturday, October 26 (Moon in Gemini to Cancer 7:09 a.m.) Avoid making commitments that you know will be difficult to fulfill. See people, places, and relationships as they are, not merely as you wish they could be. This means avoid self-deception. Pisces and Virgo will play active roles.

Sunday, October 27—Daylight Saving Time Ends (Moon in Cancer) On this Sunday, you will obtain a correct evaluation of your possessions. You will know "the cost of things." A Cancer-born family member pleads, "You can trust me and I wish you would confide in me. It would make me feel much better." Your lucky number is 8.

Monday, October 28 (Moon in Cancer to Leo 2:18 p.m.) A project that has been long delayed can be completed. Travel overseas is a distinct possibility, which could include special dealings with Aries and Libra. For some time, you've complained, "Not enough excitement." Today you get your fill of exciting developments.

Tuesday, October 29 (Moon in Leo) A relative, previously quiet, engages in colorful verbiage. Maintain your own balance. Realize that sticks and stones can break your bones, but words hurled at you need not do damage. An Aquarius, who has been out of sight, will play a marvelous role.

Wednesday, October 30 (Moon in Leo to Virgo 6:58 p.m.) Proposals are received concerning business and career, partnership and marriage. Take time to be selective. Choose what you can handle and let the others go until "next time." Cancer and Capricorn will participate in putting across a dynamic, exciting project.

Thursday, October 31 (Moon in Virgo) For most people, it will be Halloween. For magicians around the world, it will be National Magic Day. It is a day when magicians and others remember Harry Houdini. There will be inquiries concerning whether or not he "came back." Mrs. Houdini told Walter Winchell, "Houdini did come back to me during a séance."

NOVEMBER 2002

Friday, November 1 (Moon in Virgo to Libra 8:27 p.m.) On this Friday, the first day of November, you feel revitalized. Display your pioneering spirit. Make a fresh start in a new direction. Leo and Aquarius figure prominently, and will serve as inspiration. Work methods improve. You are more valued, and those in authority will let you know it.

Saturday, November 2 (Moon in Libra) With the moon in your fifth house, you exude personal magnetism and creativity. A flirtation that started innocently could be getting "complicated." Focus on children, challenge, change, and variety. Have luck with number 2.

Sunday, November 3 (Moon in Libra to Scorpio 8:09 p.m.) You will relax today. You also will laugh at your own foibles. With the moon remaining in Libra, your fifth house, you will be active in connection with children and creative projects. Sagittarius and another Gemini figure prominently.

Monday, November 4 (Moon in Scorpio) The new moon in Scorpio is in your sixth house, which relates to your general health, impassioned pleas, and contacts with people who share your basic interests. This will not be an easygoing day. But you'll overcome obstacles and objections. Taurus is represented.

Tuesday, November 5 (Moon in Scorpio to Sagittarius 8:01 p.m.)   Be ready for swift changes. Read, write, teach, and study yourself in connection with whom you want to spend the rest of your life. Focus on getting your thoughts on paper. Spend time analyzing your dreams. Tonight will be significant.

Wednesday, November 6 (Moon in Sagittarius)   Lucky lottery: 6, 13, 18, 40, 42, 51. The lunar position emphasizes cooperative efforts in connection with City Hall. The emphasis is on public relations, legal affairs, and your marital status. There will be a reunion tonight. Tears will flow—give logic equal time!

Thursday, November 7 (Moon in Sagittarius to Capricorn 10:00 p.m.)   On this Thursday, you separate fact from fancy without losing the valuable ingredient of imagination. Define terms; pay attention to real estate, to boundaries and basic costs. Pisces and Virgo will play "astounding" roles.

Friday, November 8 (Moon in Capricorn)   You've waited for this day! Focus on accounting, royalties, and banking totals. An older person wants to help and is sincere, but can't quite keep up with the times. The pressure is on due to added responsibility. Capricorn is in the picture.

Saturday, November 9 (Moon in Capricorn)   On this Saturday, look forward with anticipation. Open lines of communication. Someone in a faraway land has information to give you. Look beyond the immediate. Maintain an aura of universal appeal. Have luck with number 9.

Sunday, November 10 (Moon in Capricorn to Aquarius 3:27 a.m.)   On this Sunday, spiritual values rise. The numerical cycle number 1 relates to the sun and blends with your Mercury. Original thoughts and presentations will pay dividends. Don't wait to be told. Go your way. Stress independence and creativity.

Monday, November 11 (Moon in Aquarius)   You emerge from an aura of confusion. You are fit and in fighting form. Blend this "action cycle" with humor. You'll be asked important questions about partnership, cooperative efforts, and marriage. A Cancer plays a major role.

Tuesday, November 12 (Moon in Aquarius to Pisces 12:41 p.m.)   Forces are scattered. Nevertheless, you can select the best—emphasize quality. Remember resolutions about exercise, diet, and nutrition. Someone of the opposite sex will sidle up to you and whisper, "I can hardly keep my hands off you!"

Wednesday, November 13 (Moon in Pisces)   Racing luck—all tracks: post position special—number 4 p.p. in the fourth race. Someone in a position of authority seeks to confer with you. It's not strictly business. Be open-minded, without being naive. Scorpio is involved.

Thursday, November 14 (Moon in Pisces)   The lunar position accents promotion, production, and leadership. Get ready for quick changes. Maintain your sense of direction. A flirtation could be getting too hot not to cool down. Virgo, Sagittarius, and another Gemini play featured roles. Your lucky number is 5.

Friday, November 15 (Moon in Pisces to Aries 12:37 a.m.) Focus on harmony, especially at home. With the moon in your eleventh house, you win friends and influence people. You obtain funding for a favorite project. You'll have luck in matters of speculation, especially with these three numbers: 2, 9, 8.

Saturday, November 16 (Moon in Aries)   You will be "called in" for a consultation. The emphasis will be on the future, discarding old methods and concepts. Your pioneering spirit surfaces to your advantage. Do research on language, numbers, and symbols. During a heated debate, insist that you know what it is all about and will do something to prove it.

Sunday, November 17 (Moon in Aries to Taurus 1:22 p.m.) On this Sunday, relax with the knowledge that you did your best and favorably impressed executives. You will be told about a fresh start, a new project which will bring you more independence. Leo, Capricorn, and Cancer play spectacular roles.

Monday, November 18 (Moon in Taurus) You sense, properly so, that something is being hidden. Look behind the scenes. You are not being told the complete story. Let it be known that you are not pleased with efforts to deceive. Aries and Libra will figure in this dramatic scenario.

Tuesday, November 19 (Moon in Taurus) Leo and another Gemini have something to tell you—listen! Get ready for a fresh start. Accept new concepts. Don't ridicule ideas which appear to be "fantastic." Recall Shakespeare's lines: "There are more things in heaven and earth, Horatio, than are dreamt of in your philosophy."

Wednesday, November 20 (Moon in Taurus to Gemini 1:23 a.m.) The full moon and lunar eclipse are in Taurus, which represents your twelfth house. There is a rumble and stumble and you know for sure that something is going on backstage. Keep your emotional equilibrium, and hold off on accusations.

Thursday, November 21 (Moon in Gemini) Your cycle is high, so you put forth personal magnetism and sex appeal. Your popularity increases. A Sagittarius declares, "You have got it today!" Another Gemini asserts, "If we stick together on this, it will turn out well for both of us!"

Friday, November 22 (Moon in Gemini to Cancer 11:46 a.m.) A day made to order for you—obstacles placed in your path will be "easily" overcome. Your cycle is such that help comes from surprise sources, along with additional funding. Taurus, Leo, and Scorpio figure in this unusual scenario. Keep an open mind!

Saturday, November 23 (Moon in Cancer)   Relatives and money blend during this cycle. You will receive a "vote of confidence." A valuable article lost ten days ago will mysteriously reappear. Don't look a gift horse in the mouth. Don't ask too many questions. Lucky lottery: 5, 15, 20, 25, 35, 40.

Sunday, November 24 (Moon in Cancer to Leo 8:01 p.m.)   On this Sunday, stick close to your family, if possible. There is talk of expense in design, architecture, and further steps in beautifying your surroundings, especially at home. Keep abreast of what is happening, so that you are not off balance.

Monday, November 25 (Moon in Leo)   A well-meaning relative suggests a trip. Your response should be negative, unless you want to be caught up in a wild-goose chase. Say thanks but no thanks, perhaps next time. Make crystal clear that your time is valuable and you must receive proper, advance notice.

Tuesday, November 26 (Moon in Leo)   Results you have been hoping for will surface—this is your power play day, so take advantage of it! On a personal level, a relationship is warm at present, but could ultimately get too hot not to cool down. A Cancer is involved.

Wednesday, November 27 (Moon in Leo to Virgo 1:40 a.m.)   Have answers ready for a critical analysis likely to be put forth by Virgo. Stick to your principles, but also make intelligent concessions. A long-range forecast is involved, which could include a weather report. Aries declares, "You are the person for the job!"

Thursday, November 28 (Moon in Virgo)   On this Thanksgiving, you might be opening the door to an exciting new relationship. Be calm, but express enthusiasm for ideas and thoughts presented by a Leo. On this Thanksgiving, express gratitude for all the opportunities you had throughout the year.

Friday, November 29 (Moon in Virgo to Libra 4:53 a.m.)
Out of confusion will arise definite opinions. Trust your instincts and your heart. Those who attempt to overanalyze will be wrong. Trust your hunch. Give full play to your intuitive intellect. Cancer and Aquarius will play "sensational" roles.

Saturday, November 30 (Moon in Libra)   On this Saturday, the last day of November, the moon is in Libra. That is your fifth house, the section of your horoscope relating to creative and sexual activities. Avoid being fixed in your views. Don't insist on the answers which will reassure your ego. Have luck with number 3.

DECEMBER 2002

Sunday, December 1 (Moon in Libra to Scorpio 6:14 a.m.)
This is the last month of the year. Christmas is on the way, along with New Year's Eve. On this first day of December, there will be much soul-searching. You will be considering resolutions relating to your home, family, and marriage.

Monday, December 2 (Moon in Scorpio)   Nothing happens halfway today! Your "health problem" can be resolved if you practice moderation. This is not always easy during the holiday season. However, you have the intelligence, wit, and wisdom to do it and you will.

Tuesday, December 3 (Moon in Scorpio to Sagittarius 6:57 a.m.)   Check your details. A computer error is a distinct possibility. Double-check your bank balance, insurance, and telephone payments. Taurus, Leo, and Scorpio will play dramatic roles. Some have these letters or initials in their names: D, M, V.

Wednesday, December 4 (Moon in Sagittarius)   The new moon and solar eclipse are in Sagittarius, your seventh house. There could be plenty of action, including upsets in connection with legal affairs, public relations, and your marital status. Take notes, start a diary, and be especially aware of dreams and their symbols. Your lucky number is 5.

Thursday, December 5 (Moon in Sagittarius to Capricorn 8:38 a.m.)   Attention continues to emphasize cooperative efforts and participation in a public recognition of past and present heroes. You will be directly concerned with your public image, your legal rights and permissions, and marriage. A Libra is involved.

Friday, December 6 (Moon in Capricorn)   You will feel as if "something ominous" is in the air, and could happen at any time. Focus on hospitals, institutions, and the fall from favor of a distinguished citizen. Maintain your emotional equilibrium. Be open-minded, without being naive.

Saturday, December 7 (Moon in Capricorn to Aquarius 12:54 p.m.)   History lessons are reviewed, as you and the nation remember Pearl Harbor Day. Check the facts and figures involved. Organize your priorities. You have much to offer. There is no reason to downplay contributions. Lucky lottery: 8, 18, 24, 35, 48, 51.

Sunday, December 8 (Moon in Aquarius)   Travel to a foreign land should not be dismissed. There is a distinct possibility. Look beyond the immediate; your sense of prophecy is heightened. Predict your future. Make it come true! Aries and Libra figure in this dynamic, dramatic scenario.

Monday, December 9 (Moon in Aquarius to Pisces 8:46 p.m.)   Racing luck—all tracks: post position special—number 7 p.p. in the first race. Throughout the day, wear bright colors and make personal appearances. A love relationship might get too hot not to cool down. Avoid making demands. Ride with the tide. Leo plays a top role.

227

Tuesday, December 10 (Moon in Pisces)   You have a decision to make which involves your family or career. A secret meeting takes place. You are the subject of a discussion. Do what must be done. Be gracious about it. Cancer and Capricorn are directly involved, and feel you should follow their counsel.

Wednesday, December 11 (Moon in Pisces)   By using charm, wit you get your way, which is the "right way." Feature humor. Keep plans flexible. Make intelligent concessions. Sagittarius and another Gemini will play featured roles. Lucky lottery: 3, 7, 10, 30, 46, 50.

Thursday, December 12 (Moon in Pisces to Aries 7:57 a.m.)   Attend to details. Someone attempts to take your attention away from the essentials. Be polite, but indicate, "Thanks but no thanks, not today!" Scorpio and Taurus are involved, and might attempt to "bully you." Rebuild and rewrite. Your lucky number is 4.

Friday, December 13 (Moon in Aries)   You will be excellent at obtaining funding for a unique project. You win friends and influence people. Don't hold back! This is your kind of day. You will have luck despite "Friday the 13th." Another Gemini is in the picture.

Saturday, December 14 (Moon in Aries to Taurus 8:42 p.m.)   A family member deserves attention, even if the scheme is half-baked. Avoid being accusatory. Listen with an expression of, "I want to hear more!" This helps relieve pressure. Taurus and Libra figure in this scenario and make contributions.

Sunday, December 15 (Moon in Taurus)   Grab an opportunity to express your desires. In matters of speculation, you might find number 7 to be lucky. Visit someone temporarily confined to home or hospital. It could have been you, so be thankful! Pisces and Virgo figure in this scenario.

Monday, December 16 (Moon in Taurus)   Make this your power play day! You gain access to privileged information. Let it be known, "I'll use it if necessary!" Capricorn and Cancer will play instrumental roles. You will be provided with the material necessary to carry out a project.

Tuesday, December 17 (Moon in Taurus to Gemini 8:41 a.m.)   Maintain a universal outlook. Representatives of another nation could contact you. Be careful what you say. Say very little of consequence. Aries and Libra figure in this dramatic scenario, and have these letters in their names: I and R.

Wednesday, December 18 (Moon in Gemini)   You might be hitting yourself with sledgehammer words concerning yesterday. Today start fresh; imprint style; do not follow others. The moon in your sign represents your high cycle. Don't back down. Stand tall for your principles. Have luck with number 1.

Thursday, December 19 (Moon in Gemini to Cancer 6:29 p.m.)   Racing luck—all tracks: post position special— number 5 p.p. in the fifth race. The full moon in your sign represents the completion of a family dispute over money. Be receptive without being weak. You'll be at the right place at a special moment.

Friday, December 20 (Moon in Cancer)   Diversify; highlight your intellectual curiosity. Insist on all information, not just bits and pieces. Somehow others bend to your will. Perhaps it is due to the sincere expression you maintained for the past three days. A Sagittarius plays a major role.

Saturday, December 21 (Moon in Cancer)   On this Saturday, you get the "facts of life." Be practical where money is concerned. A Cancer family member moves to your side in an argument. Missing papers are located. This helps you put across your concepts and desires. Be a gracious winner!

Sunday, December 22 (Moon in Cancer to Leo 1:47 a.m.) Get ready for a change of scene and policy. If you are aware and move with the times, you win another major victory. A short trip is necessary to appease a family member who, if made angry, could cause trouble. A Sagittarius renders a fair decision.

Monday, December 23 (Moon in Leo)   Relatives and the protection of your property at home figure prominently. Flowers, music, and gifts are a major part of this scenario. Music plays, so dance to your own tune. A domestic adjustment is just what you want and need. Libra is in this picture.

Tuesday, December 24 (Moon in Leo to Virgo 7:04 a.m.) Spiritual values of your holiday will be much in evidence. The Leo moon represents showmanship, gifts, and expressions of goodwill. Avoid being materialistic. State your beliefs in a "believable way." If you wait, you win. Do not force issues.

Wednesday, December 25 (Moon in Virgo)   Much to your pleasure, you receive a practical gift and hear up-to-date counsel. People look to you for approval. In actuality, you are in a powerful position. Don't abdicate, despite pressure. This will be one of your most enjoyable, profitable of Christmas Days.

Thursday, December 26 (Moon in Virgo to Libra 10:52 a.m.)   You feel like you are "back home again." You are on your own turf. Others see a difference in your attitude and actions. Those who once took you for granted will change their minds. Aries and Libra will play meaningful roles.

Friday, December 27 (Moon in Libra)   Your creative juices stir. Give of yourself through reading and writing. Exciting changes are made at your behest. The holiday spirit prevails; be kind, but insist on the truth. Begin a project; highlight originality. Leo will play a dramatic role.

Saturday, December 28 (Moon in Libra to Scorpio 1:40 p.m.)   The emphasis is on partnership, cooperative efforts, and marriage. If single, that might not be for too long. If married, the spark that brought you together in the first place will reignite. Cancer and Capricorn will play memorable roles. Your lucky number is 2.

Sunday, December 29 (Moon in Scorpio)   If you don't know what to do, do nothing. You are currently in an aura of confusion. Don't rationalize. Face facts as they exist. An Aquarius means well, but advice is not valid. Sagittarius and another Gemini figure in this dynamic scenario.

Monday, December 30 (Moon in Scorpio to Sagittarius 4:00 p.m.)   A Scorpio could overturn your work schedule. Maintain your emotional equilibrium. Let it be known, "I won't scare easily!" Continue to handle details; do proofreading. Be willing to tear down in order to rebuild. A Taurus voluntarily provides vital information.

Tuesday, December 31 (Moon in Sagittarius)   Don't be in a car driven by a heavy drinker. It's a lively New Year's Eve, when many will make resolutions and promises. Don't believe everything you hear. Someone of the opposite sex, perhaps full of adult beverages, says, "I can hardly keep my hands off you!"

HAPPY NEW YEAR!

JANUARY 2003

Wednesday, January 1 (Moon in Sagittarius to Capricorn 6:42 p.m.)   During this month, you could be the "talk of the town." Travel to a foreign land is a distinct possibility. People are drawn to you; they confide problems, some of them intimate. On this first day of the new year, take the initiative and imprint your own style; don't follow others. Have luck with number 1.

Thursday, January 2 (Moon in Capricorn)   The new moon in your eighth house coincides with a revelation in connection with how much money your mate or partner possesses. Don't argue about the past. Absorb knowledge for right now. Capricorn and Cancer will play memorable roles.

Friday, January 3 (Moon in Capricorn to Aquarius 10:57 p.m.) The emphasis is on intelligence, humor, and versatility. You have a gift, Gemini, of making people laugh even through moments of grief. Sagittarius and another Gemini will play dramatic roles. Be sure of your legal rights and permissions. Be on the right side of the law.

Saturday, January 4 (Moon in Aquarius) On this Saturday, events transpire that soon will make you feel free, happy, and willing to travel. The emphasis will be on philosophy, theology, and language. Taurus, Leo, and Scorpio will be in the picture, and have these letters in their names: D, M, V.

Sunday, January 5 (Moon in Aquarius) On this Sunday, write your impressions and feelings. Important people are observing and are eager to elevate your position. Focus on advertising, publishing, and long-range communication. A Sagittarius and another Gemini will play significant roles. Number 5 is lucky!

Monday, January 6 (Moon in Aquarius to Pisces 5:56 a.m.) Focus on where you live and a possible change of residence or marital status. Music plays, so find your own rhythm and dance to your own tune. Accent diplomacy. Use your ability to make intelligent concessions without abandoning your principles. Libra is involved.

Tuesday, January 7 (Moon in Pisces) Define terms and strive to maintain your emotional equilibrium. An aura of deception is present. Above all, avoid self-deception. Don't tell all; don't confide or confess. Others will be convinced you have "psychic powers." Pisces plays a key role.

Wednesday, January 8 (Moon in Pisces to Aries 4:14 p.m.) You will be discussing "big business." What had been held back will be released in your favor. Visit someone temporarily confined to home or hospital. You will ponder, "My

232

life seems to be straightening out!" Have luck with number 8.

Thursday, January 9 (Moon in Aries)   You will be dealing with an aggressive Aries. Listen carefully; you could receive valuable hints. Open the lines of communication. Someone wants to "tell you something." Finish what you start, then toss aside preconceived notions. You are going places!

Friday, January 10 (Moon in Aries)   This is the time to make a wish come true! The moon in Aries is in your eleventh house, which means that elements of timing and luck ride with you. Past investments will pay dividends. Imprint your style. Make a fresh start in a new direction. Leo and Aquarius are in the picture.

Saturday, January 11 (Moon in Aries to Taurus 4:47 a.m.) Focus on direction, motivation, and questions about partnership or marriage. That "digestive problem" will disappear if you attend to it. You could find yourself involved with neighborhood politics. Capricorn plays an important role.

Sunday, January 12 (Moon in Taurus)   On this Sunday, there are many surprises—of a pleasant variety. Social activities increase; people share anecdotes and humor. Be generous, but not extravagant. Remember a special anniversary or birthday, then do something about it. Sagittarius is involved.

Monday, January 13 (Moon in Taurus to Gemini 5:06 p.m.)   You will find that "thirteen" will actually be your lucky number. The Taurus moon is in your twelfth house, so today you'll unveil mysteries. One "mystery" concerns a "complication in regard to finance." Tear down in order to rebuild.

Tuesday, January 14 (Moon in Gemini)   You'll experience more freedom of thought and of action. The moon in your sign highlights personality, energy, and sex appeal.

Because your cycle is high, circumstances are turning in your favor. Know it, and act as if aware of it. Virgo plays a top role.

Wednesday, January 15 (Moon in Gemini) A domestic quarrel is "smoothed over." The moon in your first house highlights your personality, originality, and excitement of discovery. Make appointments. Let people know you are alive and kicking. Attention also revolves around your home, earning power, and marital status.

Thursday, January 16 (Moon in Gemini to Cancer 2:54 a.m.) Although the moon is leaving your sign, your cycle remains fortunate. You get credit long overdue. People are intrigued! They want to be with you, and they hope you will give them an "exclusive story." Pisces and Virgo will play "astonishing" roles.

Friday, January 17 (Moon in Cancer) The lunar position favors investments, payments, and collections as well as locating lost articles. You seem down to earth, so people realize you do "mean business." This could be your power play day! Know it, and make the most of it. A Cancer figures prominently.

Saturday, January 18 (Moon in Cancer to Leo 9:27 a.m.) The full moon in your second house indicates that a financial transaction will be completed. Overcome a tendency to hit yourself with sledgehammer words. This means don't brood about what should have been or could have been. Aries and Libra play significant roles. Lucky number is 9.

Sunday, January 19 (Moon in Leo) The emphasis is on publicity, showmanship, and advertising. A short trip may be necessary in connection with a relative. Highlight versatility. Give full rein to your intellectual curiosity. You learn many things today, so be glad and thankful. Leo is in this picture.

Monday, January 20 (Moon in Leo to Virgo 1:30 p.m.) Focus on cooperative efforts, publicity, and decisions relating to partnership or marriage. Take a chance on romance; shake off emotional lethargy. Cancer and Capricorn will play productive roles. In matters of speculation, stick with number 2.

Tuesday, January 21 (Moon in Virgo)   Be analytical, make inquiries. Don't be satisfied merely to know something happened. Find out why. A member of the opposite sex declares, "You are quite wonderful, whether or not you realize it!" Sagittarius is represented.

Wednesday, January 22 (Moon in Virgo to Libra 4:24 p.m.)   A restriction is only temporary. Know it, and don't be discouraged. Rewrite, rebuild, review. Present the finished product to a superior. Be thorough when checking details. Fix things at home. Taurus and Scorpio will play essential roles. Eventual victory!

Thursday, January 23 (Moon in Libra)   Get ready for change, travel, and a variety of experiences. Read and write; learn through the process of sharing and teaching. You'll be considered attractive, quite sexy. Don't break too many hearts! A short trip will involve a relative, and a possible search for legal documents. A flirtation turns serious.

Friday, January 24 (Moon in Libra to Scorpio 7:08 p.m.) You will be asking, "Is this déjà vu?" The scenario features familiar places and faces. You experience more freedom of thought and of action. A possible change of residence or marital status is highlighted. If diplomatic, you win your way. Sound plays a role.

Saturday, January 25 (Moon in Scorpio)   You will hear many "sweet" words. Request politely, "Will you please put it in writing!" Avoid self-deception. See people and relationships as they exist, not merely as you wish they could be. Someone wants to deceive you, so protect yourself in emotional clinches.

Sunday, January 26 (Moon in Scorpio to Sagittarius 10:25 p.m.)   The employment picture commands attention. Focus on service, being sure you get credit for work done. A health problem is minor, but take care of it. Don't let it become major. Remember resolutions about exercise, diet, and nutrition. Capricorn and Cancer play roles.

Monday, January 27 (Moon in Sagittarius)   Be optimistic. Predict your future. Make it come true. Look beyond the immediate, and get ready for travel, perhaps to a foreign land. The emphasis is on universal appeal. Something you write or publish will add to your prestige. Be modest but not servile.

Tuesday, January 28 (Moon in Sagittarius)   Toss aside preconceived notions. Break from a situation that finds you being taken for granted. Find ways to negotiate a new agreement or contract. Avoid heavy lifting, and don't take on an obligation belonging to another. Leo and Aquarius are in this picture.

Wednesday, January 29 (Moon in Sagittarius to Capricorn 2:29 a.m.)   You will have more room in your living quarters. If single, you could encounter your future mate. Married or single, a domestic adjustment is essential. Maintain dietary restrictions. Your position is strong, so act as if you are aware of it. Lucky lottery: 2, 12, 20, 13, 18, 5.

Thursday, January 30 (Moon in Capricorn)   On this next to the last day of January, deal with banks and other financial institutions. Find out more about interest rates, loans, and credit. Investigate. As you make inquiries, insist on straight answers. Sagittarius and another Gemini will play outstanding roles. Lucky number is 3.

Friday, January 31 (Moon in Capricorn to Aquarius 7:44 a.m.)   On this last day of January, with the moon in Capricorn, you learn more about the intentions of those who "owe you money." Be as kind and understanding as possible. Some revision of plans will be necessary. The key is to rebuild.

Saturday, February 1 (Moon in Aquarius) You could be entertaining people from a distant city or foreign land. Include your family in this lively Saturday night. Cancer and Capricorn play dominant roles. In matters of speculation, stick with number 2. Your property value should be assessed.

Sunday, February 2 (Moon in Aquarius to Pisces 2:54 p.m.) On this Sunday, entertain and be entertained. What was long ago and far away will become available. Emphasize idealism. You will be drawn to romance. You are so attractive and witty that others comment on it. Sagittarius is in the picture.

Monday, February 3 (Moon in Pisces) Monday starts out as routine and boring. However, you will eventually rebuild and rewrite. It could be a day when the keyword is "results." Taurus, Leo, and Scorpio play sensational roles. Perfect techniques, check details, and correct a plumbing defect.

Tuesday, February 4 (Moon in Pisces) An excellent day to start a diary. Take notes on your impressions of people and places. Also, observe your dreams. They could be guideposts to the future, if properly interpreted. A flirtation will make life interesting, but know when to say, "Enough!"

Wednesday, February 5 (Moon in Pisces to Aries 12:44 a.m.) At the track: post position special—number 2 p.p. in the fourth race. Pick six—7, 6, 4, 3, 5, 1. Hot daily doubles—3 and 6, 1 and 5, 4 and 2. Away from the track, attention revolves around making your home beautiful. Strive for harmony in domestic relationships:

Thursday, February 6 (Moon in Aries) Many wishes can come true, if you so permit. In matters of speculation, stick with number 7. Married or single, romance will be featured. Avoid self-deception. See people and relationships in a realistic light. A Pisces figures prominently.

Friday, February 7 (Moon in Aries to Taurus 12:58 p.m.)
A power day, with the number 8 numerical cycle and the transiting moon in your eleventh house. Money comes like a bolt out of the blue. Elements of timing and luck ride with you. You'll be saying, "What a Friday!" Your powers of persuasion are heightened.

Saturday, February 8 (Moon in Taurus)   Lucky lottery: 16, 9, 25, 18, 1, 7. Look beyond the immediate. A financial opportunity is within your grasp. Toss aside preconceived notions. Take charge of your own future—make predictions come true. Aries and Libra will figure prominently.

Sunday, February 9 (Moon in Taurus)   What you are thinking is valid—the answer is "yes." Stress independence. Make a fresh start in a new direction. Leo and Aquarius will play memorable roles. Don't follow others; let them follow you, if they so desire. Have luck with number 1.

Monday, February 10 (Moon in Taurus to Gemini 1:44 a.m.)   A decision is made concerning your direction and motivation. Be sure you have time alone for the purpose of meditation. Something happening behind the scenes involves your family, home, and security. Dinner tonight will consist of seafood, prepared by a Cancer.

Tuesday, February 11 (Moon in Gemini)   Discipline will be lax as social activities accelerate. Turn on your charm. Introduce people to others who hold opposing views. Humor replaces formality. Persons who begin with frowns could end in smiles. Sagittarius and another Gemini play featured roles.

Wednesday, February 12 (Moon in Gemini to Cancer 12:17 p.m.)   You can overcome bureaucratic red tape. Today you will be at the right place at a crucial moment almost effortlessly. Ride with the tide; don't get in your own way. Scorpio offers critical, helpful comments. You will do the correct thing without knowing exactly how you did it.

Thursday, February 13 (Moon in Cancer)   Prepare for a series of changes; be ready for opportunities. The lunar position makes crystal clear, "Guard what is valuable!" Your cycle continues high, so some investments will pay handsome dividends. Virgo, Sagittarius, and another Gemini play dynamic roles. Lucky number is 5.

Friday, February 14 (Moon in Cancer to Leo 7:03 p.m.) On this St. Valentine's Day, you receive numerous cards making declarations of love. Take some seriously, but wait until you receive personal confirmation. Be selective when sending out your own cards. Taurus and Libra persons are involved.

Saturday, February 15 (Moon in Leo)   Find time on this Saturday night to be alone for the purpose of meditation. The answers are within, and meditation will bring them forward so that you can recognize and act on them. Maintain an aura of mystery. Don't tell all; let others play guessing games.

Sunday, February 16 (Moon in Leo to Virgo 10:23 p.m.) Spiritual values surface. The full moon in your third house points to trips, visits, and relatives. Be especially careful while driving. Steer clear of traffic jams. Someone wants your money, and is not quite subtle about it. Don't give them the satisfaction!

Monday, February 17 (Moon in Virgo)   What was supposed to be a lost cause could be just getting started. Be aware of it, and act accordingly. You'll be musing, "What goes around most certainly comes around!" Strive for universal appeal. There are more things in heaven and on earth that might fit your philosophy.

Tuesday, February 18 (Moon in Virgo to Libra 11:47 p.m.)   On this Tuesday, stress independence, creativity, and original thinking. The moon in Virgo accents home and property as well as the conclusion of a transaction. Express your own style; do not follow others. An ambitious Leo attempts to persuade you otherwise. Have luck with number 1.

Wednesday, February 19 (Moon in Libra)   Focus on the "comforts of home." The Virgo moon in your fourth house means be analytical, ask questions about property. The spotlight is on direction, motivation, and the need for meditation. A Cancer steps in as your financial adviser.

Thursday, February 20 (Moon in Libra)   Diversify, giving full play to your intellectual curiosity. The Libra moon stirs your creative juices. Focus on style and romance. Recognize that you are attractive and people also know it. Maintain your equilibrium; protect yourself in emotional clinches. Sagittarius is in this picture.

Friday, February 21 (Moon in Libra to Scorpio 1:09 a.m.) Rewrite, revise, review. A love relationship is exciting, but take nothing for granted. Focus on children, challenge, change, and a variety of sensations. Be willing to tear down for the purpose of rebuilding. People will be fascinated by you, your actions, your words.

Saturday, February 22 (Moon in Scorpio)   This will be a lively Saturday night! Remember resolutions concerning restraint. You will have the freedom to control your own destiny. Your written words receive much attention. You'll have an abundance of sex appeal. Know it, but protect yourself at close quarters.

Sunday, February 23 (Moon in Scorpio to Sagittarius 3:45 a.m.)   Harmony replaces bitterness. Focus on a domestic adjustment. There's a chance to increase your income. You'll receive a gift, which helps make your home more attractive. Taurus, Libra, and Scorpio will play dramatic roles, and have these letters in their names: F, O, X.

Monday, February 24 (Moon in Sagittarius)   A financial dispute that once was settled will be revived to your advantage. Whatever psychic qualities you possess will sur-face. Define terms, outline boundaries. Avoid self-deception. Don't give up something of value! A Pisces figures prominently.

Tuesday, February 25 (Moon in Sagittarius to Capricorn 8:10 a.m.)   Plan ahead for a financial coup. Be positive concerning the legal aspects of any venture. Get commitments in writing. Be realistic in ascertaining possibilities. If single, the topic of marriage will be discussed. Capricorn plays a top role.

Wednesday, February 26 (Moon in Capricorn)   Finish what you start. Strive for better distribution of your talent or product. Look beyond the immediate, discard preconceived notions. For you, nothing is really impossible. Know it, and exude confidence. Aries is involved. Lucky number is 9.

Thursday, February 27 (Moon in Capricorn to Aquarius 2:24 p.m.)   Shake off lethargy. Get ready for a fresh start in a new direction. Take steps into what many consider "the occult." You learn more about the finances of your mate or partner. Face the truth—it will set you free. Leo and Aquarius will play dynamic, dramatic roles.

Friday, February 28 (Moon in Aquarius)   Your extra-sensory perception is activated. You perceive the future, which includes travel, philosophy, and theology. Focus on family, home, and your marital status. Accent meditation, avoid brooding. You'll say, "There have been difficult days, but I've overcome them!"

MARCH 2003

Saturday, March 1 (Moon in Aquarius to Pisces 10:25 p.m.)   A lively Saturday night! Focus on the unorthodox in entertainment. Use your Gemini humor. People express admiration for your intellectual capabilities. Sagittarius and another Gemini will play fascinating roles. Lucky lottery: 3, 33, 8, 18, 25, 6.

Sunday, March 2 (Moon in Pisces)   People close to you return from a journey. Don't let yourself be "hypnotized." Follow your heart. You'll know what to do when time comes. Recreate a scene of domestic harmony. Taurus and Scorpio are in the picture. Don't fight progress!

Monday, March 3 (Moon in Pisces)   Your employer could be "different." Last night's new moon in Pisces represents authority, promotion, and a chance to take over the reins. It's important to write, to let others know you are articulate and talented. A flirtation starts mildly, but could soon become hot and heavy.

Tuesday, March 4 (Moon in Pisces to Aries 8:29 a.m.) You will be rewarded for past efforts. Stand tall—there's no need to be servile. Take a low bow, then proceed to "do the job." A domestic adjustment is featured. You could change your residence or marital status. Taurus and Libra will play memorable roles.

Wednesday, March 5 (Moon in Aries)   Define terms; don't confide or confess. Keep privileged information to yourself. If others want to, let them play guessing games. Avoid self-deception. See people and relationships as they are, not merely as you wish they could be. Pisces is involved.

Thursday, March 6 (Moon in Aries to Taurus 8:35 p.m.) An opportunity you missed is here again—do something about it! The focus is on power struggles, a promotion, and the pressure of added responsibility. Capricorn and Cancer will play major roles, and could have these initials in their names: H, Q, Z. Lucky number is 8.

Friday, March 7 (Moon in Taurus)   On this Friday, your powers of prophecy surge forward. The moon in your eleventh house indicates that you win friends and influence

242

people. Obtain funding for a "pet project." Elements of luck and timing ride with you. Stick with number 9.

Saturday, March 8 (Moon in Taurus) You meet interesting people this Saturday. A secret concerning finances will be revealed. Someone of the opposite sex will be bold enough to say, "At times I can hardly keep my hands off you!" Fate could take you in a new direction—don't fight it!

Sunday, March 9 (Moon in Taurus to Gemini 9:36 a.m.) Your spiritual values surface. Visit someone temporarily confined to home or hospital. You could learn more than you care to know. Imprint your own style; don't follow others. The emphasis is on home—the luxury of being able to entertain and be entertained. Cancer and Capricorn will be guests.

Monday, March 10 (Moon in Gemini) A social affair you missed last week will be made up for tonight. Your cycle is high, so you will be at the right place at a crucial moment. Sagittarius and another Gemini play significant roles. Fashion news will intrigue. Have luck with number 3.

Tuesday, March 11 (Moon in Gemini to Cancer 9:10 p.m.) Your cycle is high, so your intuition is on target. A serious discussion takes place concerning the possibility of a "name change." Interest in astrology will be heightened. Cancer, Scorpio, and Aquarius play featured roles. Revise, review, and rewrite.

Wednesday, March 12 (Moon in Cancer) Within 24 hours, you receive a financial surprise—a pleasant one. A lost valuable can be recovered, if you so permit. This means don't frighten those who want to present clues. Be calm, cool, and collected. Virgo, Sagittarius, and another Gemini play "puzzling" roles.

Thursday, March 13 (Moon in Cancer) The emphasis is on home, family, and treasured possessions. Dance to your own tune. You'll hear comments about your voice.

Developing this talent would not be a bad idea! Beautify your home. Be open to taking a chance on romance. Taurus and Libra are involved.

Friday, March 14 (Moon in Cancer to Leo 5:05 a.m.) Don't tell all! A family member who confides a secret expects you to keep it. Decorating and remodeling are on the agenda. Also, be sure to check plumbing. Look behind the scenes. Someone wants to "tell you something." Pisces and Virgo will be inextricably involved.

Saturday, March 15 (Moon in Leo) Be serious tonight! A relative is sincere, but could be sincerely misinformed. Focus on advertising, publicity, and color coordination. Capricorn, Cancer, and Leo will play "majestic" roles. In matters of speculation, stick with number 8.

Sunday, March 16 (Moon in Leo to Virgo 8:51 a.m.) On this Sunday, your spiritual values surface. Discussions include psychology, science, and theology. Look beyond the immediate. Outline the future, then make it come true. Finish what you start. Communicate with someone from a foreign land. Aries is represented.

Monday, March 17 (Moon in Virgo) On this Monday, St. Patrick's Day, you get a lot done despite the celebration. Fix things around the house. Take the initiative in making appointments. Make a fresh start in a new direction. A new, different kind of romance raises your morale. What a Monday!

Tuesday, March 18 (Moon in Virgo to Libra 9:42 a.m.) The full moon in Virgo, your fourth house, represents the completion of negotiations regarding your home or property. Focus on direction, motivation, and questions about your marital status. Cancer and Capricorn will play dominant roles. Have luck with number 2.

Wednesday, March 19 (Moon in Libra) At the track: post position special—number 5 p.p. in the third race. Pick six: 3, 4, 5, 6, 2, 3. Hot daily doubles: 6 and 4, 1 and 7, 3 and 3. Away from the track, entertain and be entertained. A pleasant surprise is due; you receive a gift that adds to your wardrobe.

Thursday, March 20 (Moon in Libra to Scorpio 9:37 a.m.) The moon in your fifth house activates your creative juices. Find ways to express yourself, especially through writing. Review details; check for the accuracy of measurements. Taurus, Leo, and Scorpio will play "complicated" roles.

Friday, March 21 (Moon in Scorpio) You will experience more freedom of thought and of action. The moon in Scorpio, your sixth house, emphasizes routine, employment, and health. Scorpio could attempt to overwhelm you. Maintain your emotional equilibrium. Another Gemini is also in the picture.

Saturday, March 22 (Moon in Scorpio to Sagittarius 10:33 a.m.) Where investments in the stock market are concerned, stay with consumer products for home and health. You receive refreshing news from a relative studying music. Be receptive yet diplomatic. Taurus, Libra, and Scorpio make you aware, "This is Saturday night!"

Sunday, March 23 (Moon in Sagittarius) On this Sunday, spiritual values will be much in evidence. The number 7 numerical cycle equates to mystery, which means journeys into the unknown. Discuss and defend your beliefs. Pisces and Virgo will play distinctive roles.

Monday, March 24 (Moon in Sagittarius to Capricorn 1:48 p.m.) A day of production and promotion. Capricorn and Cancer help make this an exciting Monday. Focus on priorities, organization, and distribution. Your feelings are intense—you practically demand a display of affection. Don't demand too much!

Tuesday, March 25 (Moon in Capricorn) Focus on occult, bizarre situations and people. Someone will ask if you are aware of the zodiacal sign of Charles Atlas. Surprisingly, you answer, "The world's most perfectly developed man was a Scorpio, what else!" Libra plays a key role.

Wednesday, March 26 (Moon in Capricorn to Aquarius 7:50 p.m.) Make a fresh start. Emphasize independence of thought and action. The Capricorn moon is in your eighth house, which represents other people's money, including your partner or mate. Be aware of percentages; get the most for your money. Leo figures in this scenario. Lucky number is 1.

Thursday, March 27 (Moon in Aquarius) On this Thursday, get ready for a meeting tomorrow by having the facts at hand. A quiet time alone tonight would not hurt matters at all. The answers will come from within via meditation. Capricorn and Cancer will answer an emergency call.

Friday, March 28 (Moon in Aquarius) There's plenty of entertainment as well as good news on this Friday! An excellent day for trying on clothes, for improving your appearance, for keeping resolutions about exercise, diet, and nutrition. Sagittarius and another Gemini figure prominently. Have luck with number 3.

Saturday, March 29 (Moon in Aquarius to Pisces 4:25 a.m.) Focus on distance, communication, and language. Refuse to be inveigled into a senseless dispute involving religion or politics. Finish what you start. Don't rely on preconceived notions. Taurus and Scorpio insist on main roles.

Sunday, March 30 (Moon in Pisces) The moon at the top part of your chart indicates promotion, possibly through consultation with a superior. Read and write; learn through the process of teaching. Virgo, Pisces, and another Gemini will be available, if you will but toss aside false pride. A journey to another land is closer to reality than you imagined.

Monday, March 31 (Moon in Pisces to Aries 3:04 p.m.)   On this last day on the month, you receive a unique honor. Express thanks without being obsequious. Your family is involved. A domestic adjustment works out for the best. Be diplomatic, and make intelligent concessions. Taurus and Libra are in today's scenario.

APRIL 2003

Tuesday, April 1 (Moon in Aries)   The new moon in Aries represents your house of hopes and wishes. Your powers of persuasion are heightened. You won't be anybody's fool. In matters of speculation, stick with number 4. Taurus, Leo, and Scorpio play significant roles, and have these letters in their names: D, M, V.

Wednesday, April 2 (Moon in Aries)   Your creative abilities surface! People important to you take note of your writing skills. You could also find yourself in the role of teacher or speaker. Get ready for change, travel, variety, and adventure. A flirtation turns serious, so don't play games!

Thursday, April 3 (Moon in Aries to Taurus 3:19 a.m.)   On this Thursday, you make an important domestic adjustment, which could include a change of residence or marital status. A mystery is building. In 24 hours, you will be faced with decisions about what is happening "backstage." Dance to your own tune!

Friday, April 4 (Moon in Taurus)   Don't be afraid to wait! Do not equate delay with defeat. At first, you may not believe it, but time is on your side. Pisces and Virgo will fill in the blanks. Define terms; get promises in writing. You'll be told of a real estate deal.

Saturday, April 5 (Moon in Taurus to Gemini 4:23 p.m.) On this Saturday, nothing happens halfway—it will be all or nothing. A secret meeting takes place, involving Taurus and Scorpio. Credit long withheld will be granted. You could be placed on a pedestal! Have luck with number 8.

Sunday, April 6—Daylight Saving Time Begins (Moon in Gemini)   On this Sunday, welcome a family member who has been "at sea." In your high cycle your judgment and intuition are on target. Take the initiative when making appointments and arranging consultations. Complete a project that was started two months ago. Aries will play a fascinating role.

Monday, April 7 (Moon in Gemini)   Take the initiative! Welcome a chance to take a cold plunge into the future. Emphasize originality. Take yet another chance on romance. Imprint your own style; don't follow others. Leo and Aquarius step up to the plate on your behalf.

Tuesday, April 8 (Moon in Gemini to Cancer 5:35 a.m.)
You will feel as if something has been taken away from you. That will be temporary. The focus moves to family and home, also to the realization that your love is not unrequited. The sale or purchase of property could be on today's agenda. A Cancer is involved.

Wednesday, April 9 (Moon in Cancer)   The moon position reveals the location of a lost article as well as the opportunity to increase your income. A family member helps. Be gracious, without being obsequious. The future is bright, so don't worry about the past. You could invent a game that brings fun and smiles to people.

Thursday, April 10 (Moon in Cancer to Leo 2:52 p.m.)
By attending to details, you could "win money." In matters of speculation, stick with number 4. Your losing streak ends—this could be the beginning of a winning streak. Taurus and Scorpio are in the picture, and will serve as reliable guides.

Friday, April 11 (Moon in Leo)   Give full play to your intellectual curiosity. Another Gemini provides inspiration. Serious discussions involve your family, the possibility of twins. Someone who claims to "know it all" confronts you, issuing a challenge. Maintain your sense of humor and emotional equilibrium.

Saturday, April 12 (Moon in Leo to Virgo 8:05 p.m.)
Stick close to home this Saturday night. There will be plenty of traffic accidents, so drive with care if you do leave home. Avoid scattering your forces. This means focus on the main objective. Taurus, Libra, and Scorpio play featured roles. Lucky lottery: 12, 18, 33, 24, 1, 7.

Sunday, April 13 (Moon in Virgo)   Play the waiting game. A property sale will be more beneficial, if you are willing to practice restraint. On this Sunday, a relative decides, "I must leave you!" Be gracious, but find out what the score is and whether you can do anything about it.

Monday, April 14 (Moon in Virgo to Libra 9:40 p.m.)   This is your lucky day, both for romance and finance. Execute a power play with skill. Capricorn and Cancer will be first to give you long-deserved credit. Today's scenario features complications and challenges. Get down to business early.

Tuesday, April 15 (Moon in Libra)   You will be thinking, "This sure is one unusual Tuesday!" You could receive an invitation to travel to a foreign land. Aries and Libra will play significant roles. Let go of a burden that was not your own in the first place. Your fortunate number is 9.

Wednesday, April 16 (Moon in Libra to Scorpio 9:15 p.m.)   The full moon is in your house of creativity and sexuality, making this an unforgettable day. Focus on romance, initiative, originality—the ability to imprint your own style. Some suggest that you follow them. Don't! Let others follow you, if they so desire.

Thursday, April 17 (Moon in Scorpio)   Skin care is important. Emphasize glamour and home improvement. A decision is reached concerning motivation and direction. Cancer and Capricorn will play paramount roles. Don't overlook an opportunity that involves entertainment or music. Don't be overly modest.

Friday, April 18 (Moon in Scorpio to Sagittarius 8:51 p.m.)   The moon position emphasizes health care, employment, and ways to keep resolutions about exercise, diet, and nutrition. Laugh at your own foibles. Make inquiries, giving full play to your intellectual curiosity. Sagittarius and another Gemini play dramatic roles.

Saturday, April 19 (Moon in Sagittarius)   Steer clear of fire hazards. There could be an explosion, which might be associated with a firecracker. Be thorough, without being tiresome. Taurus, Leo, and Scorpio will play memorable roles. In matters of speculation, have luck with number 4.

Sunday, April 20 (Moon in Sagittarius to Capricorn 10:21 p.m.)   Questions arise about cooperative efforts, partnership, and marital status. Be sure you are on the right side of the law. The moon in your seventh house involves your reputation, credibility, and legal affairs. Books play a role; information is found in occult literature.

Monday, April 21 (Moon in Capricorn)   Be calm this Monday, if your family discussions become heated. Maintain your emotional equilibrium. It becomes obvious that a domestic adjustment is required. There could be a change of residence or marital status. Libra will play an unforgettable role.

Tuesday, April 22 (Moon in Capricorn)   Be conservative. Take no unnecessary risks. Someone who claims to be a "master of the occult" should not be taken seriously. Pisces and Virgo will play astonishing roles. Delve deep into mysteries—you will solve them!

Wednesday, April 23 (Moon in Capricorn to Aquarius 2:58 a.m.)   At the track: post position special—number 1 p.p. in the first race. Pick six: 1, 3, 4, 5, 8, 6. Hot daily doubles: 1 and 1, 3 and 7, 4 and 6. Away from the track, a relationship will involve extra responsibility, possibly an addition to your family in the not-too-distant future.

Thursday, April 24 (Moon in Aquarius)   Focus on distance, publishing, and advertising. Look beyond the immediate. People seek your help in solving problems, some of them quite intimate. By helping others, your own dilemmas dissolve. However, know when to say, "enough!"

Friday, April 25 (Moon in Aquarius to Pisces 11:02 a.m.) You are right in rhythm! Be aware, confident. Wear bright colors when you make personal appearances. Dance to your own tune, follow your heart. Someone who proposes a love affair could have selfish reasons. Protect yourself; back off and wait for another time.

Saturday, April 26 (Moon in Pisces)   Include a family member in this Saturday night's celebration. Your professional superior makes a surprise appearance. Be gracious, not servile. You will hear news about the "shifting of gears, of positions." Express amazement, but be receptive.

Sunday, April 27 (Moon in Pisces to Aries 9:54 p.m.) Entertain and be entertained. As your spiritual values surface, you will have more confidence. You will be more sure about your direction, motivation, and career path. Someone who helped guide people pays you a meaningful compliment. Express thanks. Plan activities for the evening, including dining out.

Monday, April 28 (Moon in Aries)   This will not be an ordinary Monday. It will be necessary to revise, to rewrite, to rebuild. Taurus, Leo, and Scorpio will play dynamic roles. If thorough, you win. If you don't attend to minor details, you lose. Have luck with number 4.

Tuesday, April 29 (Moon in Aries)   Trust a hunch. Your intuitive intellect serves as a reliable guide. The moon in Aries, your eleventh house, tells of winning friends and influencing people. You could obtain funding for a project that had been neglected. Virgo is involved.

Wednesday, April 30 (Moon in Aries to Taurus 10:25 a.m.) On this last day of the month, join your family in celebration. Your popularity increases and some people suggest that you should run for political office. Don't agree or disagree. Timing and luck ride with you. In matters of speculation, choose number 6.

MAY 2003

Thursday, May 1 (Moon in Taurus) Important persons stand behind you. They have faith in you, and will demonstrate it. The new moon in your twelfth house means that negativity will be knocked out by positive results. An excellent day for communicating. The written word plays a major role. Sagittarius is in the picture.

Friday, May 2 (Moon in Taurus to Gemini 11:26 p.m.) You learn once again, "All that glitters is not gold." A domestic adjustment is featured, and could involve where you live and with whom. The question of your marital status looms large. Today's scenario features flowers, music, and luxury items. Home is beautiful!

Saturday, May 3 (Moon in Gemini) On this Saturday, take special care in traffic. Stay away from crowds, if possible. An element of deception is present. Verify the facts, get promises in writing. Pisces and Virgo will play outstanding roles. Lucky lottery: 7, 25, 18, 30, 14, 22.

Sunday, May 4 (Moon in Gemini) Your cycle is high. Therefore, your judgment and intuition will be on target. Accent your personality. Make special appearances. Be willing to participate in an "adventure." An engineering project "calls to you." Don't underestimate your own value. Let it be known you have a price, and it is high.

Monday, May 5 (Moon in Gemini to Cancer 11:40 a.m.) This will not be a blue Monday. You finish a project. Your personality is highlighted. Your sex appeal is heightened. Be confident; there is no need to be servile or obsequious.

What a Monday! Someone who owes you a favor and wants to repay it will invite you to dinner.

Tuesday, May 6 (Moon in Cancer)   Make a fresh start. Don't brood about someone who might be left behind. A lost valuable is retrieved. Your financial cycle is high. Money could come from a surprise source. You'll be dealing with a temperamental Leo or Aquarius. Don't hesitate to praise and show your appreciation.

Wednesday, May 7 (Moon in Cancer to Leo 9:44 p.m.) At the track: post position special—number 2 p.p. in the seventh race. Pick six: 1, 5, 3, 2, 4, 8. Hot daily doubles: 1 and 4, 2 and 7, 3 and 8. Away from the track, a decision is made about your goals, home, and marital status. A Cancer is involved.

Thursday, May 8 (Moon in Leo)   This could be one of your most pleasant Thursdays! The moon is in your third house, so check priorities and realize your own worth. The spotlight is on your home, finding comfortable living quarters, and romance. Sagittarius and another Gemini could participate in a "comedy routine."

Friday, May 9 (Moon in Leo)   Tear down in order to rebuild. Emphasize color coordination and showmanship. You attract people and have the ability to "win them over." Be aware of details; check plumbing. Stand tall for your principles. Taurus, Leo, and Scorpio figure in today's action.

Saturday, May 10 (Moon in Leo to Virgo 4:29 a.m.) You could have good fortune in matters of speculation by sticking with number 5. A Leo relative spins some strange tales. Listen, evaluate, be entertained. A flirtation that started off innocently might be getting too hot not to cool down.

Sunday, May 11 (Moon in Virgo)   Attention revolves around your home, family, and the value of a building. The key is to be diplomatic. If you attempt to force issues, you lose. There will be music. Find your rhythm and dance to your own tune. Libra says, "I wish I could be near you more often!"

Monday, May 12 (Moon in Virgo to Libra 7:41 a.m.)
A sense of creative criticism is heightened. Make inquiries, ask questions. Insist on answers, not evasions. A deception is involved. See people and relationships as they are, not merely as you wish they could be. Pisces plays a key role.

Tuesday, May 13 (Moon in Libra)   You might be saying to yourself, "Everything is going too well and I feel too good. I wonder what is happening!" Focus on creativity, sex appeal, and the ability to adapt yourself to changing conditions. Capricorn and Cancer play formidable roles.

Wednesday, May 14 (Moon in Libra to Scorpio 8:12 a.m.)
Look beyond the immediate. Forgo previous beliefs. Let go of a burden that was not yours to carry in the first place. A relationship that sizzled needs to be given more attention. Whatever you want to happen will happen—if you so permit!

Thursday, May 15 (Moon in Scorpio)   Take care of a problem that seemed minor, relating to health or employment. Keep resolutions, especially those concerned with your diet. Make a fresh start. Display independence of thought, and of action. Leo and Aquarius could become good and true friends.

Friday, May 16 (Moon in Scorpio to Sagittarius 7:42 a.m.)
Last night's full moon and lunar eclipse in Scorpio activate your sixth house. This could bring about major changes in your job, where you live, and dietary restrictions. A coworker who befriends you is sincere. Be receptive, giving a smile to get a smile. Capricorn is involved.

Saturday, May 17 (Moon in Sagittarius)   This could be a lively Saturday night! The moon in Sagittarius, your seventh house, warns you to play the waiting game. There are legal aspects to an enterprise of which you are not aware.

A romantic liaison tonight should not be taken too seriously. Lucky number is 3.

Sunday, May 18 (Moon in Sagittarius to Capricorn 8:03 a.m.) Any frustration you experience you bring on yourself. The number 4 numerical cycle represents red tape as well as the need to revise, to review, and to rewrite. Ride with the tide. Don't fight your fate! Taurus, Leo, and Scorpio will figure in this challenging scenario.

Monday, May 19 (Moon in Capricorn) Prepare for change, travel, and a variety of sensations. The Capricorn moon is in your eighth house, which represents other people's money as well as mystery, the occult, and revelations. An excellent time for reading and writing, perhaps starting a diary.

Tuesday, May 20 (Moon in Capricorn to Aquarius 11:01 a.m.) Money could be made available to make your home beautiful. Let go of preconceived notions. With your Gemini wit, you can get almost anything desired! What seemed out of reach will suddenly be possible. Taurus and Libra are represented.

Wednesday, May 21 (Moon in Aquarius) Lucky lottery: 11, 20, 2, 7, 5, 8. Define terms. Avoid flying if possible. The world will not be what it looks like. Some persons overindulge; stay away from them! Pisces and Virgo make it possible to balance the sheet.

Thursday, May 22 (Moon in Aquarius to Pisces 5:40 p.m.) Things happen! You could be on the receiving end of some startling news. Be receptive without being naive. A business transaction is huge enough to make news—you could ultimately be involved. You'll be recognized, even applauded for your ideals.

Friday, May 23 (Moon in Pisces) Focus on promotion, distribution, and pressure due to added responsibility. No matter what causes this pressure, you will be up to it. Many express surprise at your being able to stick to one thing until it is completed. Aries is represented.

Saturday, May 24 (Moon in Pisces)   Don't fight unless you expect to win. A fresh start with a new attitude is featured. Lead the way; do not follow others. Wear bright colors when you make personal appearances. If married, the spark that brought you together in the first place will reignite. Lucky number is 1.

Sunday, May 25 (Moon in Pisces to Aries 3:58 a.m.) Within 24 hours, you will reach a zenith of popularity! You will win friends and influence people. You will obtain funding for a pet project. There is nothing to fear, although of late you have been excessively timid. Capricorn is involved.

Monday, May 26 (Moon in Aries)   Highlight versatility and humor. Realize you are capable of winning friends and influencing people. The Aries moon is in your eleventh house. That means you'll have luck in matters of speculation, especially by sticking with number 3. Elements of timing ride with you, so don't get in your own way.

Tuesday, May 27 (Moon in Aries to Taurus 4:31 p.m.) Although some bureaucrats may attempt to hinder your progress, you will overcome and be victorious. Handle the details with equanimity. This could be one of your extraordinary days—you revise, rebuild, repair. Scorpio, Leo, and Taurus figure in this scenario.

Wednesday, May 28 (Moon in Taurus)   Keep plans flexible. Do what you can and do it well. The Taurus moon indicates you will recover a lost article and possibly make successful investments. Virgo, Sagittarius, and another Gemini figure prominently. Your lucky number is 5.

Thursday, May 29 (Moon in Taurus)   Be careful about directions and names. Deception could be caused by your insistence on seeing things only your way, not the way they really exist. Attention revolves around home, family, and the ability to obtain "superior" living quarters.

Friday, May 30 (Moon in Taurus to Gemini 5:30 a.m.)
Rectify errors made 24 hours ago. A relative will be involved. Avoid pouting or brooding. You'll be told what a fine person you are. Indicate, "I know it!" Pisces and Virgo will play sensational roles. Exercise care near water!

Saturday, May 31 (Moon in Gemini)   There is a blue moon and solar eclipse in your sign! Be careful about making claims or agreeing to commitments. Focus on a power play, having something of value up your sleeve. Capricorn and Cancer edge themselves into today's exciting scenario. Lucky number is 8.

JUNE 2003

Sunday, June 1 (Moon in Gemini to Cancer 5:26 p.m.)
Your vitality makes a comeback. Spiritual values surface. Do your own thing; don't follow others. A fascinating Leo lends spice to your life. The focus is also on your home, residence, and marital status. You'll receive a gift, possibly a luxury item. Accept it as a "peace offering."

Monday, June 2 (Moon in Cancer)   There is an aura of confusion today. Play the waiting game. Get a definition of terms in writing. Perfect techniques. Look beyond the immediate. Don't tell all. A gain is indicated if you maintain an aura of mystery. Let people play guessing games. Pisces figures prominently.

Tuesday, June 3 (Moon in Cancer)   Guard your personal possessions. Someone wants something for nothing, and you could be the prime target. Refuse to give up something of value. The emphasis is on power, authority, promotion, and different ways of distribution. A relationship intensifies, and could lead to an exciting adventure.

Wednesday, June 4 (Moon in Cancer to Leo 3:23 p.m.)
It will be better to finish rather than start. A financial burden is relieved. Within 24 hours, you get cheering news. A long-distance communication confirms opinions, and could

lead to an invitation to visit a foreign land. Aries and Libra play major roles. Lucky number is 9.

Thursday, June 5 (Moon in Leo)   Shake off your fears and doubts. A relative, in a surprise decision, will support your ambition. Emphasize versatility, without scattering your forces. Leo and Aquarius will be in the picture, helping with showmanship and publicity. You are going to win!

Friday, June 6 (Moon in Leo to Virgo 10:49 a.m.)   On this Friday, decide upon direction and motivation. Agree with yourself through meditation. If single, a relationship is serious and could lead to a business partnership or marriage. Answers come from within, and that's why you will be meditating.

Saturday, June 7 (Moon in Virgo)   The emphasis is on art and literature as well as the ability to "pick winners." Have luck today by sticking with number 3. There's a surprising amount of social activity. Maintain goodwill and humor. Keep recent resolutions concerning exercise, diet, and nutrition.

Sunday, June 8 (Moon in Virgo to Libra 3:28 p.m.)   Be analytical. Refuse to be satisfied merely to know something occurred—find out why it happened. Someone who once did you a favor wants again to be close. This relationship is favorable, so be responsive. Scorpio and another Gemini play leading roles.

Monday, June 9 (Moon in Libra)   Read and write, teach and learn. Someone of the opposite sex confides, "You attract me very much!" The answer to a perplexing problem could be found in arcane literature. Investigate, learn, and report. Many will depend upon your findings. Virgo is in the picture.

Tuesday, June 10 (Moon in Libra to Scorpio 5:38 p.m.) Stick close to home, since the temptation is to go far afield in distance or relationship. This is no time to be playing games. Conditions exist to make your home beautiful.

Funding will be forthcoming. Taurus, Libra, and Scorpio figure in today's dramatic scenario.

Wednesday, June 11 (Moon in Scorpio)   There is no need to "back off." The employment picture changes in your favor. See people and relationships as they are, not merely as you wish they could be. Maintain your aura of mystery and intrigue. Pisces and Virgo will figure prominently.

Thursday, June 12 (Moon in Scorpio to Sagittarius 6:11 p.m.)   Those who attempt to persuade you to quit do not have your best interests at heart. Superiors and the law are on your side. Be confident, and proceed accordingly. Don't get in your own way. Stand tall for your principles and beliefs. A Cancer is in this picture.

Friday, June 13 (Moon in Sagittarius)   This day is not unlucky for you! You gain recognition and perhaps an invitation to travel. You'll be relieved of a burden not your own in the first place. Aries and Libra play dominant roles. Get rid of preconceived notions. Nothing for you is impossible!

Saturday, June 14 (Moon in Sagittarius to Capricorn 6:37 p.m.)   Wear bright colors, including yellow and gold. Focus on legal agreements, partnership, marriage. Be aware of public relations, reputation, credibility. People you admire express faith in you. Accept graciously, without being obsequious. Leo is in the picture.

Sunday, June 15 (Moon in Capricorn)   A recent disappointment boomerangs in your favor. You'll unlock a mystery and be given credit for doing so. Check details, including measurements. Focus on accuracy and the willingness to stand by what you consider "the truth." Capricorn is in this scenario.

Monday, June 16 (Moon in Capricorn to Aquarius 8:41 p.m.)   Diversify! Accent your ability to laugh at your own foibles. Your popularity is on the upswing. People want to be with you; some want to wine and dine you. Luck rides with you. In matters of speculation, stick with number 3. Sagittarius is featured.

Tuesday, June 17 (Moon in Aquarius)   A promise you thought was broken will be mended. Do not equate delay with defeat. You will be let in on a financial transaction. Be discreet; don't confide or confess. Taurus, Leo, and Scorpio play major roles and have these letters in their names: D, M, V.

Wednesday, June 18 (Moon in Aquarius)   At the track: post position special—number 1 p.p. in the third race. Pick six: 2, 4, 5, 6, 3, 1. Hot daily doubles: 1 and 2, 8 and 5, 3 and 2. Away from the track, a relationship is serious, and could lead to partnership or marriage. Start a diary!

Thursday, June 19 (Moon in Aquarius to Pisces 1:57 a.m.) Today's favorable lunar aspect coincides with long-distance communication. A family member, in an excited way, suggests a journey abroad. You may remark, "We don't even speak the language." In response you'll hear these words, "We will learn!"

Friday, June 20 (Moon in Pisces)   Almost everything is done in a "secret manner." Backstage activities dominate. The focus is on mystery, intrigue, and questions concerning, "Should I tell it all?" Keep your promise to be discreet. Do not tell all! Pisces and Virgo play "persuasive" roles.

Saturday, June 21 (Moon in Pisces to Aries 11:05 a.m.) What you have been waiting for will arrive. Someone in a position of authority finally sees things your way. Focus on power, distribution, and promotion. A relationship is intense, but maintain your emotional equilibrium. Lucky lottery: 8, 17, 47, 3, 13, 5.

Sunday, June 22 (Moon in Aries)   Spiritual values dominate. The moon position indicates you can win friends. Your powers of persuasion are heightened. In matters of speculation, stick with number 9. A relative away from home for at least a year returns in a surprising way. Aries is involved.

Monday, June 23 (Moon in Aries to Taurus 11:14 p.m.) Make a fresh start. Realize people depend on you to "win for them." Major wishes will be fulfilled. You do have power, so wish for what you need, not merely luxury items. Leo and Aquarius help you make a decision concerning your goals and motivation.

Tuesday, June 24 (Moon in Taurus) Take advantage of sudden "good fortune." You have luck in matters of finance today. A partner or mate shows trust in your intuition. Now, trust yourself! Cancer and Capricorn help smooth the path, as you attempt to fulfill obligations.

Wednesday, June 25 (Moon in Taurus) Lucky lottery: 25, 2, 12, 18, 6, 3. What was secret will be revealed. You will be trusted with information. Be subtle; maintain your emotional equilibrium. You could be tested and questioned. Sagittarius and another Gemini will play humorous, important roles.

Thursday, June 26 (Moon in Taurus to Gemini 12:11 p.m.) Though your cycle continues high, check the details and do basic research. Someone did not tell the whole truth about an automobile or other property. Find out the reasons why. Let it be known you mean business. You eventually win by rewriting, describing what is expected.

Friday, June 27 (Moon in Gemini) Your cycle is high, so you will be at the right place at a crucial moment almost effortlessly. You exude personality and sex appeal. Be careful; don't break too many hearts! Focus on reading, writing, and teaching. You reap a reward based on recent efforts.

Saturday, June 28 (Moon in Gemini to Cancer 11:50 p.m.) Attention revolves around making the home beautiful as well as improved relations with family. Make appointments; let people see that you are alive and kicking. Beat the odds.

Do what others term "the impossible." Rest assured: "Everything will turn out right!" Your lucky number is 6.

Sunday, June 29 (Moon in Cancer)   Serious discussions take place about a possible "change of names." Be flexible; give serious thought to numerical value. Pisces and Virgo play important roles. See relationships as they exist, not merely as you wish they could be.

Monday, June 30 (Moon in Cancer)   On this last day of June, you could be part of a financial coup. Get your fair share; count your change. Guard your possessions. Don't give up something of value. Capricorn and Cancer play memorable roles. Have luck with number 8.

JULY 2003

Tuesday, July 1 (Moon in Cancer to Leo 9:11 a.m.) Keep your main objective in mind. The financial situation will ease. You could find what you want in connection with your living quarters. Property is evaluated—good news! Define terms. An element of deception is involved in your love life.

Wednesday, July 2 (Moon in Leo)   What started out as defeat will be turned into a rousing victory. A Leo relative will be part of this exciting scenario. Pick and choose, be selective, insist on quality. Capricorn and Cancer figure in today's complicated, dynamic scenario. Have luck with number 8.

Thursday, July 3 (Moon in Leo to Virgo 4:15 p.m.)   At the track: post position special—number 1 p.p. in the seventh race. Hot daily doubles: 4 and 5, 3 and 7, 1 and 1. Away from the track, finish a project, then look beyond the immediate. A journey to a foreign land is a distinct possibility. Aries plays a role.

Friday, July 4 (Moon in Virgo)   On this holiday, read and write. Be analytical. Ask questions, receive answers.

Maintain this holiday's spirit by reviewing historical documents. The Declaration of Independence should be read aloud. Your personality and sensuality are highlighted. Leo is represented.

Saturday, July 5 (Moon in Virgo to Libra 9:19 p.m.)
Property value represents good news. Cancer and Capricorn will play dramatic roles. Be cooperative, but do not abandon your principles. You hold the trump card; know it and act accordingly. The answer to a question will be found in special reading material.

Sunday, July 6 (Moon in Libra)   Within 24 hours, your creative juices will stir. A request is granted. You'll have more freedom of thought and of action. Read and write; share knowledge by teaching. Sagittarius and another Gemini figure prominently. You will receive an invitation to a unique social gathering.

Monday, July 7 (Moon in Libra)   Be aware of details; check plumbing facilities. Be willing to rewrite and to rebuild. The Libra moon in your fifth house equates to creativity, change, travel, and a variety of sensual experiences. Those who want you to be a "prisoner of mediocrity" will be vocal.

Tuesday, July 8 (Moon in Libra to Scorpio 12:42 a.m.)
The emphasis is on reading, writing, teaching, exploring. An excellent day to start a diary. Write your impressions of places and people. But keep it locked away; don't be self-conscious about what you write. Virgo, Sagittarius, and another Gemini figure in this scenario.

Wednesday, July 9 (Moon in Scorpio)   What had been hanging on as a threat to your security will be removed. Focus on a possible change of residence or marital status. Be diplomatic, if you expect to win. A Libra individual professes love. Show gratitude without being obsequious. Have luck with number 6.

Thursday, July 10 (Moon in Scorpio to Sagittarius 2:47 a.m.) Attend to a minor health problem before it becomes major. Conditions at your workplace are subject to change, which eventually proves favorable. Look beyond the immediate; make predictions about your future. Pisces will play a mysterious role.

Friday, July 11 (Moon in Sagittarius) A long-distance communication involves a possible "change of name." Your intuitive intellect is on target. Don't be persuaded to do what you don't want to do. Keep your emotional equilibrium. Your morale gets a boost. Capricorn and Cancer play outstanding roles.

Saturday, July 12 (Moon in Sagittarius to Capricorn 4:20 a.m.) What you have been waiting for is actually here, if you will only look. Meantime, lie low; be patient and persistent. Be aware of legal aspects, and stay on the right side of the law. The question of your marital status looms large. Lucky lottery: 42, 11, 17, 1, 5, 16.

Sunday, July 13 (Moon in Capricorn) The full moon in Capricorn represents your eighth house. This means you will be dealing with a mysterious person who is in charge of a considerable amount of money. Loan percentages will be discussed. You will meet someone who physically attracts you. Be careful; don't start anything you cannot finish.

Monday, July 14 (Moon in Capricorn to Aquarius 6:37 a.m.) On this Monday, your vitality makes a comeback. A decision is reached about where you want to live and with whom. Be truthful within—heed the voice of conscience. Cancer and Capricorn play dominant roles. Listen to your heart; it tells the truth.

Tuesday, July 15 (Moon in Aquarius) Focus on distance, language, and the ability to make your dreams come true. What seems far away and long ago will be available. It can make you happy, if you so permit. Keep resolutions about exercise, diet, and nutrition. Another Gemini insists on playing a top role.

Wednesday, July 16 (Moon in Aquarius to Pisces 11:14 a.m.) Focus on packaged goods, emphasizing color coordination, showmanship, and advertising. Tear down in order to rebuild. Open the lines of communication. Someone in a foreign land wants to "tell you something." Taurus plays a major role.

Thursday, July 17 (Moon in Pisces) Someone in a position of authority "backs your play." Don't be shy about accepting help. Read, write, teach, share knowledge. A relationship is serious; know it and act accordingly. Virgo and another Gemini intend to stay until the "bitter end."

Friday, July 18 (Moon in Pisces to Aries 7:19 p.m.) Focus on diversity, appreciation of beauty, flowers, music, and romance. A change of residence or marital status might be in the cards. Be receptive, not weak. Taurus and Libra show their affection for you. In matters of speculation, stick with number 6.

Saturday, July 19 (Moon in Aries) For a time, you will feel euphoric. After all, that is better than brooding. Avoid self-deception. Perceive people, places, and relationships as they are, not merely as you wish they could be. Pisces and Virgo play mysterious roles.

Sunday, July 20 (Moon in Aries) Power play! The pressure will be on, but you will be up to it. The Aries moon relates to your eleventh house, so be aggressive in fulfilling your hopes and wishes. Elements of timing and good fortune ride with you. In matters of speculation, stick with number 8.

Monday, July 21 (Moon in Aries to Taurus 6:47 a.m.) Look beyond the immediate. Strive for universal appeal. With your wit, wisdom, and intelligence, you can make this a day when you are on the precipice of fame and fortune.

A burden will be lifted; it was not your own to carry in the first place. Aries is in this picture.

Tuesday, July 22 (Moon in Taurus)   Join forces with Leo. Emphasize independence and originality. A love relationship heats up, and could get too hot not to cool down. Don't follow others; let them follow you, if they so desire. Wear bright colors, including yellow and gold.

Wednesday, July 23 (Moon in Taurus to Gemini 7:41 p.m.)   You receive gifts, perhaps jewelry. A secret meeting is taking place even as you read these words. Taurus is involved, and much has to do with finance. People talk about you. Your popularity rises. You can win your way! Lucky number is 2.

Thursday, July 24 (Moon in Gemini)   At the track: post position special—number 3 p.p. in the fifth race. Hot daily doubles: 3 and 5, 5 and 5, 2 and 4. Away from the track, your social life accelerates and popularity increases. The moon is in your sign, so your judgment and intuition will be on target.

Friday, July 25 (Moon in Gemini)   Your cycle continues high, so do your own thing. Don't follow others. Be willing to tear down for the ultimate purpose of rebuilding. Be thorough, check details. What you overlooked two days ago will once again command attention. Scorpio is involved.

Saturday, July 26 (Moon in Gemini to Cancer 7:22 a.m.) Grab an opportunity while it exists—read and write, teach and learn. A flirtation is getting more serious than you expected. Since you do not deliberately want to hurt anyone, make your intentions crystal clear. Another Gemini is represented.

Sunday, July 27 (Moon in Cancer)   What appeared to be a setback will boomerang in your favor. The lunar position relates to your income, including payments, collections, and the ability to increase your earnings. Taurus, Libra, and Scorpio play major roles, and could have these letters in their names: F, O, X.

Monday, July 28 (Moon in Cancer to Leo 4:15 p.m.) On this Monday, practice restraint. You will hear about many investment schemes. However, you're not hearing the complete story. Protect your valuables. Bargain hunting at this time is not likely to succeed. Play the waiting game.

Tuesday, July 29 (Moon in Leo)   The new moon in Leo is in your third house. In turn, that represents relatives, trips, visits, and a new attitude toward those close to you. Capricorn and Cancer play important roles. Make clear, "I intend to live my own life!"

Wednesday, July 30 (Moon in Leo to Virgo 10:25 p.m.) Finish what you start. A temperamental Leo relative claims, "You have been neglecting me!" Focus on advertising, publicity, and showmanship. Drive carefully; stay out of traffic jams. Someone of the opposite sex will make a declaration of love.

Thursday, July 31 (Moon in Virgo)   On this last day of July, be very careful that you don't blemish your material by unconsciously copying others. The key is original thinking, independence of thought and of action. A different kind of love is on the horizon. A Leo figures prominently.

AUGUST 2003

Friday, August 1 (Moon in Virgo)   Obtain prices of building material. Take charge of your own destiny. Capricorn and Cancer will play significant roles. Don't let go of your creative control. The emphasis is on basic issues, employment, and your general state of health.

Saturday, August 2 (Moon in Virgo to Libra 2:46 a.m.) Imprint your style. Do things your way, which will be the right way. Ignore naysayers. Let go of a burden not your own to carry. You will hear news about a possible journey to another land. Libra and Aries play dynamic, dramatic roles.

Sunday, August 3 (Moon in Libra)   Spiritual values surface. The focus will be on children, challenge, change, and variety. On this Sunday, recoup, gather your forces, permit energy to make a comeback. You'll be given a compliment by one you admire. Take it seriously—you've earned it.

Monday, August 4 (Moon in Libra to Scorpio 6:11 a.m.) Banter with associates or neighbors will vary from the comic to the serious. The range will cover gossip and government. Whatever you do, stay on top of the situation. Focus on local politics, cooperative efforts, partnership, and marriage.

Tuesday, August 5 (Moon in Scorpio)   Highlight versatility. Get things done in an efficient way. Some people might tell you, "You work too hard!" Give that serious consideration. It might be that you don't work hard enough where creativity is concerned.

Wednesday, August 6 (Moon in Scorpio to Sagittarius 9:10 a.m.)   Keep a wait-and-see attitude. You'll be relieved of many details, but a legal challenge could await. Double-check your rights and permissions. Someone whose loyalty has been proven should be rewarded. Taurus is represented.

Thursday, August 7 (Moon in Sagittarius)   The emphasis is on public relations, partnership, and contracts. Also important is the ability to work with and understand the law. Words are key, so read, write, and teach; communicate information in writing. Another Gemini, a Virgo, and a Sagittarius will play significant roles.

Friday, August 8 (Moon in Sagittarius to Capricorn 12:02 p.m.)   Be diplomatic. Make a necessary domestic adjustment. You could change your residence or marital status. If kind and diplomatic, you will win. If attempting to force issues, you will lose. The choice is yours. Libra will play a defining role.

Saturday, August 9 (Moon in Capricorn) Let go of preconceived notions. What did not go through two months ago will now be enthusiastically accepted. Strive for universal appeal. Avoid self-deception. See people and places as they exist, not merely as you wish they could be.

Sunday, August 10 (Moon in Capricorn to Aquarius 3:23 p.m.) Deal with someone who has much to do with finance. Although it is Sunday, you could have a conversation with a friend or associate in the banking business. You'll learn more about who has the money, as contrasted to who does the talking.

Monday, August 11 (Moon in Aquarius) Let go of an obligation not your own in the first place. Focus on distance, communication, and comprehension of what is truly important to you. Aries and Libra will play major roles, and could have these initials in their names: I and R.

Tuesday, August 12 (Moon in Aquarius to Pisces 8:18 p.m.) Just after midnight last night the full moon in Aquarius accented your ninth house. So you will experience the thrill of learning another language, of seeing how other people live, of viewing cultural differences. Participate in a humanitarian project. People will be drawn to your blend of entertainment and wisdom.

Wednesday, August 13 (Moon in Pisces) A dramatic reunion takes place. You'll give serious consideration to partnership or marriage. Put aside preconceived notions; let new ideas surface. The focus is also on direction, motivation, and your ability to meditate. Good news: A lost valuable will be returned.

Thursday, August 14 (Moon in Pisces) Leave details for another time. For now, handle a "big project." The focus is on style, fashion, and the ability to demonstrate and model. Remember this philosophy: To get a smile, give a smile. A Sagittarius plays an outstanding role. Lucky number is 3.

Friday, August 15 (Moon in Pisces to Aries 3:59 a.m.)
Many of your desires will be fulfilled. Ask for what you need, as well as luxury items. You will have luck in matters of speculation, especially by sticking with number 4. Taurus, Leo, and Scorpio will play "sensational" roles.

Saturday, August 16 (Moon in Aries) You will be given more creative freedom. Read and write. Make suggestions that show you are capable—an original thinker. Someone of the opposite sex says, "I can hardly keep my hands off you!" Be careful; don't believe everything you hear. Virgo is involved.

Sunday, August 17 (Moon in Aries to Taurus 2:52 a.m.)
Within 24 hours, you learn a secret that had been kept from you. Be tolerant; don't argue to place the blame. Don't fear the unknown. Welcome additional information. Be gracious. Give and receive affection. Libra figures in this scenario.

Monday, August 18 (Moon in Taurus) You could be called into a "secret meeting." Focus on payments, collections, and an insistence on getting a fair deal. Your cycle is moving up; you've seen and heard the worst of it. From now on, it is all to the good. Pisces plays a role.

Tuesday, August 19 (Moon in Taurus) A romance that was hidden will be revealed, unless you take special care to be discreet. Focus on theater, hospitals, and various institutions of confinement. You could provide a service that will be helpful to others and will gain you a profitable enterprise.

Wednesday, August 20 (Moon in Taurus to Gemini 3:40 a.m.) A day you have been waiting for—show what you can do. Participate in charitable and political activity. People will be drawn to you, feeling that you can resolve their dilemmas. Cooperate and help, but know when to say, "Enough!" Aries is involved.

Thursday, August 21 (Moon in Gemini)   Get ready for a fresh start with added independence. Put into operation your original thoughts and ideas. Focus on romance and creativity as well as your ability to win friends and influence people. Wear bright colors, including yellow and gold. A different kind of romance is featured.

Friday, August 22 (Moon in Gemini to Cancer 3:43 p.m.) You might be asking, "Is this déjà vu?" Today's scenario features familiar places and faces. A relationship that went asunder could be back in place, if you so permit. The emphasis is on food, cooking, and restaurant management. Be near water, if possible.

Saturday, August 23 (Moon in Cancer)   Celebrate! This could be a Saturday night live. Money owed will be paid. Your credit rating is good; keep it that way! The spotlight is on a reunion, cooperative efforts, and your marital status. Another Gemini will play a fantastic role. Lucky number is 3.

Sunday, August 24 (Moon in Cancer)   On this Sunday, handle details. Give assurance that you are sensitive to the feelings of a loved one. This could be your "makeover" day. Revise, review, rebuild. Taurus, Leo, and Scorpio will play essential roles. Avoid a display of temperament!

Monday, August 25 (Moon in Cancer to Leo 12:46 a.m.) You can "figure out" your life up to now and where it is going from here. Face yourself and the music. The written word will figure prominently. Virgo and another Gemini play outstanding roles. Be analytical. Get your thoughts on paper. If necessary, start a diary!

Tuesday, August 26 (Moon in Leo)   Home, children, challenge, and a variety of experiences are featured. You will enjoy this day. Take advantage of the chance to read, write, teach. A family member confides, "I want to sing!" Be tolerant; don't say "yes" or "no." Listen carefully!

Wednesday, August 27 (Moon in Leo to Virgo 6:25 a.m.) The new moon in your fourth house places emphasis on home, property, and the sale or purchase of hard goods. Refuse to give up something of value. Hold tight to sentiment and basic needs. Pisces and Virgo play outstanding roles. Lucky number is 7.

Thursday, August 28 (Moon in Virgo) A business transaction takes place. You are in the driver's seat. There is no need to be servile. Bring forth facts and figures. On a personal level, love is hot and heavy. If merely playing games, move on. Cancer and Capricorn play sensational roles.

Friday, August 29 (Moon in Virgo to Libra 9:40 a.m.) Take advantage of "space." Within 24 hours, you'll be concerned with legal rights and permissions. Today and tonight, you'll have the time and space to fulfill commitments. A question relating to marriage looms large. Aries and Libra figure in this scenario.

Saturday, August 30 (Moon in Libra) Take a chance on romance! Make a fresh start in a new direction. Wear bright colors that include yellow and gold. Make personal appearances. Your Gemini wit and humor will get you in and out of tight spots. Take more than ordinary care in traffic. Lucky number is 1.

Sunday, August 31 (Moon in Libra to Scorpio 11:59 a.m.) On this last day of August, be especially careful in connection with legal rights and permissions. Partnerships and marital status figure prominently. Be with your family, if possible. A gourmet dinner tonight helps raise your morale. A Cancer provides the "missing link."

Monday, September 1 (Moon in Scorpio)   You will be "amazed" by events that happen on this Monday. Look beyond the immediate. Take control of your own destiny. Separation from a loved one is temporary. A wild celebration takes place when a reunion occurs. Aries is in the picture.

Tuesday, September 2 (Moon in Scorpio to Sagittarius 2:31 p.m.)   On this Tuesday, resolve to make a fresh start. Let go of a burden not really your own. Give yourself time to enjoy life, to travel, and to participate in romance. Some will ask, "Why should you have those things?" A Leo figures prominently.

Wednesday, September 3 (Moon in Sagittarius)   Focus on direction, motivation, and the need for meditation. If single, you could meet your future mate. If married, the spark that brought you together reignites. Accent food, survival, and creative projects. Cancer and Capricorn play authoritative roles.

Thursday, September 4 (Moon in Sagittarius to Capricorn 5:50 p.m.)   Make this a social time. Give full play to your intellectual curiosity. Lie low where legal affairs enter the picture. Be a counterpuncher. Have facts and figures available. Marriage figures prominently. Sagittarius is in this scenario.

Friday, September 5 (Moon in Capricorn)   On this Friday, the puzzle pieces are "trying" to fall into place. If patient, and if you keep the faith, all will turn out well. From now on, be positive about what you print, publish, or broadcast. Taurus, Leo, and Scorpio play dominant roles.

Saturday, September 6 (Moon in Capricorn to Aquarius 10:14 p.m.)   Get ready for change, travel, variety. Write your impressions of places and people. A money deal will be made with a Capricorn. Be discreet; don't tell all. A romantic episode lends spice to your life. Know when to say, "Enough!" Lucky number is 5.

Sunday, September 7 (Moon in Aquarius)   On this Sunday, spiritual values will be seriously discussed with family. Avoid self-deception. See people and places as they are, not merely as you wish they could be. Maintain an aura of intrigue and mystery. Libra is in the picture.

Monday, September 8 (Moon in Aquarius)   Be discreet! Don't tell all; don't confide or confess. The Aquarius moon represents that section of your chart relating to travel, publishing, and "inner feelings." Your psychic impressions should be taken seriously. Hold tight to your values and principles.

Tuesday, September 9 (Moon in Aquarius to Pisces 4:06 a.m.)   Business deals dominate. A long-distance call may be necessary. Open the lines of communication! Someone wants to provide pertinent information. You could be dealing with someone who speaks a foreign language. Capricorn and Cancer will play paramount roles.

Wednesday, September 10 (Moon in Pisces)   Discussions revolve around the mantic arts and sciences, including astrology. People celebrating birthdays want to know more about Leo. This could open the door to a fascinating hobby at the very least. Lucky lottery: 9, 12, 18, 23, 7, 4.

Thursday, September 11 (Moon in Pisces to Aries 12:09 p.m.)   At the track: post position special—number 1 p.p. in the seventh race. Pick six: 4, 1, 3, 2, 8, 4. Hot daily doubles: 1 and 4, 3 and 7, 5 and 3. Away from the track, make a fresh start. Realize your love is not unrequited. Take a chance on romance!

Friday, September 12 (Moon in Aries)   Many of your hopes and wishes will be fulfilled, if you so desire. Take necessary risks to achieve your goal. Your powers of persuasion are heightened. Obtain funding for a project that is not exactly popular. Cancer and Capricorn play meaningful roles.

Saturday, September 13 (Moon in Aries to Taurus 10:49 p.m.)   The answer to your question: Highlight versatility and diversity, make inquiries, attend a social affair. Express your humor in ways that enable you to laugh at your own foibles. You will entertain and be entertained. Have luck with number 3.

Sunday, September 14 (Moon in Taurus)   Leave yourself open to "spiritual experiences." Your cycle is moving up, so be patient and keep the faith. Within 48 hours, gloom will become a stranger. Remember, to get a smile, give a smile. Taurus, Leo, and Scorpio will figure prominently.

Monday, September 15 (Moon in Taurus)   With the moon in your twelfth house there are likely to be "secret dealings" in connection with finances. Keep your emotional equilibrium. Hold tight to your principles. Don't give up something of value for nothing. Another Gemini is in the picture.

Tuesday, September 16 (Moon in Taurus to Gemini 11:31 a.m.)   Secrets concerning your home or family are on top of the agenda. What you learn is more mysterious than startling. Express thanks for finally being told. But add this, "Let us not in the future keep secrets from each other!"

Wednesday, September 17 (Moon in Gemini)   Your cycle is high, so trust your judgment and intuition. Define terms. Watch for a real estate opportunity. Don't deceive yourself; see people and relationships in a realistic way. Separate illusion from fact. Pisces and Virgo will play fantastic roles.

Thursday, September 18 (Moon in Gemini)   Take the initiative in making contacts and arranging appointments with bigwigs. Focus on power, authority, promotion, and added responsibility. The pressure is on, but you will be up to it. Capricorn and Cancer play memorable roles. Have luck with number 8.

Friday, September 19 (Moon in Gemini to Cancer 12:06 a.m.)   Make an adjustment so that you can be objective about an opportunity you once missed "long ago and far away." Let go of an obligation you need not have carried in the first place. A chance exists to visit a foreign land. Focus on publishing, advertising, and publicity.

Saturday, September 20 (Moon in Cancer)   A rare opportunity exists to increase your income. Good news: A lost valuable will be found or retrieved. Be grateful, without being obsequious. You will feel, correctly so, that you are being given another chance to ring the bell of prosperity. Have luck with number 1.

Sunday, September 21 (Moon in Cancer to Leo 10:00 a.m.) Be close to the family; share experiences and aspirations. Someone close to you provides secret information that could be the key to success. Be discreet, without becoming a hermit. A picnic-style dinner tonight provides an opportunity for humor and wisdom. A Cancer is involved.

Monday, September 22 (Moon in Leo)   You wake up this Monday with an optimistic view. People want to be with you, and will make it obvious. Be sociable, but don't neglect basic issues. Make inquiries. Give full play to your intellectual curiosity. Keep up with fashion news.

Tuesday, September 23 (Moon in Leo to Virgo 4:03 p.m.) Today may seem to pass slowly, filled with details and minor tasks. Tell yourself, "It must be done and I will do it!" A relative wants your company on a short trip. Perhaps going is okay, but don't get involved in a wild-goose chase. Taurus is in the picture.

Wednesday, September 24 (Moon in Virgo)   Focus on property and living quarters as well as intense dealings with a Virgo. You will feel attracted to Libra and vice versa. Read, write, teach. A flirtation is serious, so protect your interests. The emphasis is on advertising, publicity, and distribution. Have luck with number 5.

Thursday, September 25 (Moon in Virgo to Libra 6:48 p.m.)   You might be saying (about me), "That astrology fellow has written my diary in advance!" Focus on a possible change of residence or marital status. If diplomatic, you win. By attempting to force issues, you lose. Taurus, Libra, and Scorpio are in this picture.

Friday, September 26 (Moon in Libra)   The new moon in your fifth house starting late last night spells flirtation, physical attraction, and the stirring of your creative juices. You could try your hand at learning a musical instrument. Don't deceive yourself in connection with a relationship. It is better to be safe than sorry.

Saturday, September 27 (Moon in Libra to Scorpio 7:51 p.m.)   Focus on children, challenge, and a variety of experiences. A business organization seeks a consultation. Accept, but don't go hat in hand. This could be your power play day! Capricorn and Cancer play instrumental roles. Lucky lottery: 8, 28, 18, 15, 2, 5.

Sunday, September 28 (Moon in Scorpio)   On this Sunday, predict the future—you can make it come true! Emphasize universal appeal. Look beyond the immediate. Participate in a humanitarian political project. Write your impressions; take note of your dreams. Aries and Libra will figure in today's exciting scenario.

Monday, September 29 (Moon in Scorpio to Sagittarius 8:56 p.m.)   A serious discussion occurs over a possible "change of name." It could be personal or business or both. Make a fresh start. An excellent day for beginning an enterprise. Love will not be a stranger! If married, the spark that brought you together reignites.

Tuesday, September 30 (Moon in Sagittarius)   On this last day of September, be willing to wait. In fact, play the waiting game. Circumstances are not right for a full plunge into the future. Additional information will be forthcoming. The spotlight is on legal affairs, public relations, and your marital status.

OCTOBER 2003

Wednesday, October 1 (Moon in Sagittarius to Capricorn 11:21 p.m.)   On this first day of October, the aspects are fine for a new start. Imprint your own style; don't follow others. Be ultracautious about legal rights and permissions. Take the initiative, but be sure you are on the right side of the law. Leo is in the picture.

Thursday, October 2 (Moon in Capricorn)   Focus on where you are going and your motivation. The question of marriage looms large. Remember recent resolutions about your general health that include exercise, diet, and nutrition. Cancer and Capricorn play outstanding roles.

Friday, October 3 (Moon in Capricorn)   Be willing to experiment, to give full play to your intellectual curiosity. Make inquiries about payments, loans, percentages. What had been a mystery will be revealed to your advantage. Sagittarius and another Gemini play fantastic roles.

Saturday, October 4 (Moon in Capricorn to Aquarius 3:45 a.m.)   Attempting to skip details today would be wrong. Become thoroughly familiar with the task at hand. Tear down in order to rebuild. Make this your "makeover" day. Steer clear of traffic jams and crowds. Remove fire hazards from your home and workplace.

Sunday, October 5 (Moon in Aquarius)   Take a philosophical view of current happenings. Focus on psychology, meditation, and theology. The moon in your ninth house highlights your ability to reach more people and to find effective ways of distribution. The emphasis is on teaching, learning, reading, and writing.

Monday, October 6 (Moon in Aquarius to Pisces 10:20 a.m.)   Music plays. Find your rhythm, dance to your own tune. You could change your residence or marital status. Be diplomatic, even to those who seem to be aching for a fight. Your voice sounds different, and people comment, "You could go very far if you exploit that voice!"

Tuesday, October 7 (Moon in Pisces)   You might be asked to do a job you have not been trained to do. Don't pretend. Say what you think, then let the chips fall where they may. A superior expresses admiration for your honesty. Say thank you without being obsequious. Pisces is involved.

Wednesday, October 8 (Moon in Pisces to Aries 7:07 p.m.)   What appeared to be a defeat will boomerang in your favor. A superior or "the boss" looks upon you admiringly. Accept more responsibility; do what must be done. You will be rewarded. Capricorn and Cancer will play "distinguished" roles.

Thursday, October 9 (Moon in Aries)   Look beyond the immediate. Turn on your Gemini charm to win friends and influence people. The Aries moon represents your eleventh house. That means luck, especially in matters of speculation. Stick with number 9. Libra plays a top role.

Friday, October 10 (Moon in Aries)   Elements of timing and luck ride with you. The full moon in your eleventh house emphasizes creativity, style, and speculation. An excellent day for fund-raising, for winning allies, and for getting your way despite the odds. Leo and Aquarius figure in this scenario.

Saturday, October 11 (Moon in Aries to Taurus 6:04 a.m.) Grab any opportunity to shine. Don't miss a chance for fame or fortune. A secret meeting takes place, even as you read these words. An important person stands up for you, and for that be thankful. Capricorn and Cancer play roles.

Sunday, October 12 (Moon in Taurus)   On this Sunday, you'll be intrigued by the history of various religions. Give full play to your curiosity. Make inquiries. Maintain a pleasant, humorous attitude. Accept social invitation. By so doing, you can win adherents to your cause.

Monday, October 13 (Moon in Taurus to Gemini 6:44 p.m.)   Try on a new wardrobe. It does fit, and you look great. Be willing, however, to laugh at your own foibles. You possess the gift of making others laugh, even through their grief. Taurus and Scorpio will play "mysterious" roles.

Tuesday, October 14 (Moon in Gemini)   Judge not lest you be judged. This means give others the benefit of the doubt. If lenient in this way, you win over persons who might have been against you. A flirtation is serious. Be aware of what it could lead to! Protect yourself in close quarters.

Wednesday, October 15 (Moon in Gemini)   In your high cycle, puzzle pieces fall into place. This relates especially to where you live and your marital status. Be diplomatic. Listen closely to musical scores. You are going places, likely to surprise yourself! Lucky lottery: 6, 16, 36, 18, 40, 13.

Thursday, October 16 (Moon in Gemini to Cancer 7:39 a.m.)   A financial opportunity is present. Define terms. Avoid self-deception. There's an aura of mystery and intrigue. So don't tell all, don't confide, and don't confess! Pisces and Virgo will play fantastic roles. At times, the dishes seem to fall out of your hands.

Friday, October 17 (Moon in Cancer)   Obtain the facts and figures about a financial enterprise. You might be amazed at how well you fit in. The assignment will be received. Focus on organization and recognition of priorities. Capricorn and Cancer will play leading roles.

Saturday, October 18 (Moon in Cancer to Leo 6:40 p.m.)   What appeared to be lost will be recovered. Take this as a warning—don't trust too many people! Reach beyond the immediate to perceive potential. Love plays a role; you'll know once and for all that your love is not unrequited. Have luck with number 9.

Sunday, October 19 (Moon in Leo)   On this Sunday, participate in lively discussions with friends or neighbors. Much could be based on politics, but mainly on the mantic arts and sciences. Discussions will range from spiritualism to numerology and astrology. Leo plays a featured role.

Monday, October 20 (Moon in Leo)   Give serious consideration to such subjects as partnership and marriage. You will locate comfortable living quarters. Cancer and Capricorn will play premier roles. If you meditate, many dilemmas will resolve. Keep the faith!

Tuesday, October 21 (Moon in Leo to Virgo 1:59 a.m.) Highlight versatility. Become more familiar with subjects before debating them. Your popularity is on the rise. People vie to see who can wine and dine you. Check the building material to remove safety hazards. A celebration later would be in order.

Wednesday, October 22 (Moon in Virgo)   Check the plumbing, iron out the details—you possibly found the "right place." Perhaps you've found it, but might not be aware of it. Look beyond the immediate. Dig deep for information. Do not equate delay with defeat. What you've been waiting for arrives tonight.

Thursday, October 23 (Moon in Virgo to Libra 5:26 a.m.) Give full play to your intellectual curiosity. You exude personality and sex appeal. A flirtation gets serious, but don't break too many hearts. Virgo, Sagittarius, and another Gemini play major roles, and have these letters or initials in their names: E, N, W.

Friday, October 24 (Moon in Libra)   Attention revolves around the necessity for staying at home. Emphasize romance—with flowers, music, and courtly behavior. One who disappointed you will more than make up for it. Be diplomatic in accepting an apology. Libra figures prominently.

Saturday, October 25 (Moon in Libra to Scorpio 6:07 a.m.) Use your sense of showmanship. Advertise and publicize. The new moon in Scorpio relates to your sixth house, which includes employment, basic issues, and getting things done. See people as they are. Avoid self-deception. Protect yourself at close quarters.

Sunday, October 26—Daylight Saving Time Ends (Moon in Scorpio) A power play day! Nothing happens halfway. It will be all or nothing. A temperamental coworker creates mischief. Steer clear of controversy, if possible. Spiritual values dominate; be receptive. Capricorn and Cancer play outstanding roles.

Monday, October 27 (Moon in Scorpio to Sagittarius 4:54 a.m.) Lie low, play the waiting game. Be sure of your legal rights and permissions. Emphasize public relations, reputation, and credibility. Take care in dealing with Sagittarius. Aries will also figure in this dramatic scenario. Lucky number is 9.

Tuesday, October 28 (Moon in Sagittarius) You will get help in solving a long division mathematical problem. Refuse to be stymied by those who say, "It can't be done!" Imprint your own style. Don't follow others. A different kind of romance is on the horizon. A Leo figures prominently.

Wednesday, October 29 (Moon in Sagittarius to Capricorn 5:36 a.m.) You'll be asking, "Is this déjà vu?" Today's scenario features familiar places and faces. Questions loom large concerning partnership or marriage. You will be oriented despite some persons who wish otherwise. Direction and motivation will be made crystal clear.

Thursday, October 30 (Moon in Capricorn) Highlight social activities. Find out where you stand percentage-wise in a financial transaction. Some envious people will accuse you of being in the playground of the occult. Keep them guessing! Don't tell all; don't confide or confess.

Friday, October 31 (Moon in Capricorn to Aquarius 8:41 a.m.) This is not only Halloween, but also National Magic Day in memory of Harry Houdini. Read about and discuss his amazing feats. People will consult you, their curiosity aroused. They want you to talk about Houdini. Taurus is in the picture.

NOVEMBER 2003

Saturday, November 1 (Moon in Aquarius) You may be pondering "long ago and far away." Get your thoughts on paper. Open the lines of communication. Someone in a faraway place wants to tell you something. Be receptive, without being naive. Cancer and Capricorn will play fascinating roles.

Sunday, November 2 (Moon in Aquarius to Pisces 2:52 p.m.) What a Sunday! The number 3 numerical cycle equates to Jupiter, planet of luck. Ask questions, make inquiries. A spiritual leader will be complimented, if you ask and dig deep for the answers. Wear your new wardrobe; you'll be complimented on your appearance.

Monday, November 3 (Moon in Pisces) On this Monday, arrange to fix things. Check plumbing and attend to details previously overlooked. Taurus, Leo, and Scorpio will figure in this scenario, and could have these letters or initials in their names: D, M, V. Lucky number is 4.

Tuesday, November 4 (Moon in Pisces) Read and write. Participate in a contest based on skill with words. Virgo, Sagittarius, and another Gemini figure prominently. Someone in an executive position confides, "I think you are very attractive, and we should get to know each other!"

Wednesday, November 5 (Moon in Pisces to Aries 12:02 a.m.)   Attention revolves around your home, music, domesticity, and a possible change of residence or marital status. An opportunity exists for promotion—permit your words to speak out loud. The pressure is on, but you will be up to it. Have luck with number 6.

Thursday, November 6 (Moon in Aries)   At the track: post position special—number 1 p.p. in the seventh race. Pick six: 1, 4, 7, 3, 8, 2. Hot daily doubles: 1 and 4, 2 and 6, 2 and 5. Away from the track you'll be surprised by a guest who entertains you with illusions and magic tricks.

Friday, November 7 (Moon in Aries to Taurus 11:28 a.m.)   Your hopes and wishes are fulfilled. You have luck in speculation by sticking with number 8. Your popularity increases, and people express the desire to wine and dine you. Exhibit humor and an ability to laugh at your own foibles. Capricorn is in the picture.

Saturday, November 8 (Moon in Taurus)   A relationship begins or ends—it's up to you which one it will be. Money is involved, a lost article located. A Taurus comes up with a surprise of the pleasant variety. Finish what you start. Look behind the scenes for answers.

Sunday, November 9 (Moon in Taurus)   Don't let people take you for granted. You do have money coming to you. Persist in getting your fair share. Don't follow others. Accent originality, daring, and a pioneering spirit. Leo and Aquarius will play astonishing roles.

Monday, November 10 (Moon in Taurus to Gemini 12:13 a.m.)   Ask questions. Prepare answers for questions that will be asked of you. Cooperative efforts, partnership, and marriage will top the agenda. A disappearing pet will once again show affection. Capricorn and Cancer will play meaningful roles.

Tuesday, November 11 (Moon in Gemini)   Give full play to your intellectual curiosity. Your cycle is high, so

284

your judgment and intuition serve as reliable guides. People who previously shied away now express the desire not only to be with you but also to entertain you. Sagittarius figures prominently.

Wednesday, November 12 (Moon in Gemini to Cancer 1:09 p.m.) Rewrite, rebuild, review, and, if necessary, start anew. Puzzle pieces are ready to fall into place. A mathematical problem will be solved. You'll excel at word games. Taurus, Leo, and Scorpio play important roles, and have these letters in their names: D, M, V.

Thursday, November 13 (Moon in Cancer) What seemed to be long ago and far away will practically be at your doorstep. Someone of the opposite sex confides, "I had to track you down because of the attraction I have for you!" Virgo, Sagittarius, and another Gemini figure in this scenario.

Friday, November 14 (Moon in Cancer) On this Friday, stick close to home, if possible. Focus on music, diplomacy, and an important domestic adjustment. Find your own rhythm, dance to your own tune. This message becomes crystal clear tonight. You receive a gift, perhaps a luxury item that helps make your home beautiful.

Saturday, November 15 (Moon in Cancer to Leo 12:46 a.m.) A financial pressure is relieved. See people and places as they are, not merely as you wish they could be. Trust your psychic impression. A romantic illusion causes no harm. Enjoy it! Pisces and Virgo work their way into today's scenario.

Sunday, November 16 (Moon in Leo) Focus on promotion, production, and distribution. The Leo moon represents your third house, which means relatives, trips, and visits. People ask favors; oblige them if what they ask is practical. Know when to say, "Enough!" A romantic relationship is intense, and might get too hot not to cool down.

Monday, November 17 (Moon in Leo to Virgo 9:34 a.m.)
Finish what you start. Arrange with a Leo relative to "explore the unknown." Give full play to your intellectual curiosity and to your love of mystery. You are going places, but you require further directions. Aries and Libra figure in this scenario.

Tuesday, November 18 (Moon in Virgo) Bright lights shine! An area of home previously dark gets more light. Don't follow others; let them follow you. Wear bright colors that include yellow and gold. A different kind of romance is on the horizon. A Leo figures prominently.

Wednesday, November 19 (Moon in Virgo to Libra 2:40 p.m.) You'll be dealing with structures and buildings, also the home. You will be "in touch" with an older individual who befriended you. Cancer and Capricorn play scintillating roles, and could have these letters or initials in their names: B, K, T.

Thursday, November 20 (Moon in Libra) The Libra moon relates to your fifth house, which means creative juices are activated. Find an outlet to display your talents. Give a smile to get a smile. Focus on fun and social graces as well as the possibility of a journey. Sagittarius and another Gemini figure in this dynamic scenario.

Friday, November 21 (Moon in Libra to Scorpio 4:22 p.m.) Revise, review, rebuild! What had been rejected could now be accepted. The focus is on creativity, challenge, children, and physical attraction. Someone of the opposite sex confides, "I can hardly keep my hands off you!" Scorpio is involved.

Saturday, November 22 (Moon in Scorpio) On this Saturday, check the structure of a creative project. Don't skip the details. A flirtation is serious, so respond accordingly. Virgo, Sagittarius, and another Gemini figure in this dynamic scenario. Be analytical. Get your thoughts on paper. Lucky number is 5.

Sunday, November 23 (Moon in Scorpio to Sagittarius 4:02 p.m.)   The new moon and solar eclipse fall in Scorpio, your sixth house. There could be stunning changes in connection with employment. Keep resolutions about exercise, diet, and nutrition. Today's scenario features a possible change of residence or marital status.

Monday, November 24 (Moon in Sagittarius)   Look beyond the immediate. Lie low; check legal rights and permissions. A Sagittarius attempts to force you into a situation that is uncomfortable, possibly illegal. Be alert and aware; maintain creative control.

Tuesday, November 25 (Moon in Sagittarius to Capricorn 3:31 p.m.)   On this Tuesday, play the waiting game. All information has not been provided. There could be legal ramifications that thwart your efforts. Capricorn and Cancer will play mysterious, productive roles. Have luck with number 8.

Wednesday, November 26 (Moon in Capricorn)   Lucky lottery: 10, 8, 18, 5, 12, 17. What had been a threat will be removed. The answers to many questions will be found in arcane literature. A romantic relationship is fiery. Protect yourself in emotional clinches. Money is involved.

Thursday, November 27 (Moon in Capricorn to Aquarius 4:48 p.m.)   An original "setting" helps make this a memorable Thanksgiving. Sharp retorts are featured; debates ensue about the true meaning of the holiday. Leo and Aquarius will play featured roles. For you, neither encourage nor discourage debates.

Friday, November 28 (Moon in Aquarius)   Get to the heart of matters. Ask questions and receive answers, not evasions. Focus on cooperative efforts, partnership, and marital status. Leftovers from Thanksgiving will be "delicious." Capricorn and Cancer play holiday roles.

Saturday, November 29 (Moon in Aquarius to Pisces 9:26 p.m.)   You'll enjoy this Saturday, but don't believe everything you hear. The air is filled with compliments. Social activities increase. Wear a new wardrobe, with a "different look." Sagittarius and another Gemini help make this day "outstanding."

Sunday, November 30 (Moon in Pisces)   Within 24 hours, you get news revealing promotion is just around the corner. You'll be dealing with important people who recognize your best qualities. Avoid being obsequious—move and write with confidence. Taurus plays a dramatic role.

DECEMBER 2003

Monday, December 1 (Moon in Pisces)   On this first day of December, with the moon in Pisces, you step forward to battle fears, doubts, and superstitions. Your popularity zooms. You will be up-to-date in fashion. Sagittarius and another Gemini play significant roles.

Tuesday, December 2 (Moon in Pisces to Aries 5:55 a.m.) Someone in authority commends you, giving you extra work. Rewrite, review, rebuild. People comment on your looks, mostly favorable. A lost scarf or necktie will be returned tomorrow. Taurus, Leo, and Scorpio figure in today's scenario.

Wednesday, December 3 (Moon in Aries)   Many of your hopes and wishes come true. You have good fortune in matters of speculation by sticking with number 5. If single, you could meet your future mate. If married, the love spark reignites. Another Gemini inspires you to finish a creative task.

Thursday, December 4 (Moon in Aries to Taurus 5:29 p.m.)   It is not too early to prepare for the holidays. Make a list of the people you want to be with. There is no need to lower your standards. Attention revolves around your "house beautiful." Do some speaking or singing. Taurus and Libra help you over the rough spots.

Friday, December 5 (Moon in Taurus)   Define your terms, especially in connection with real estate. A secret relating to finance will be disclosed. A mystery about numbers will be resolved. Don't give up your valuables. Protect your assets. An element of deception is present, so protect yourself in emotional clinches.

Saturday, December 6 (Moon in Taurus)   Suddenly you learn more about expenses and budgeting. Handle it with aplomb. If startled, don't show it. You will be in the driver's seat. Visit someone temporarily confined to home or hospital. Capricorn will play a distinctive role.

Sunday, December 7 (Moon in Taurus to Gemini 6:25 a.m.)   Memories of Pearl Harbor haunt. Look beyond the immediate. Toss aside preconceived notions. An opportunity will exist to travel, perhaps to a foreign land. You are gaining recognition. Aries and Libra will play dramatic roles.

Monday, December 8 (Moon in Gemini)   What a Monday! The full moon is in Gemini, your sign. This high cycle features romance, creativity, and style. Invade places where it is said angels fear to tread. A new, different kind of romance is on the horizon. Leo and Aquarius play top roles.

Tuesday, December 9 (Moon in Gemini to Cancer 7:10 p.m.)   Your cycle is high, so emphasize your Gemini personality. Make use of drama and showmanship. The spotlight is on cooperative efforts, local politics, partnership, and marriage. Keep resolutions about exercise, diet, and nutrition. A digestive problem proves minor, if you don't neglect it.

Wednesday, December 10 (Moon in Cancer)   On this Wednesday, grasp an opportunity that you let slip by last month. Make personal appearances. Express your views in a dynamic way. There is no need to be servile or obsequious. Bring forth artistic tendencies. Have luck with number 3.

Thursday, December 11 (Moon in Cancer)   A serious discussion takes place relating to names and whether or not to change them. You'll be concerned with the mantic arts and sciences that include numerology and astrology. Your intuition, honed to razor-sharpness, will serve as a reliable guide.

Friday, December 12 (Moon in Cancer to Leo 6:39 a.m.) A lost valuable is retrieved. Check your assets. Get your priorities in order. An excellent day for reading and writing, learning through process of sharing, and teaching. A member of the opposite sex confides, "At times I cannot keep my hands off you!" Don't believe everything!

Saturday, December 13 (Moon in Leo)   Transform your home into a "showplace." Whether or not you actually do it, at least make an effort. An important visitor will be your guest—you learn this in a surprising way. Focus on flowers, art, music, and romance. Lucky number is 6.

Sunday, December 14 (Moon in Leo to Virgo 4:05 p.m.) Spiritual values surface. This could be a day of self-revelation. Be analytical. Protect yourself in romantic clinches. Someone wants something for nothing, and you could be the prime target. Perfect techniques, streamline procedures. Pisces is in the picture.

Monday, December 15 (Moon in Virgo)   Lie low, play the waiting game. The emphasis is on public relations together with legal rights and permissions. The spotlight is also on questions concerning partnership or marriage. Capricorn and Cancer have been waiting to surprise you. They mean well, so don't be resentful.

Tuesday, December 16 (Moon in Virgo to Libra 10:44 p.m.) Be aware of property values. Let go of a burden you should not have carried in the first place. Think on an international scale. Don't limit yourself. Aries and Libra claim they can "fill the bill." Have luck with number 9.

Wednesday, December 17 (Moon in Libra)   Make a fresh start. Emphasize your originality and pioneering spirit. The lunar position stirs your creative juices. Read and write, teach and learn. A flirtation gets hot and heavy. Wear bright colors when you make personal appearances. Lucky lottery: 1, 11, 18, 22, 2, 24.

Thursday, December 18 (Moon in Libra)   You might be asking, "Is this déjà vu?" Today's scenario features familiar faces and places. If single, you could meet your future mate. If married, the love spark reignites. The spotlight is on your home, cooking, and restaurant management. A Cancer figures in this scenario.

Friday, December 19 (Moon in Libra to Scorpio 2:18 a.m.)   Get basic chores out of the way early. An invitation to celebrate comes almost at the last minute. You might be asked to hop on a plane. Open the lines of communication. Highlight sociability. Laugh at your own foibles and help make others laugh, too. Sagittarius is involved.

Saturday, December 20 (Moon in Scorpio)   What starts as an apparent defeat will boomerang in your favor. Taurus, Leo, and Scorpio play significant roles. Be aware of details; check for correct measurements. You'll be asked to help solve a mathematical problem. You'll do it, and also excel at word games.

Sunday, December 21 (Moon in Scorpio to Sagittarius 3:14 a.m.)   On this Sunday, realize your potential. Become familiar with the basics of a foreign language. An excellent day for writing, possibly to start a diary. Steer clear of people who take you for granted. You are an exciting personality, so act as if you're aware of it.

Monday, December 22 (Moon in Sagittarius)   The lunar position highlights people who might oppose your ideas. Check for legal rights and permissions. The spotlight is also on cooperative efforts, partnership, and marriage. You could change your residence or marital status. If so, locate new living quarters.

Tuesday, December 23 (Moon in Sagittarius to Capricorn 2:55 a.m.) The new moon in Capricorn represents your eighth house. This indicates that you discover a "money secret." You also learn the truth about percentages in borrowing and lending. Define terms; get promises in writing. Pisces is involved.

Wednesday, December 24 (Moon in Capricorn) On this Christmas Eve, you fathom some of the mysteries of the holiday in a deeper way than previously. Speak and write about it. Among gifts received will be one that is heavy to carry, possibly involving water. Capricorn plays a role.

Thursday, December 25 (Moon in Capricorn to Aquarius 3:13 a.m.) Merry Christmas! The moon position highlights spirituality. The numerical cycle emphasizes universal appeal with added recognition. Participate in a humanitarian project. Let others become aware of your "spiritual glow." An Aries figures prominently.

Friday, December 26 (Moon in Aquarius) You feel renewed. Your vigor makes a dramatic comeback. Optimism replaces gloom, if you so permit. Visit people, wearing bright colors that include yellow and gold. You are a winner, so act as if you are aware of it. You will be a role model for young persons.

Saturday, December 27 (Moon in Aquarius to Pisces 6:09 a.m.) What had been a limitation turns out to be an asset. Do not equate delay with defeat. A family member who has been obstreperous will become cooperative. You'll have almost everything, including love, money, and health. A Cancer is in this picture.

Sunday, December 28 (Moon in Pisces) Entertain and be entertained. Someone you respect will return the compliment. If you must speculate today, stick with number 3. A relative in a faraway place telephones concerning travel, fashion, or romance. Keep resolutions about basic health, exercise, diet, and nutrition.

Monday, December 29 (Moon in Pisces to Aries 1:09 p.m.) Don't wait until the last minute for New Year's Eve plans. You will be invited to attend a prestigious celebration. Be receptive, without being obsequious. Show gratitude, without being servile. Taurus, Leo, and Scorpio will play key roles.

Tuesday, December 30 (Moon in Aries) The Aries moon relates to your eleventh house. This coincides with the ability to make wishes come true. Elements of timing and luck ride with you. Take it easy on adult beverages. Don't drive with a heavy drinker. Virgo, Sagittarius, and another Gemini play fascinating roles.

Wednesday, December 31 (Moon in Aries) On this New Year's Eve, don't stray too far from home. Accept a party invitation with the inner understanding that you will remain sober. A romantic liaison will prove memorable, and could relate to the future. Taurus, Libra, and Scorpio are part of this holiday.

HAPPY NEW YEAR!

ABOUT THE AUTHOR

Born on August 5, 1926, in Philadelphia, Sydney Omarr was the only person ever given full-time duty in the U.S. Army as an astrologer. He also is regarded as the most erudite astrologer of our time and the best known, through his syndicated column (300 newspapers) and his radio and television programs (he was Merv Griffin's "resident astrologer"). Omarr has been called the most "knowledgeable astrologer since Evangeline Adams." His forecasts of Nixon's downfall, the end of World War II in mid-August of 1945, the assassination of John F. Kennedy, Roosevelt's election to the fourth term and his death in office . . . these and many others are on the record and quoted enough to be considered "legendary."

ABOUT THE SERIES

This is one of a series of twelve
Day-by-Day Astrological Guides
for the signs of 2003
by Sydney Omarr.

The Ultimate Guide to Love, Sex,
and Romance

SYDNEY OMARR'S ASTROLOGY, LOVE, SEX, AND YOU

SYDNEY OMARR

Whether your goal is a sexy seduction, finding your
soulmate, or spicing up a current relationship, this all-
in-one volume will guide you every step of the way—
with a little help from Sydney and the stars.

Includes:
- An in-depth description of each sign for men and women
- Compatibilty forecasts
- A fantastic section on romantic dinners for two, featuring
a complete kitchen-tested menu for each sign
- Myths and symbols associated with each sign
- An introduction to each sign's shadow
- Ratings on which signs are the most passionate
- and much more

206932

Available September 2002

To order call: 1-800-788-6262